To Tomatra Scott (Scotty)

Best Wishes,

Robert Staples

The World
of
Black Singles

Recent Titles in
Contributions in Afro-American and African Studies
Series Adviser: HOLLIS R. LYNCH

"Keep A-Inchin' Along": Selected Writings of Carl Van Vechten about
Black Arts and Letters
Bruce Kellner, editor

Witnessing Slavery: The Development of Ante-bellum Slave Narratives
Frances Smith Foster

Africans and Creeks: From the Colonial Period to the Civil War
Daniel F. Littlefield, Jr.

Decolonization and Dependency: Problems of Development of African
Societies
Aquibou Y. Yansané, editor

The American Slave: A Composite Autobiography Supplement, Series 2
George P. Rawick, editor

The Second Black Renaissance: Essays in Black Literature
C. W. E. Bigsby

Advice Among Masters: The Ideal in Slave Management in the Old South
James O. Breeden, editor

Towards African Literary Independence: A Dialogue with Contemporary
African Writers
Phanuel Akubeze Egejuru

The Chickasaw Freedmen: A People Without a Country
Daniel F. Littlefield, Jr.

The African Nexus: Black American Perspectives on the European
Partitioning of Africa
Sylvia M. Jacobs

Freedom and Prejudice: The Legacy of Slavery in the United States
and Brazil
Robert Brent Toplin

The World of Black Singles

CHANGING PATTERNS OF MALE/FEMALE RELATIONS

Robert Staples

CONTRIBUTIONS IN AFRO-AMERICAN AND AFRICAN
STUDIES, NUMBER 57

GREENWOOD PRESS
Westport, Connecticut • London, England

Library of Congress Cataloging in Publication Data

Staples, Robert.
    The world of Black singles.

    (Contributions in Afro-American and African studies;
no. 57 ISSN 0069-9624)
    Bibliography: p.
    Includes index.
    1.   Afro-American single people—California—San
Francisco Bay region—Case studies.   2.   Afro-American
single people. I. Title. II. Series.
HQ800.4.U62S267   305   80-1025
ISBN 0-313-22478-1 (lib. bdg.)

Library of Congress Catalog Card Number: 80-1025
ISBN: 0-313-22478-1
ISSN: 0069-9624

First published in 1981

Greenwood Press
A division of Congressional Information Service, Inc.
88 Post Road West, Westport, Connecticut 06881

Printed in the United States of America

10 9 8 7 6 5 4 3 2 1

TO MY FATHER, AMBROSE STAPLES
AND MY UNCLES, JOHN AND JAMES ANTHONY
WHO PROVIDED ME WITH POSITIVE ROLE MODELS
OF HUSBANDS AND FATHERS

Contents

Tables

Preface

The number of people who assisted me in carrying out this project are too numerous to mention. I can only hope they will accept a collective thank you for their help. I wish to acknowledge a special debt of gratitude to Wendell Brooks, Velma La Point and Alan Vaughn who were among the people most involved in the project from start to finish. Of the individuals who assisted me in one way or another during the research phase, I want to thank Barbara L. Carter, Elaine Mayberry, Marie Peters, Patricia Bell Scott, and Peter Stein.

Among the individuals who read all or parts of the original draft of the manuscript and made valuable suggestions were Cheryl Cromwell, Carolyn Greene, Jeanette Jennings, and Terry Jones. Julie Jamerson and Mona Scott provided me with moral support during the five years I worked on the book. Doris Bowman and Sally Maeth typed and edited the manuscript. And, I want to acknowledge the contribution of Cynthia, who exemplifies all the contradictions of singlehood.

Last, but not least, I thank all those people who distributed the questionnaires for me, especially those who were so careful in monitoring their return. The most important group of all were the individuals who told me in person or in writing about their single lives. This was a voluntary, unremunerated effort on their part, and some of it was very painful. The only way I could hope to repay them was by producing a book that shed some light on their condition. If this work does not accomplish that goal, I accept all the responsibility for its failure.

Introduction

Unmarried people have suddenly become this nation's largest minority group. If we count individuals who have never married, and those who are divorced, separated, and widowed, they account for more than a third of America's population over the age of fourteen, and their numbers are growing.[1] This group has been neglected in the literature because of their transient status—most would eventually enter the ranks of the married population. Increasingly, however, Americans are beginning to view singlehood as a way of life. Some will choose it voluntarily, others will be forced into making the "choice."

Singlehood or marriage is more likely to be a dilemma for Afro-Americans. As a group they are proportionately more likely to be unmarried, divorced, separated or widowed. Approximately 52 percent of the black population over age 18 is single. Moreover, singlehood poses special problems for them because of the excess number of women, the different cultural traditions under which they were raised, fewer institutional supports for coping with unmarried life, and the inevitable complications stemming from their status as a racial minority. Hence a book dealing with the reasons for and nature of black singlehood is long overdue. Nowhere in the literature is this subject directly dealt with, despite the magnitude of the black singles situation in America.

The purposes of this book are to delineate the characteristics of black singles, their coping mechanisms for dealing with singlehood, and the black single life-style. To make it a viable effort, we will concentrate on certain segments of the black singles population, primarily those between the ages of 25 and 45, with a college education, and living in large metropolitan areas. This allows us to avoid the awesome implications of poverty, singleness in small or rural communities, and the more prosaic dating patterns of black college youths. Beyond the age of 25 and in metropolitan areas where people are often isolated from community and kin supports and pressures, singleness often becomes a unique way of life. Hence, we can view singlehood in all its different contours and the various ways in which individuals handle it.

Confining our study to blacks who have a college education may be perceived as too narrow to understand the single life-style among all blacks. After all, they represent only 13 percent of the black population between the ages of 25 and 45.[2] Several factors entered into the decision to concentrate on such a group. While the primary purpose of our investigation is to explore the life-styles of black singles, it is also an exposition of the process of acculturation. The differences between the black and white singles' existences are more a matter of degree than kind. This should make the study of interest to a general audience as well as to the black middle class. Concentrating on the middle class group allows us to focus on the sociocultural aspects of singlehood. It is otherwise difficult to separate those aspects from the economic forces that impinge on the variations in marital status among lower class blacks. In essence, this is a comparative study of black and white singles, with similar levels of education and income but different social realities.

The study is based on one hundred personal interviews in the metropolitan area around San Francisco. An additional 400 self-administered questionnaires were returned from the larger metropolitan areas in the United States. Our analysis is qualitative in nature. We believed that understanding black singlehood was more important than methodological rigor. This book is written without much professional jargon, but sociological theory and insights permeate the analysis. The book should be appropriate and relevant to a general reading audience, to classes in the family, race relations, and ethnic studies as well as to family scholars.

Since our intentions are to present a sociological account comprehensible to the mass public, a variety of methodologies will be employed. They will be sociological studies, newspaper and magazine stories, census data, questionnaires, interviews, and participant observation. The overall purpose is to present a picture of black singlehood as seen through diverse available sources. The benefit of such a book is that it permits us to study black life from a somewhat normative perspective. That is, we can see blacks as normal human beings coping with the pervasive problems posed by singlehood without focusing on their roles as individuals besieged by oppressive forces. This does not mean that race or racial oppression are a negligible element. These factors are always central to the black condition. But our focus is on the black single's lifestyle, not the conditions which may have originally produced the problem.

The idea for a study of black singles arose out of my personal situation and academic interests. For most of my adult life I have been unmarried. During that same period of time I also spent nine years in college and lived in eight different cities. With my time occupied by academic activities, I hardly noticed any problem in being single. A very mobile career pattern had prevented my noticing the formation of a black singles world. Five years ago, after the waning of my writing efforts and my settlement in San Francisco, I observed the large numbers of my friends and colleagues who were unmarried or formerly married. Many of them were in the dating game. What they reported to me was an endless set of frustrations: men who did not want to make a commitment and who had fragile egos, men and women who did not show up for dates, some who were undergoing identity crises and had a strong sense of ambivalence about sex. Being somewhat puzzled, I wrote to my confidant and mentor, Paul Rosenblatt at the University of Minnesota. Complaining to him that both marital and single life were problematic, I wondered which was worse. His answer was: "whichever you are in at the time."

While such an answer leaves much to be desired and even more to be explained, it poignantly describes the dilemma of many Americans. Many whites and some married blacks may be surprised at this plight of single blacks. They probably assume that single blacks are free to pick and choose from the large numbers of available singles. People simply do not believe that singles are often at home alone on Friday and Saturday nights. Even more incredulous to them would be the fact that I spend many weekend nights with three or four black male friends, all of them highly educated, creative and sensitive men. They have, for all practical purposes, dropped out of active involvement in the dating game. All of them, to my knowledge, are heterosexuals, and they do interact with women, but on a selective and qualitatively different basis.

Since this is not an autobiography, I will not dwell on my personal life. Suffice it to say that I bring an experiential insight into the world of black singles. As a student of the black family for ten years, I also am concerned with what is happening to that unit. In a sense it is very difficult for me to undertake a study which basically focuses on conflict between black males and females. All these years I have written on the strengths of black families. It is still my belief that it is a strong institution albeit a different one from the middle class white family. In a way these middle class black singles are facing problems because they too closely approximate middle class whites. Yet they are not white and must deal with all the ramifications of that irrefutable fact.

Having come upon the idea of studying black singles, I discussed it with a number of my friends and associates. Everywhere it was mentioned, eyes lit up with interest. Even married couples were eager to learn about the subject, some out of a hidden envy and curiosity about the presumed "good life" of single people, others because they had unmarried friends who were experiencing some difficulty. In the past five years one of the most popular sessions in black professional meetings has been on male-female relations. It was a topic of immense interest everywhere I went. People called and asked me to speak on it, and seminars were organized to discuss the issue.

Several things have happened between the time I began the study in 1975 and now. In that five-year span there has been a dramatic increase in the proportion of singles, female-headed families, and teenage pregnancies among blacks. Obviously, the trend toward black singlehood was not abating. During the winter of 1979 I taught a course at the University of Michigan on black male/female relationships. Despite the fact that the course was not listed in the schedule of classes, it attracted over 100 students, all of them black. Most of them were from Detroit (between the ages of 18 and 22) and had some difficulty in their relationships with the opposite sex. When I gave them a modified version of my questionnaire, I discovered most wanted to marry someday; they were more sexually conservative than the older singles and had an idealized concept of love and marriage. Some of the problems they had were unique to their age group and circumstances. Others were remarkably similar to those of their older counterparts.

With increasing awareness of the growing number of black singles and concern about their problems and the implications of these problems for society, the subject has received media attention and attempts at resolution. Two of the major Black magazines, *Jet* and *Ebony*, have devoted a regular section to the sexes in their issues. The leading black intellectual journal, *The Black Scholar*, deviated from its typical issues on politics and economics to publish a special symposium on black male/female relationships. Most of the major news weeklies and daily newspapers have published articles on the subject. Nathan and Julia Hare have established a new bimonthly journal, *Black Male/Female Relationships*. While this has led to charges of the media magnifying the problem, the statistic which shows that a majority of adult blacks are not married and living with a spouse speaks for itself.

Fortunately, efforts are underway to deal with the situation. In every major city there are teams of therapists bringing black men and women together to discuss their relationships. Mental health organizations are gearing up to help single individuals and cohabiting couples. Black singles organizations are cropping up in the larger cities as are singles bars. Courses on the subject are being taught at a number of colleges. Before any of these efforts can meet with any success, it is necessary to understand the origin, cause, and nature of the problem. That was my purpose in formulating and implementing this study. I became aware of the issue of singlehood while attending the Groves Conference on Marriage and the Family in Dubrovnik, Yugoslavia, in 1975. It was in a session on singlehood that I heard Peter Stein, author of the book *Single*, say that singles were America's largest minority group.[3] Upon returning home, I checked the census data and found blacks overrepresented among singles. Obviously, it was a subject which required further serious investigation.

To embark on the study I sought out a female collaborator—to balance my perspective with the female view. Having helped me develop the strategy and formulate the questionnaire, she was forced to drop out by her demanding schedule as an administrator, professor, lecturer and wife. We had decided to base the study on interviews, a national questionnaire, personal observation and the published relevant data and literature. A combination of these measures was necessary since one alone would not be sufficient. With only a small research grant from the Graduate Program in sociology at the University of California and my own personal funds, there were limitations in the scope of the study. Fortunately, the interest of many blacks was translated into a very generous amount of help and cooperation.

Specifically, an open-ended questionnaire was developed and sent off to key people who were asked to distribute it to unmarried blacks between 25 and 45 years old, with at least four years of college that were living in a metropolitan area. Out of 1,500 questionnaires distributed, approximately 400 were completed and returned. I and two trained interviewers, a male and female, conducted one hundred in-depth interviews. In addition, I visited some of the cities with large black populations and talked to people about black single life-styles in cities not visited. I had the advantage of having lived in Los Angeles, Detroit, Minneapolis-St. Paul, Nashville, Washington, D.C. and Jackson, Mississippi. To supplement these measures, I also talked to a number of black and white professionals who worked with singles. The author of a study of white singles, Peter Stein, was particularly helpful in sensitizing me to the similarities and contrasts between white and black singles.

All of the personal interviews were conducted in what is known as the Bay Area, the most prominent city in it being San Francisco. It is a metropolitan area of around 4.1 million people with blacks composing about 437,000 of its total population. The greatest concentration of blacks are in the cities of Oakland, San Francisco, Richmond and Berkeley. Its middle class black community is smaller, proportionally, than in such cities as Atlanta, Washington, D.C. and Los Angeles. Here one finds a more liberal ethos, especially in Berkeley and San Francisco, than in other large cities of America. San Francisco is also the only major city where the majority of the population is unmarried.

Establishing contacts for the personal interviews was relatively easy. Despite my earlier comments about the isolation of the black elites, they are in certain ways a closely connected group. In any group of ten middle class blacks, it is possible to find a mutual acquaintance. Many of them went to the same college or know each other through social or professional contacts. We used the referral system to recruit interviewees. Starting off with our personal friends, the names of their friends were solicited and contacted. The interest in the study was so great that some people asked if they could be interviewed. The self-administered questionnaires often were snapped up like free tickets to a jazz concert. We distributed them at conferences, lectures, parties, etc., any place where black singles congregated. As a result, our sample approximates the universe of middle class black singles.

The interview process was of interest in itself. When it commenced, only the male interviewer and I were involved. He was 28 and single; a Ph.D. candidate in psychology. Our first interviewees were all women. The interviews reflected certain dynamics of male-female relationships in general. Some women assumed we were not serious about doing any kind of study but were using this as a way "to get over." As a result a number of them cancelled out and a few insisted on meeting in neutral places like restaurants or their office. In most cases we met in their home. Each one I interviewed offered me wine, sometimes cheese, and in a few instances invited me to stay for dinner (an offer I always declined). All the homes were immaculate and the women fashionably dressed. A few of them were openly flirtatious and seductive. One woman, dressed in a skimpy outfit, never took her piercing brown eyes off me during the entire interview. Some of them were very hostile and wary.

A similar situation might have developed if our female interviewer had interviewed male singles. However, she was assigned only to female subjects in order to determine if the gender of the interviewer differentiated the responses to our questions. A careful reading of the interview data indicates that the skill of the interviewer, not gender, is the important variable. Many of the interviews were quite painful for the subjects, as they were forced to relive traumatic experiences and focus on their situation. At one point I had to take a brief hiatus from doing them because they were taking up to five hours, and I was emotionally drained after nine straight hours of listening to and empathizing with two subjects.

On the other hand the men I interviewed were considerably less accessible and cooperative. Unlike the women, they insisted on being interviewed in their office. Many were very paranoid about the purposes of the study and were less than open in their answers. A well-known local social scientist, who was head of an organization engaged in several research projects, was very arrogant and hostile in refusing to be interviewed. We had been forced to make an extra effort to personally interview men, since there was almost an 8 to 2 ratio of women over men returning the self-administered questionnaires.

In addition to the above, I visited a number of places where singles were known to gather. As a departure from my habitual solitary life, I solicited and accepted invitations to house parties. My purpose was not to initiate a new life-style but to make a systematic observation of who went to these places and the kind of interaction that took place in them. I made it a point to strike up conversations with many of the participants. As a result of this study, I broadened many of my contacts in this elite black community. Since I am an academic person, our paths may never have crossed in the normal course of events. Although some of the analysis and interpretation that follows may seem a bit harsh—even negative— most people were quite simpatico with me and their responses were, in the main, the most honest ones they could muster or handle. As a member of the group being studied, there is little solace for me in the quandary we are in, except to hope that it will be a temporary phase in our lives.

All of the quotations and case histories cited come from the interviews or questionnaires unless otherwise identified. I have not used the real names of any person involved and have changed other details if it would in any way reveal the identity of the study's participants. Most of the respondents are women, which reflects the fact that the majority of black singles are women. The data were collected between 1975 and 1979.

This chapter outline describes, in brief, the contents of the book. Chapter one deals with the demographic characteristics of the black singles population, that is, age, sex, region, income, and so forth. In chapter two, we focus on where black singles meet, how they encounter each other, and what types of individuals they meet in certain settings. The third chapter discusses the practice of dating, its changing form and dynamics. Problems unique to random dating are delineated.

Chapter four will examine how singles feel about commitment and marriage, what their expectations are, and their past experiences in handling this question. The fifth chapter analyzes how sex is handled, or avoided, by both men and women, the pattern of sexual behavior, attitudes toward it, and its role in the singles' life style.

In chapter six, the role of friends, both of the same sex and the opposite sex, in the life of black singles will be viewed. What are the positive and negative elements in opposite sex friendships? Are the same sex friendships an equally compensating relationship for romantic involvement? Crossing the color line (chapter seven) will be an examination of the increasing practice of interracial dating, how black males and females view it, the reasons for it, and its dynamic and problematic aspects. The chapter on single parents involves a study of their unique situation and the problems of having children and trying to participate in the dating game. In the alternative life styles chapter we look at how some individuals cope with singlehood via a career orientation, homosexuality, cohabitation, single parenthood, polygyny, and so forth. The final chapter sums up the problems as well as the benefits of singlehood. Finally, we look at the future direction of this phenomenon.

NOTES

1. U.S. Bureau of the Census, Current Population Reports, Series P-20, *Marital Status and Living Arrangements, March 1978* (Washington, D.C.: U.S. Government Printing Office, 1979), p. 1.

2. Approximately 21 percent of black men and women 18 to 24 years old are presently enrolled in college. Cf. U.S. Bureau of the Census, *The Social and Economic Status of the Black Population in the United States: An Historical View, 1790-1978* (Washington, D.C.: U.S. Government Printing Office, 1979), p. 86.

3. Peter Stein, *Single* (Englewood Cliffs, N.J.: Prentice-Hall, 1976).

The World of
of
Black Singles

Single and Black in America   1

A decade ago our society was caught up in debating the validity of traditional marriage, and more especially, in debating the roles of women in marriage. It was a period in our history when alternative life-styles to traditional marriage were receiving a great deal of media coverage. "To live a carefree single life, being true only to one's self" seemed to be the popular philosophy of the day. Whatever we may think about this period and related concerns about the family, there is little question that our views and even theoretical precepts have been altered. Until that time the sociological explanation of marriage and family life within this society had been a fairly standard and predictable justification of the nuclear family and of its relationship to the larger social order. Furthermore, emphasis was placed on a number of well-defined functions that were attributed to marriage and the resulting nuclear family unit. George Murdock explained that marriage was that structure through which relationships were established and normalized.[1] Others with similar views included Malinowski who viewed marriage as being a universally accepted means through which parenthood was legitimated.[2] Spiro also followed in this same tradition by asserting that the nuclear family is universal—that regardless of the outward structure, the essence of all families is nuclear.[3]

Others viewed marriage and family life as being rather "fixed" in its relationship to the larger social order. Parsons, for example, has attempted to show that the structure of the nuclear family was the best possible in this highly industrialized, urbanized, and complex society.[4] Furthermore, many of these theorists shared the view that any exception to the perceived norm was not simply considered as being different, or even seen as representing acceptable alternatives, but they rather tended to see "exceptions" as being deviant or unacceptable to the normal functioning of society. The major emphasis from both social scientists and from the popular media was that marriage was and should be the goal of most people in our society at some point in their lives. The fact that the American family was faced with a multitude of problems even at that time appeared to have little effect on the popular emphasis that marriage and the nuclear family represented the best of all possible worlds.

Now what is most interesting in this area is the widespread discussion and increasing acceptance of alternative life-styles, and it is within this context that "singlehood" has taken on new dimensions.

Singlehood is, of course, not new. This society and in fact most societies have in some form provided for an acceptable state of being single—usually within some religious context. "Natural" periods of being single also have been acceptable in our society; adolescence, early adulthood, and a period of time following the death of a spouse. It seems clear, however, that few if any provisions were made for singlehood outside of some very clearly defined institutional boundaries. Looking at this in another way, one could say that being single had little or nothing to do with the wishes and desires of the individual, but it was rather a category or status with well-defined parameters. The whole issue of establishing a life-style is a rather recent aspect in American life. Historically the concept of singlehood was not nor could it have been considered.

The whole issue of individual identity is relevant to this discussion. There was, for most societies in the past, no socially accepted identity outside the context of the family or some other prescribed and accepted group; and marriage was, therefore, not merely a union of two individuals, but rather a union of representatives from socially established groups. Again, the issue of free choice was not something to even be considered. It has only been since the transformation of the family from a rural to an urban setting and the combined effects of industrialization and its by-products—the weakening of the economic base of the family and its traditional system of support as well as the increasing advent of leisure time—that we begin to set the stage for the discussion at hand.

Although the times, "they are a changing," it is hard to imagine a society in which large numbers of people reject the idea of marriage. In fact, one can hardly envision such a society being able to perpetuate itself. America's forefathers obviously considered singlehood a threat when they imposed a special tax on men who insisted on remaining bachelors. As we look at contemporary America, we see how far we have come from the days when birth, marriage, and death were the three supreme experiences in life. The proportion of never-married adults in the United States continues to increase. In the 1960s the average American got married between the ages of 20 and 24. In 1977 we found 45 percent of women in that age range still single. In 1960 only 28 percent of women were still unmarried. In 1977 about 64 percent of the men were still bachelors at the age of 24 compared to 53 percent in 1960. It would be easy and comforting to assume that Americans are delaying marriage until a later age. But the proportion of singles has also increased for the 25 to 29 age group. While many will eventually marry, it is conceivable that a large proportion will remain single throughout their entire lives. Moreover, if we consider the number of individuals divorced, separated, or widowed, over 50 million Americans or about a third of all people over the age of 18 are, theoretically, in the state of singleness.[5]

Obviously, attitudes toward marriage have changed in the past twenty years. Although these changes in marital patterns are historically unprecedented among the population at large, the alteration of marital patterns among Afro-Americans is even more pronounced. The increase in black singlehood is consistent with the conventional wisdom that marriage failed to take on an institutional character among blacks. Due to the vicissitudes of slavery, generally, people have believed the formal and legal aspects of marriage were never a strong norm in the Afro-American community. Upon further historical examination, this assumption does not withstand the scrutiny of objective data. It is true that blacks were not allowed to have a legal marriage during the period of slavery. Marriage was, and is, essentially a contractual relationsnip, and the bondsmen were not permitted to consummate legal contracts for any purposes. However, there were relationships between male and female slaves that were recognized socially, if not legally. After slavery ended, the freedmen went to great lengths to have their relationships legalized. A legal marriage was a status symbol to a group deprived of such rights for a couple of centuries. They married in record numbers and the majority of blacks were lodged in nuclear families by the beginning of the twentieth century.[6]

Due to the black middle class's values of culture and respectability, marriage was regarded as essential to the functioning of this group. Failure to marry would undermine the basis of status in the Afro-American community. Marriage and family respectability was the foundation of high status in black culture.[7] One indication of the black value of marriage is the fact that more black women eventually entered into a marital union than their white counterparts. In 1973 among black women 65 years and over, only 3.5 percent had never married in comparison to 6.9 percent of white women.[8]

CHARACTERISTICS OF BLACK SINGLES

In a fifteen-year period the proportion of blacks married and living with a spouse has undergone a steady decline. In 1960, 63 percent of all black men 14 years and over were recorded as married. By 1975 this had dropped to 53 percent. Among similar black women the proportion declined from 60 to 49 percent. In 1978 the proportion of blacks married and living with a spouse was a distinct minority (48 percent). During the age at which most people marry or remain single (35 to 44), 7 percent of black men were still single and 8 percent of black women had never married. A slightly higher proportion of men living in the North and West (12 percent) had never married in comparison to men residing in the South (10 percent). The reverse was true for black women living in the North and West (7 percent) in contrast to women of the South (9 percent).[9]

Among the group of blacks that has the greatest interest to us, (middle-class blacks ages 25 to 45) a clear picture emerges. As the income level rises, so do the number of men who are married and living with their wife. Many are still married to their first wife, and those who have divorced subsequently remarry.[10] On the other hand, black women who have graduated from college are the least likely to have married by the age of thirty.[11] Among those who do marry, especially those who have five or more years of college, their divorce rate is higher, and remarriage rate lower, than black women with less education. Ironically, the black men who are least likely to marry or remarry are those who have less than a high school education.[12] This suggests that marriage rates are a function of education (or status) for black men and women, but in different directions. And it also points out a basic problem for middle-class black women: the men who have a similar status are married, and the largest number of black men in the eligible pool are those who have a much lower status.

An understanding of the history of blacks helps to illuminate the causes of this situation. For a number of years, the proportion of black women graduating from college exceeded the proportion of men. When blacks were still located in the rural South, many black families preferred to send the daughter to college because a wider variety of occupations were open to men. The women, in turn, could only become college-educated schoolteachers or domestic servants. Moreover, because blacks were an agrarian people for much of this century, the sons were kept on the farms and involved in agriculture. Thus, we find that in 1956, 62.4 percent of all the college degrees awarded to blacks were granted to women.[13] As a result in the year 1975 there were 411,000 black women with four years or more of college compared to only 342,000 black males.[14] In the years 1965 to 1975 the gap between male and female college graduates began to narrow. However, in 1977 there were over 84,000 more black women enrolled in college than black men. Among whites there were 672,000 more college men than women.[15]

There are other factors which operate in the world of middle-class black singles. Based on our reading of the data, there is a ratio of two women for every male in this age and class cohort, a much more imbalanced sex ratio than the ratio of female to male college graduates would warrant. The pool of eligible male cohorts is further decreased by a number of other factors. Many college-educated black men marry women with less education. It is estimated that the number of black male homosexuals greatly exceeds that of female lesbians. We know that black men marry outside their race at a rate three times higher than do black women, and most of those men are members of the higher socio-economic level. The greatest number of black men in the eligible pool do not fall in the same class grouping as single women. A strange paradox is that many of the eligible men do not have the opportunity to marry due to their low level of education and income and the women fail to marry because of their high level of education and income.

TYPES OF SINGLES

Singles are not a monolithic grouping. The categories used by the United States Census Bureau are the never-married, the widowed, the separated, and the divorced. Among blacks the largest number (in the 25 to 45 age group) are the separated. Lower-income blacks have long used physical separation as a form of marital dissolution. The expense of a divorce has generally deterred many of them from seeking legal recognition of a union torn asunder. Yet very few middle-class black singles allow a marital disruption to remain in a legal limbo. The time between physical separation and divorce proceedings is typically brief except in those cases where ambivalence about the termination of a marriage exists. Among some men it is often a ploy to ward off pressures for marriage from a future consort. Those who are only separated do not differ greatly from the divorced except for a reduced desire to marry again. Of course, this is contingent on the length of time a person has been separated.

The divorced form the second largest category in our age cohort and may be qualitatively different from the never-married. Usually they are older, and many have children. The number with children is less than might be expected. College-educated black women have the lowest fertility rate of all women. Only 14 percent of black children live in single-parent households that have an annual income of $15,000 and over.[16] Actually, the majority of middle-class black singles were formerly married. It is only within the age range below thirty that most are never married. We would expect to find some difference between the never married and formerly married with children. The divorced persons with children often have attenuated families and carry out most functions, as other nuclear families do. The pull of marriage may not be as great as among childless singles.

Very few of the age and class cohort were among the widowed. While the average black widow loses her husband at an early age,[17] only a very small number of middle-class black singles had lost a spouse through death. The never-married group is much larger in numbers and proportion. Men and women under the age of thirty were more likely to be never married as were women that had five years or more of college.[18] While the tendency of the younger group to remain single is understandable, the high rate of singlehood among the highly educated women is not. Apparently, the higher the educational level of the woman, the more improbable is her chance of marrying. The reverse is true for men. In part we have already explained how this situation emerged. While the proportion of black men with five years or more of college exceeds that of black women, the men have generally married women below their educational level, while the women futilely seek men who are status compatibles. With a very small pool from which to choose, it becomes an elusive goal.

While we consider all individuals who are not married and living with a spouse as part of our singles category, not all of them are single in the same way. Stein, for instance, has developed a four-celled typology containing the features of voluntariness and permanence. His four types of singles are classified as (1) permanent and voluntarily single, (2) permanent, but involuntarily single, (3) temporarily and voluntarily single, and (4) temporarily, involuntarily single.[19] While these categories might be useful as a unit of analysis, they imply certain value assumptions about singlehood which we do not share. Considering that our age cohort of singles is all under the age of 45, to posit their singlehood as a permanent status would seem premature. As for the voluntary nature of their single status, that is impossible to determine. Although a number of our single women reported receiving marriage proposals, the reasons for their refusals appeared to be the rejection of the particular males, not the institution of marriage. The self-conception of our black singles may, instead, reflect their need to avoid cognitive dissonance. When there is an inconsistency between a status and a belief system, the individual may reduce the dissonance by altering her beliefs.[20]

To insure self-acceptance, many single women declare themselves happy and voluntary in their single status.

Our study of black singlehood would be more valid if we used the concept of a singles career. This concept designates objective movements that one may make through the singles world. Within these movements are manifest changes in self-conceptions that accompany relocations in that milieu. The most common, and of greatest interest to us, is the free-floating single. This type of single is totally unattached to any other person and dates randomly, with or without the purpose of seeking a committed relationship. Another type is the individual in an open-coupled relationship. This person has a relatively steady partner, but the relation is open enough to encompass other individuals in a sexual or romantic relationship. Sometimes it is an open-coupled relationship in a unilateral sense with one of the partners deceptively pursuing other parties. Occasionally it is merely the failure to define the relationship explicitly by either of the partners. A related type is that of the closed-coupled relationship.[21] In this case the partners look exclusively to each other for their sexual and affectionate needs. By mutual agreement fidelity is expected and the partners are emotionally bound to each other.

We could call this next group the committed singles. They would be those individuals who are cohabitating in the same household, are engaged to be married, or otherwise have an agreement to establish a permanent relationship. In many ways they do not share the singles life-style which we will study. The cohabitators often maintain the existence of married couples, sans the legal validation. Those committed to a permanent relationship are so emotionally bound to each other that they spend most of their leisure time together and encounter few of the problems that perplex other singles.

Another singles stage through which people may pass (or stop at) is accommodation. There are two types of accommodations; temporary and permanent. In one group of singles (under age 45) the accommodation to their single status may be temporary. They will lead a solitary existence except for friendships. For many women, it can mean refusing all dates and, for men, failing to pursue any heterosexual contacts. Certainly, people in this stage are asexual and cease all sexual activity. Some accommodationists may temporarily adopt an alternative life-style or sublimate through work, school, or religion. The permanent accommodationist will generally be in an older age cohort. We limited our study to singles under the age of 45 because we believed those over that age to be more permanently resigned to their single status. While this demarcation of singles may be disputed, we surely know that they are in the singles world in a very different way. Past the age of 45, many of the women will be widows and do not plan to remarry. Others have been formerly married, have borne children who are now adults, and devote themselves to the grandparent role.

THE PUSH AND PULL TOWARD SINGLEHOOD

People may be temporarily single for a variety of reasons. In his study of white singles, Stein identifies the pushes and pulls towards singlehood and marriage. The pulls would be those positive aspects of singlehood which propel the individual away from marriage. The pushes would be negative forces which force individuals to remain single.[22] While any combination of push and pull factors could maintain a person in the single status, certain ones seem paramount among black singles. First and foremost of the push factors, is the imbalance in the sex ratio and the ramifications thereof. There is an estimated excess of one million women in the black population, resulting in a ratio of 90 males per 100 females. The ratio is even lower in the marriageable years (18 to 35) and in the large cities. Much has been made of the census undercount of black males, and a statistical correction for the undercount places the "real" ratio at 95 males per 100 females.[23] Although the quantity may increase when the correction is made, it hardly compensates for the "quality" of men available. Many of the black men not counted are transient and unemployed and, hence, unacceptable to most of our middle-class black singles.

The imbalance in the sex ratio is due to a number of sociological factors. Young black men have a comparatively high mortality rate, and many are confined to prisons, mental hospitals, and military bases. The higher rate of homosexuality and interracial marriage among black men deducts a large number from the eligible pool. Only the latter two factors are relevant to our middle-class group. Moreover, the sex ratio is subordinate to the class parameters drawn around the eligible pool. Because of their higher level of income, most single black women could choose a mate from the pool of men at the lower socioeconomic level. In the past they did so, but fewer are now inclined to "marry down." For many of them the pool is restricted to those men who are on a comparable or higher status level. Thus, large numbers are pushed into singlehood by the lack of men with the requisite characteristics.

Another push factor, linked to the sex ratio, is the inability to find a compatible mate. Because black men are able to pick and choose, they may act more cavalier toward women than they might otherwise be inclined to. Certainly the men have the option to screen out certain types of women among the abundant number in the eligible pool. Among those most likely to be screened out are the very assertive, independent women, and the physically unattractive. Of course, the standards which women set for a mate may be unrealistic, given the quantity and quality of the available pool. Too often the attributes desired in a mate are notably absent in most men. It is typical of women to desire a sensitive, supportive, and affectionate mate. Men, however, are socialized into a self-conception that values success, leadership, and sexual performance. The incongruity between child socialization and adult needs will continue to present a problem.

There could be any number of forces that operate as a pull toward singlehood. Marriage, in general, can mean sacrifices, compromises, and sharing, which are anathema to many single individuals. The tendency to avoid those acts might best be summed up as the culture of narcissism.[24] It is the triumph of individual needs over group prerequisites. As modern-day capitalism shifted its emphasis from production to consumption, materialist values were promoted by encouraging the pursuit of an individualistic life-style. The virtues of individual materialism were inconsistent, to some, with the tedium and responsibility associated with marriage. As blacks ascended into the affluent middle class, many acquired those same values. The success of a black liberation movement, based on group unity, turned into a cult of the self. One sage observer noted:

A movement whose strength had been its non-materialism, a movement fueled by the black church and rooted in Southern folkways and national black culture was turned into its opposite by America's concessions. . . . In the scramble nearly everyone was dancing to the Isley Brothers' tune, 'Do your own thing, do what you want to do' . . . pursuing his or her own interest to the exclusion of all else.[25]

How many of our black singles succumbed to the materialist temptations of middle-class America, we do not know. The imbalanced sex ratio makes it difficult to sort out the voluntary and involuntary single women. Certainly, it is clear that many of our black singles have determined that marriage, and the commitment and responsibility it entails, is incompatible with their pursuit of the good life. Not every black single, of course, is devoted only to self-satisfaction. Many will continue to involve themselves with social movements and civic activities because they have the resources and time to do so. Others visit the children's home society regularly or spend time, money, and emotions on nieces, nephews, and cousins. Some take under their wing a little sister or brother via the Big Brother and Sister Associations. It is incumbent upon us to note that participating in these activities is confined to only a minority of middle-class black singles.

THE CASE FOR AND AGAINST MARRIAGE

One of the biggest push factors in singlehood is the fear of an unhappy marriage. Although there is some evidence that marriage is an unhealthy institution for many who inhabit it, especially women, Jessie Bernard cites studies which reveal that fewer single than married women show mental health impairment. She also notes that more married women report themselves as happy than single women do.[26] Other studies confirm the stress marriage places on some persons. One investigation found that of all the possible sources of stress, marriage and family problems rank as the primary stress inducer.[27] At the same time, other studies show the family to be the greatest source of satisfaction to Americans. Again, the suicide rates, which were formerly lower for married women, are beginning to be higher than those of single women.[28] Studies continue to show that the higher the income of women in the labor force, the greater the likelihood that they are unmarried.[29]

Obviously, marriage is a mixed blessing for some people. When one views the studies of black attitudes toward marriage, it appears to be more of a curse. From the onset of adolescence, many black men express a desire to shun the institution. Black women are more likely to express their dislike for it after having experienced marriage. Available research consistently shows the black housewife to be more dissatisfied with her marriage than her white counterpart.[30] Much of this disenchantment is due to the complications of racism and poverty that impact on marital happiness. As income rises, so does marital happiness. Given a divorce rate twice as high as whites, the distaste for marriage among blacks is understandable.

Although the partisans of singlehood have pointed to the negative impact of marriage on mental health, there is another side to the argument. The available data on rates of mental disorder (as measured by admissions to mental institutions or outpatient psychiatric care) show single people to have higher rates of mental illness. This is true for both blacks and whites, men and women.[31] The National Center for Health Statistics found that the overall measures of health status indicate that married persons had fewer health problems than non-married persons.[32] In one of the most extensive and thorough investigations of the impact of marital status on health, Dr. James Lynch discovered that people at every age who live alone have death rates two to three times higher than those of married individuals. Among non-whites, for instance, in the critical ages between 25 and 50, twice as many who are divorced or widowed die from hypertensive heart disease as married persons of comparable ages. His conclusion is that individuals who live alone are more susceptible to physical and emotional illnesses because they continuously lack the tranquilizing influence of human companionship during life's stresses.[33]

Marriage, moreover, is nothing more than a contract between two consenting adults to work together toward the achievement of mutually defined goals. It was not originally created as an institution designed to provide personal happiness. Until the twentieth century the family was an economic unit in which the arm of production was lodged. Along with the group production of goods and services came the reproduction of children, sexual access, and socialization. Love and happiness were afterthoughts which came to full expression in the twentieth century. Those qualities have to be sought and worked out by a conscious and joint effort. The imperfections of most humans will forever make their achievement a challenging task. Marriage is the most intricate arrangement humans can enter into, particularly since the guidelines of tradition are no longer present. As two sage students of the subject concluded: "Perhaps many disappointments could be avoided if people only realized that institutions and life-styles are only as good as the people involved. Happiness and satisfaction are not determined by institutions or life-styles, but rather they come from within individuals and depend on the quality of relationships between people."[34]

THE RISE OF FEMINISM

Feminism as an organized social movement has attracted very few black women. But its impact on attitudes toward the woman's role has been noticeable and is increasing. In part it is responsible for the reluctance to marry. Whatever the virtues of marriage, it is evident that it is an institution that favors men. It is typically women who bear the brunt of the demands of marriage. They are the ones who must subordinate their career mobility to the males, who must carry most of the burden of housework and child care, and who have their friendships, movements, and activities confined by their marital status. Although some black single women speak to the need to have an egalitarian marriage, it is a demand that can hardly be placed before black men who operate as buyers in a buyers' market. Ergo, some single women refuse to consider joining an institution where their needs have a low priority.

Other signs of feminism are more visible. A number of black women's organizations devoted to women's issues have been formed in recent years. Some are more feminist in ideology than others. One group of black women issued a manifesto that declared sexism to be a destructive and crippling force within the black community.[35] The book *Black Macho and the Myth of the Super-*

woman by Michelle Wallace contained a strident and acrimonious attack on black male sexism.[36] It attracted a large black female audience as did the play "For Colored Girls Who Have Considered Suicide" by Ntozake Shange. While not a feminist play, the negative portrayal of black males has an ad hominem appeal to its largely female audience. These rumblings of feminism have a different origin in their black female proponents. Rather than being a protest against black male political and economic domination, which is largely nonexistent, they reflect, instead, tensions in interpersonal relationships. Even a black female writer felt compelled to assert:

The problem is that the personal pain which forms the subtext of many white and now black feminist pronouncements, a pain which is being experienced most acutely in the area of male/female interaction, has social origins that have little or nothing to do with sexual politics. People are in pain because their personal lives are being ravaged as the warfare of the marketplace increasingly filters into the social order.[37]

Hard-core feminism represents a no-win situation for black women. If it is full political and economic equality they want, it will have to be granted by the ruling elite of this country, a group composed exclusively of white males. It will hardly be granted before the grievances of white women are redressed and their sheer numbers make such a possibility unlikely. Few, indeed, expect black women to achieve equality independent of the race as a whole. Since problems in male/female interaction fuel the feminist thrust among black women, their stridency in attacking black males is hardly calculated to net them much gain in this area. It is conceivable, of course, that their protests may generate some constructive dialogue between the sexes and sensitize black males to their needs. A more likely response will be defensiveness, anger, and wariness on the part of black men. Many may, as currently is the practice, use their vast array of options to exclude women of a feminist orientation from the pool of eligible mates. Subsequently the political and economic inequality of black women will remain since black males have little control over its distribution, and the problems of interpersonal relationships will continue by default. In the words of Jean Carey Bond, "To the extent that feminists are promoting the very conflict between men and women that they profess to abhor by peddling perspectives which obscure the socio-economic causes of male/female antagonism, the movement is functioning more as a part of the problem than as an instrument of the solution."[38]

Black women are, of course, the victims of sexist values and practices emanating from within and outside the black community. It is, however, a qualitatively different brand of sexism than that faced by white women. There is less inequality of income between black women and men. In general, black women earn 80 percent of the income that black men earn (white women only earn 56 percent of the income white males earn). College-educated black women actually have a higher median income than college-educated white women and earn 90 percent of the median income of college-educated black males.[39] Still, in the complex interplay of racism and sexism, black women are placed in the intractable dilemma of professional success and interpersonal failure. Increasingly they are becoming victims of a social system that rewards their professional skills in the work world but penalizes them for their achievements in the dating and marriage marketplace.

SINGLEHOOD AND THE BLACK COMMUNITY

Those who support singlehood as a viable alternative to a monogamous marriage appear to be misreading the relationship of the individual to his/her culture. The family is the keystone of social organization in most societies. In the black community it is largely the only institution in which the hopes and values of blacks are anchored. To view singlehood as a matter of personal choice is to ignore the family's vital role in the maintenance of a cohesive cultural entity. Whether individuals marry or not may not be the critical issue but rather in what kind of structure can certain vital functions essential to a group's survival be most expeditiously and effectively carried out. Perforce, singlehood as an ideological preference represents the primacy of individual needs over cultural prerequisites. Hence, at some point it will be incumbent upon us to do a cost-benefit analysis of singlehood as a way of life.

Some delineation of the causes of singlehood and class variations is necessary for an understanding of its implications to the black community. The causes of singlehood may be dichotomized into those which represent ideological preferences and cases which reflect structural restraints. Much of black singlehood among the lower classes is due to structural restraints. The societal destruction of lower-class black men is so massive that the women of that class are left with few desirable mate choices. These women, however, do not pursue a life of self-indulgence. Most marry and bear children which they raise with the support of the absent father and an extended family system. In every sense of the word they are carrying out the vital functions of a family. Their attenuated structure, however, prevents them from maximizing the advantages of the nuclear family.

The disadvantages of the single-parent family are reflected in its impact on class mobility. When lower-class black families were intact, the pooling of resources through the joint efforts of the husband and wife enabled many of them to increase their class's life chances. Because of the decline in the nuclear family unit, that coping technique is not as available. In 1978 black families accounted for 10 percent of all families and only 7 percent of all married-couple families.[40] This decrease is responsible in part for the increase in the gap between black and white family income. From 1970 to 1973 black family income declined from 61 percent to 58 percent of white family income, due primarily to the reduction in the number of blacks married and living with a spouse. As further evidence of the monetary value of the nuclear family, the U.S. Bureau of the Census reports that young black husband-wife families (husband under 35 years of age) in the Northeast and West had achieved income parity with their white counterparts.[41]

Changes in their marital patterns will have to await larger changes in the social structure. On the other hand, many of the middle-class black singles maintain their status via an ideological preference. A troublesome singlehood is preferred to compromising their standards for a mate. The implications of this "choice" contains some serious implications for the black community. A crucial function of the family is the bearing and rearing of children. College-educated black women have the lowest fertility rate of all groups in the United States and most of the middle-class singles are childless.[42] While blacks as a whole have a higher fertility rate than whites, the bulk of those children are being born out-of-wedlock and increasingly to teenage mothers. The black middle-class is not even replacing itself through reproduction. In sum, this group has defaulted on the time-honored task of educating and socializing children. Whether singlehood is a matter of individual choice or not, its ramifications must be borne collectively. The main purpose of this study, however, is to examine the dynamics of the black single life-style.

NOTES

1. George Murdock, *Social Structure* (New York: MacMillan, 1949).

2. Bronislaw Malinowski, Parenthood, the basis of social structure, in *The New Generation*, eds. V. Calverton and Schmalhaven (New York: Macaulay, 1930), pp. 113-168.

3. Melford Spiro, Is the family universal? *American Anthropologist* 56 (October 1954): 839-846.

4. Talcott Parsons and Robert Bales, *Family, Socialization and Interaction Process* (Glencoe, Ill.: The Free Press, 1955).

5. U.S. Bureau of the Census, *Marital Status and Living Arrangements: March 1977* (Washington, D.C.: U.S. Government Printing Office, 1978).

6. Herbert Gutman, *The Black Family in Slavery and Freedom 1750-1925* (New York: Pantheon, 1976).

7. St. Clair Drake and Horace Cayton, *Black Metropolis* (Chicago: University of Chicago Press, 1945).

8. U.S. Bureau of the Census, *Marital Status and Living Arrangements: March 1973* (Washington, D.C.: U.S. Government Printing Office, 1974).

9. U.S. Bureau of the Census, *Marital Status and Living Arrangements: March 1977*.

10. Paul C. Glick and Karen Mills, *Black Families: Marriage Patterns and Living Arrangements* (Atlanta: Atlanta University, 1974), p. 9.

11. Alan Bayer, College impact on marriage, *Journal of Marriage and the Family* 34 (November 1972): 600-18.

12. Glick and Mills, *Black Families*.

13. Jean Noble, *The Negro Woman College Graduate* (New York: Columbia University Press, 1956), p. 108.

14. U.S. Bureau of the Census, *Money, Income and Poverty Status in 1975 of Families and Persons in the United States and the West Region, by Divisions and States* (Washington, D.C.: U.S. Government Printing Office, 1978), pp. 21-22.

15. Number of blacks attending college triples in decade, *The Washington Post*, June 10, 1978, p. A1.

16. U.S. Bureau of the Census, *The Social and Economic Status of the Black Population in the United States: An Historical View 1790-1978* (Washington, D.C.: U.S. Government Printing Office, 1978), p. 108.

17. Ruth Gossett, Black widows, in *The Sexually Oppressed*, eds. H. and J. Gochros (New York: Association Press, 1977), pp. 84-95.

18. U.S. Bureau of the Census, *Marital Status and Living Arrangements: March 1977*.

19. Peter Stein, A typology of singlehood (Paper presented at the National Society for Women in Sociology Meeting, San Francisco, August 1978).

20. Leon Festinger, *A Theory of Cognitive Dissonance* (New York: Harper and Row, 1957).

21. The terms open and closed coupled relationship is borrowed from Bell and Weinberg's typology of homosexual relationships. Cf. Alan Bell and Martin Weinberg, *Homosexualities* (New York: Simon and Schuster, 1978).

22. Peter Stein, *Single* (Englewood Cliffs, New Jersey: Prentice-Hall, 1976), p. 65.

23. U.S. Bureau of the Census, *The Social and Economic Status of the Black Population*, p. 16.

24. Christopher Lasch, *The Culture of Narcissism* (New York: Norton, 1979).

25. William Strickland, The rise and fall of black political culture: or how blacks became a minority, *Monthly Report of the Institute of the Black World*, May/June 1979, p. 3.

26. Jessie Bernard, *The Future of Marriage* (New York: Bantam Books, 1973), pp. 28-58.

27. Norval Glenn, The contribution of marriage to the psychological well-being of males and females, *Journal of Marriage and the Family* 37 (August 1975): 594-599.

28. Jesus Velasco-Rice and Elizabeth Mynko, Suicide and marital status: a changing relationship, *Journal of Marriage and the Family* 35 (May 1973): 239-244.

29. Elizabeth Havens, Women, work and wedlock: A note on female patterns in the United States, in *Changing Women in a Changing Society*, ed. J. Huber, (Chicago: University of Chicago Press, 1973), pp. 213-19.

30. Robert Blood and Donald Wolfe, *Husbands and Wives* (Glencoe, Ill.: The Free Press, 1960); Karen Renne, Correlates of dissatisfaction with marriage, *Journal of Marriage and the Family* 32 (February 1970): 54-67.

31. Roger Bastide, *The Sociology of Mental Disorder* (London: Routledge and Kegan Paul, 1972), pp. 154-55; M. Harvey Brenner, *Mental Illness and the Economy* (Cambridge, Mass.: Harvard University Press, 1973), pp. 11-81.

32. Unwed healthier than married, *The San Francisco Examiner*, 20 June 1976, p. 1.

33. James J. Lynch, *The Broken Heart* (New York: Basic Books, 1977), pp. 42, 52, 53.

34. Nick Stinnett and Craig Birdsong, *The Family and Alternate Life Styles* (Chicago: Nelson-Hall, 1978), p. 204.

35. Statement of the National Black Feminist Organization, 1973.

36. Michelle Wallace, *Black Macho and the Myth of the Superwoman* (New York: Dial Press, 1978).

37. Jean Carey Bond, Two views of "Black Macho and the Myth of the Super-woman," *Freedomways*, First quarter 1979, p. 20.

38. Ibid.

39. Cf. Diane K. Lewis, A response to inequality: Black women, racism and sexism, *Signs: A Journal of Women in Culture and Society*, Winter 1977, pp. 339-61.

40. Single-woman American households are increasing, census reports, *The Washington Post*, 14 August 1978, p. A24.

41. U.S. Bureau of the Census, *The Social and Economic Status of the Black Population*, pp. 26-27.

42. U.S. Bureau of the Census, *The Social and Economic Status of the Black Population*, p. 129.

Where the Action Is 2

Where to meet a potential mate poses a problem for many black singles. Unlike whites, they do not have a network of institutions which they inhabit and control. A young, single, white woman is in a more desirable position. In most large cities, she has the advantage of numbers on her side. During the course of her normal activity, she will meet fairly large numbers of eligible men. And, because there are more white male college graduates than females, many of the men she meets will be of an equal or higher socioeconomic status. On the other hand, the professional black woman faces a shortage of men on her status level and may not come into contact very often with suitable men. Due to racial tokenism in hiring practices, it is not uncommon for blacks to work in isolation. In certain cities they may live in isolation. Since work contacts often form the basis for social relations, they must confront the problem of where to go to meet a potential mate.

This was not always the case. As a cohesive community in the South, contacts between the sexes were easily made. Racial and class segregation facilitated the congregation of blacks from every walk of life. Frequently men and women made their initial contact in the first grade of the public school. However, our black singles face a different set of circumstances. Many of them left their hometowns to attend college. After graduation they followed the jobs to larger cities away from their close friends and relatives. As they moved to these cities, some settled in middle-class black enclaves, and others were dispersed throughout different sections of the city. One may hear that all the blacks in a particular city are organized into separate cliques and are not hospitable to strangers. What this means is that the earlier black settlers in a city have formed stable friendships based on common interests, similar life experiences and longevity in the same place. Still, this only begs the question: where's the action?

RETURN TO THE SOURCE

Traditional meeting places for blacks still exist. Generally they were institutions which had other functions besides pairing off eligible men and women. The most common and oldest social center was the black church. Before any other institution emerged as a source of social activity, the church dominated the social life of most blacks. It was the one place where blacks congregated in a period when white facilities were off-limits. A black journalist reminisced about the importance of the black church:

It was a time when the "social life" of kids centered on the church and, as you grew older and started "noticing girls," the "most popular churches" were those which attracted the prettiest teenage girls and had the best programs for young people. You were really on some time if you, and your pals, got to "walk home" a popular girl after evening church activities. The fact that you might have to wait hours to get home on the old "J" streetcar, or some other means of public transportation meant nothing if you got to hold hands on the way home.[1]

As a meeting place the church may continue to be significant in the rural South and still has some significance in the urban South. However, in the main, many young black people wrote off the black church as a useful institution in the black community about fifteen years ago. In a visit to some black churches, we found most of the congregation to be middle-aged, with a sex ratio of 80 percent female to 20 percent male among the adults. The men generally were over 50 years-of-age and held some sort of office in the church. The young people who were in attendance tended to be either female, married men with their families, or single men who were rumored to be gay. Researchers on the black church report that a greater mix of young black men and women can be found in those institutions that are somewhat secular in nature and devoted to social action.[2]

Another important source of romantic partners for black people was the school. Until the desegregation of schools in the sixties, most blacks attended the very few schools set aside for them. Since black singles in this study have already gone through college, the schools obviously did not provide a mate for many of them. According to one psychologist, they missed the best opportunity for finding a mate they will ever have. Bernie Zilbergeld declares:

> They find they already had the best place to meet. It was high school or college. Things go downhill after that. One problem is that as you get older, over age 22, you start to develop your own sense of who you are, what you can live with, and what you're prepared to deal with. You reduce your pool of eligibles. In high school or college, almost anyone will do. As you get older, you're more selective.[3]

Of course, some of the singles studied did find mates in college and were subsequently divorced or the relationship terminated. College would seem the ideal place to meet a potential partner. It is the one place where most individuals are single, belong to the same class, and can meet easily in a nonthreatening situation. Still, the statistics show that black women who graduate from predominantly black colleges are the most likely to reach the age of 30 without having married.[4] One reason is that the sex ratio at many black colleges is very imbalanced. At Tougaloo College in 1976, for instance, there were six female students for every one male student. Another factor is the different maturity level of the sexes. Black women often complain that the men, even those a few years older, are simply not ready to take on any responsibility or to make a commitment. More recently, at predominantly white colleges, black college students of the opposite sex do not come into contact with each other. The women continue to major in the humanities, education, and liberal arts field, while the men have tended to go into business and the physical and natural sciences. On some campuses the black student organizations that existed in the early seventies are defunct or their meetings are not well attended.

Some of the surveyed black singles are still in graduate school. But this is a different situation. Many have returned to school after a long absence and are much older. While there may be more black men in college on the graduate level, most are married or living with a woman. They, moreover, may not be looking for or want women with the same level of education or in the same discipline. One person, a 34-year-old male doctor, believes that women seeking more education were putting themselves at a further disadvantage in finding a husband. According to him

Many of the women in our medical school chose to go into medicine because they couldn't find a husband. Once they get a medical degree, it's even harder to find one. Where can a black female M.D. find a black man that won't be threatened by her status, or more importantly, where can she find one of comparable status who will accept the demands on her time? Now, we have them coming back for residency training or to become specialists in some field. Getting more training just puts them deeper in the hole.

While the assumptions of this man could be regarded as sexist, since they are based on the theory that securing a husband and not an education is the main objective of black women, they still reflect the dilemma of many black women who want a career and a husband. Undoubtedly some black women pursue a graduate degree in lieu of a husband and willingly admit to doing so. But not everyone is in agreement with the thesis that further education hinders a woman's chance of finding a husband. Another view is held by this 31-year-old female college professor:

That may be true statistically but not individually. For example, that individual woman may go to law school and have classmates who are primarily men, provide herself with a higher income with more money to adorn herself and travel. The nature of her job would expose her to a different circle of friends and may provide her with more contact with potential marriage partners than she would have had in an elementary classroom as a teacher.

Despite her Pollyanish view, large numbers of black women exit from graduate school with "nothing more than a degree." Those who wanted something else will have to look on. Once they are out of college an old standby for black folks is the house party. The purely social party may be an effective medium for meeting eligible people, but it is one that has to be negotiated with care. Parties have some value, especially for blacks, because they bring people of a similar status (for example, socioeconomic and marital) together in an atmosphere of congeniality. Ostensibly individuals go there to have fun, but it is the one place which is more oriented toward meeting members of the opposite sex than any other outside of the singles bar. Parties are basically for people who are free-floating singles and feeling out the market. Those who are in committed relationships tend not to be frequent party goers, and married couples generally socialize with other marrieds.

Singles are able to meet each other at parties; the problem is one of not meeting people with similar motivations and traits. Parties are often events that do not allow for assessing a person's character and intentions. The whole atmosphere of parties is superficial, where interaction between men and women is seductive and a play on emotions, the attraction of dress, and personality. Depending on who decided upon the guest list and other contingencies, the sex ratio at a party may be awkwardly skewed toward one sex, pitting the excess members of one gender into competition for the available dance or sexual partners. A common scene at parties is the lineup of the sexes on opposite sides of the room until captivating music or a heavy consumption of libations breaks the ice. Meeting and talking to a potential mate requires certain social skills which people may or may not possess. Women may have to wait to be approached, and men have to know how to do the approaching. Lately people are beginning to complain that the distance between the sexes is never broached, and the sexes remain segregated behind the facade of aloofness and shyness.

We might raise the question of who goes to parties and their reasons for doing so. Many women go on occasion because they are without a man, and it is better than staying home alone. Men, with an abundance of women to choose from, do not need to go to a party to find a female companion. Those who go are in many cases men who enjoy the thrill of nightlife, drinking, drugs, and chasing women. Or so report the women who meet them in such situations. A 31-year-old female social worker said:

Most of the men I date I meet in work-related activities, usually in civic and/or professional activities. Since we have a basis for our relationship other than strictly social, these persons generally remain friends. The majority of relationships I've had with men whom I've met in strictly social settings (parties) usually don't last. Most were near dilettantes, both on and off the job. I figure that a man who is successful in life doesn't have that much time or interest in going to parties. You have to meet them elsewhere.

The one exception to her generalization may be the "nonsocial" party, where a group of people in similar occupations or with similar interests come together primarily for conversation. These parties often lack the awkwardness of the social parties where dancing and music dominate the scene. The sexes intermingle easier and conversation initially centers around the concerns of their profession and group. Men are more skillful at initiating dialogue about such matters, and women do not perceive their approach as a "come on." It is a comfortable setting in which to meet other people and not feel driven to "come on" to the opposite sex. The disadvantages of this setting for black singles are that such gatherings tend to be few and far between, their professions are often dominated by whites, there are few blacks to meet at such events, and single black males are rarely abundant in these contexts. What is lacking in quantity, however, may be more than compensated for by the caliber of person they meet.

PUBLIC PLACES

When singles first arrive in a city, there are few places to meet other eligible singles. For those without any social contacts, singles bars and discos are readily available. This is a relatively recent meeting place for middle-class blacks. Discos were not in vogue until the last five years, and singles bars for blacks were nonexistent. Bars existed, but they were patronized primarily by men. Now we find a network of black-oriented singles bars exist in cities such as Los Angeles, New York, Chicago, and Washington, D.C. It must be noted that there are salient differences between black and white singles bars. Blacks, for example, rarely refer to their places as singles bars; they are just places where middle-class blacks can go and relax with each other. While it certainly happens more often than some may admit, one-night stands with women encountered in such settings are not common. Although singles meet in such places, and contacts are initiated, they are not places of sexual congress.

One of the problems with participation in the bar scene is the presence of "undesirable" elements. To reduce or eliminate their presence, blacks have established the membership club. Requiring individuals to have certain qualifications and pay a membership fee is a form of quality control. One such club has gained national recognition among blacks. Known as Foxtrappe, it is located in Washington, D.C. The connotation of the term, Foxtrappe, in black parlance implies it is a place to meet attractive young women. A visit confirms that some of Washington's most attractive professional black women frequent the place. We can assume that the majority of them are single, although the owners claim that slightly more than half of the female membership is married.[5] On any given night a large number of those in attendance are not members. Due to the heavy travel in and out of Washington and the tourist attraction of the club, it serves a transient clientele.

Singles bars are a last resort for many women. If they want to meet a man in order to form a serious relationship, the singles bar is the least likely place to find one. Yet most women go to singles bars for that purpose. There seems to be no reason for an attached woman to frequent a singles bar. The men, however, attend for other reasons. Estimates are that nearly half the men who go to singles bars are married.[6] Many of them are there only to see whether they still have what it takes to attract women. The single men are there to try for a quick sexual conquest. Because some of the women are very lonely, a man's chances of success are better than in other settings. If the male meets a woman whose objective matches his own, a sexual liaison may ensue. Otherwise games of various kinds are played. Some of the women may only want to solicit free drinks from male patrons. Others may simply want to test their sex appeal by the number of men who approach them. As a 29-year-old male businessman reported, "I've found the worst places to make friends are at the so-called singles bar and parties. The people are just too plastic, the situation forces them to be."

Discos are a slightly different story. They are not solely a source of singles pairing. Many people attend, sometimes as a couple, just for the fun of it all. The composition of the participants is diverse. Probably the ones most blacks frequent are multiracial and contain different social classes. The high volume of the music precludes any serious conversation between men and women. Emphasis, then, has to be placed on physical factors such as clothes, dancing ability, and looks. Discos are a habitat of the younger group of black singles. Still, singles do meet and pair off in such places. After a brief conversation, names and phone numbers are exchanged. In some cases a rendezvous may take place the same night. The success rate of relationships formed in such arenas are predictable, and low, considering the circumstances under which people meet.

Meeting people in public places gives rise to problems endemic to them, the most serious problem being the presence of pretenders on the scene. Since these people are met "on the spot," there is no independent verification of basic facts about them. Men are more likely to be pretenders, although women are increasingly resorting to this ruse. A common pretense is that of being unattached when, in reality, one may be seriously involved in another relationship. The motivation of male pretenders is generally the desire for sexual variety outside the primary relationship. Women's acts of deception are more complex. Some do it because men have monopolized this practice, and they feel a turnabout is fair play. Others may hide the fact that they are involved elsewhere because they are interested in finding somebody "better" and realize that this revelation could discourage other men. In some cases women have a considerable amount of leisure time because the primary man in their life is either married, too busy, or living in another city.

Male pretenders may deceive women about many facets of themselves. A common tactic is to upgrade their educational or occupational level. The nurses aide becomes a medical doctor, the community college graduate confers upon himself a Ph.D. Other status-enhancing techniques include mentioning close friendships with celebrities and renting a luxury car for the night. We were told about the case of one man who was unemployed. He spent most of his unemployment insurance income on a luxury apartment. His strategy was to tell women that he was an executive with one of the airlines. Most of the women were, themselves, in very prestigious, high-paying occupations. Being a handsome man, about six feet two inches tall, he attracted a lot of women, but he believed his unemployed status would be a disadvantage. Generally, he achieved his goal of sexual conquest and sometimes borrowed money which he never repaid. Eventually he was discovered to be an unemployed, former laundry worker. By that time he had gotten all the market could bear.

Of course, the biggest pretenders are the pseudo-singles, that is, married men. By the estimates of black women, as many as 75 percent of the men found in certain gathering places are married. As a 38-year-old female researcher informed us, "When you go to some of these places and see all these men, you have to wonder why there are so many lonely black women. After asking around, you find out most of them are married. There aren't many opportunities for single blacks to congregate in the same setting. A lot of married men are out looking for companionship, creating problems for single women." Not all of the pseudo-singles are men. There has been a discernible increase in married women seeking to meet men in public places. One man reported meeting a woman three times in different locations and having engaged in rather lengthy conversations before she admitted to being married. Many of the female marrieds are not motivated by the desire to have an extramarital sexual affair, but want to test their sex appeal, socialize with men, or feel out the market for a "better" partner.

There are women who are receptive to the overtures of married men who do not attempt to hide their status. And some women consider them fair game as potential husbands. This attitude can and does pose some problems for the black community. The "liberation" of a married man from his wife and children simply puts another woman into the singles category and renders the children fatherless. It contributes to the feelings of distrust and insecurity about black men in general, and specifically to the feeling that they cannot be counted on to remain faithful to a woman. However, it is typically the single woman who is the loser in an extramarital liaison. One study reveals that the majority of married men (about 80 percent) who have affairs have no intention of leaving their wives.[7] In most cases one- or two-night stands are the longest duration of such affairs. When they last longer the single woman will be subject to all the constraints of such a relationship. Married men often cannot spend much money on her, are unable to take her out in public, leave her alone on holidays, and are irregular or unpredictable about the time they can spend together.

Married men, however, constitute the most successful, and in some ways the most accessible, of black men that single black women encounter. As a 34-year-old female government employee said, "One reason why single women may deal with married men is because if you're lonely, it's 'better than nothing'. Sometimes women don't know a man is married until they are emotionally involved; then it becomes much harder to extricate oneself from the relationship, especially if all else looks dismal." Another woman, a 38-year-old sociologist, took a calculated view of the role of married men in the singles world:

> Whether married men constitute a problem or not depends on how you look at it. Clearly, relationships between married men and single women are fraught with tensions and difficulties, but free-floating married men serve an important social function in a group with an imbalance in the sex ratio. Of course, many feminists and others as well, might call this particular interpretation sexist. But what we're seeing is really nothing more than the operative process of the dialectic and the contradiction that notion implies. The answer to a particular problem contains in its solution the seeds of new conflicts and problems. It's a simple truth we too often forget.

THE ORGANIZATION

Those who wish to avoid the superficiality and pretense of parties, discos, and singles bars can, in many cities, turn to other resources to meet members of the opposite sex. There is a slow but growing trend toward the formation of black singles organizations; groups whose primary purpose is to bring unmarried black men and women together in a convivial setting. We discovered the existence of two such organizations after a black man wrote the following letter to a newspaper, "A black woman, not indifferent, wrote to say that in the two years since her divorce, she has met only a handful of men, and she wants to know where and how to find more companionship. I'm a black man, in my 50s and divorced and I would like to meet this woman."

In response to his query the newspaper suggested that:

Perhaps you, she and others who are seeking social exchange would be interested in checking into "Swinging Singles,"* a predominantly black organization for single people, 23 and up. The group meets the first and third Saturdays of the month for dancing, games, travel, etc. A charge of five dollars per meeting covers food and non-alcoholic beverage.

The newspaper printed the names of two black singles organizations. When we contacted the head of one of them, she explained that her organization had not scheduled any meetings for a number of months and was not planning anything in the near future until they found a building in which to hold their activities. In the ten years of its existence, she claimed eight couples had met their spouse through her organization. When the founder of this organization was contacted, she responded with a curt note saying that she no longer was associated with the singles club. After calling the director of "Swinging Singles," she refused to give any information to us over the phone. Upon receiving a letter written on university stationery, she wrote a friendly note asking us to call again.

When we spoke to her again on the phone, she talked of the problems she had in running a black singles organization.

I am running this club out of the goodness of my heart. I want people to come together and have a good time. We have been in existence since 1971. Many marriages and lasting friendships have occurred during that time. We have ceased our activities lately because of the low attendance at our events. In the beginning of our operation, we attracted more women than men. These women thought they would meet large numbers of eligible and attractive men. But the few men who came were looking for women in their twenties and thirties. Now, I tell women not to come here with high expectations of meeting their ideal man but only to meet people and make friends, even if they are of the same sex.

Subsequently she sent us a form letter that stated the club would be reactivated, and affairs were scheduled for the first Saturday of

---

*A fictitious name. The two singles organizations are located in a large midwestern city.

each month. At the bottom of the letter was the warning, "These affairs are for SINGLES ONLY. Do not attend if married and do not bring friends who are married (living with wife/husband)." When this author arrived at the club, he paid the five dollar entrance fee and was given a name tag on which his first name was written. The director greeted me warmly and escorted me into the back room where I was introduced to many of the female patrons.* The place was partitioned into two sections, the front room where people danced to disco music and the back room where there were tables and food and beverage. During the early part of the evening most people were seated at the tables. The eighty-five patrons were about 75 percent female, with an approximate age of 48. Most of the men appeared to be over the age of fifty. I would characterize these singles as upper-lower class and lower-middle class. Most of the men were blue-collar workers, and the women worked as salespersons, clerks, and secretaries. Many of the women were seated together at tables playing bingo, cards, and keno. The few men there were dispersed throughout the room playing cards and other games. From their outward appearance few would be characterized as attractive or having any refined social skills.

Although the club was ostensibly a place to meet eligible singles, most of the women maintained they were not there to meet men for romantic purposes. A similar image management has been noted by other observers of organized singles organizations.[8] None of the women I talked to were involved in a relationship with a man. Most had been previously married, and their children were now independent adults. The men I talked to stated they came here because it was a comfortable place to be and devoid of the "young thugs" that frequented other places. Some hoped to meet a "nice woman," but admitted that in the history of their involvement in this club they had not established a serious relationship. Some believed the women felt they were too good for them. Few people whom I interviewed believed that coming to a singles club was a humiliating or degrading experience. The atmosphere was congenial; people intermingled and danced together with ease. As a place

---

*I had informed her that I was a professor at the University of California and was doing a study on black singles. Not every patron was given the same treatment.

to enjoy human companionship, it was very adequate. To meet and mate with members of the opposite sex, it would be best to look elsewhere.

Other organizations bring singles together in a more de facto manner. The singles apartment complex so common among whites in California exists among blacks but generally does not contain the structured activities designed to facilitate their interaction. Due to the large numbers of black singles, any apartment complex which they inhabit in large numbers is for all practical purposes a singles apartment building. Since such apartment complexes rarely schedule activities for their tenants, many singles never meet, or meet only in passing. Where possible, they may meet in a laundromat, swimming pool or tennis court on the premises. One deterrent to meeting people in a singles apartment complex is the reluctance of many singles to become romantically involved with their neighbors. Being entangled with a fellow tenant is a risky matter. A single person may lose some freedom of association and movement if the partner is inclined toward jealousy or possessiveness. We have reports of women being forced to move elsewhere after having dissolved a relationship with a neighbor. There were stories of unexpected visits by a former lover and even harassment of her male visitors.

There are other organizations to turn to for limited assistance. Fraternities and sororities often sponsor dances which attract a large number of black singles. We were told that some black sorority chapters keep a list of eligible men who will serve as escorts for their members. These men are generally in their forties, and the women may be expected to bear part or all of the expenses. Another organization worth mentioning is "Jack and Jill," one of the most selective and oldest black social organizations. It has 148 chapters in the United States and provides activities for black youths according to age groups. Dances, picnics, recreation, and cultural activities are among the activities scheduled to facilitate the contact of middle-class black children. According to a leader of this organization, "roughly one third of the Jacks and Jills have married each other since the organization began."[9] This, of course, is functional only for young blacks, and the Jack and Jill organization has been severely criticized as being elitist.

Among the best organizations for matching up black singles are professional organizations. While they exist, theoretically, to disseminate and exchange information on issues in specific disciplines, they are also social gatherings. At some of their annual meetings there are often social functions which provide a congenial atmosphere for purely social interaction. Some local or regional chapters of black professional organizations regularly schedule parties, cocktail receptions, disco dances, and other social events. While it is certainly a convenient way in which to meet people, it has its disadvantages. One may see more men than women in such groups, but typically the men are married and the women are not. Even among the eligible singles, fewer matches than would be expected actually take place. Some people do not wish to marry members of the same profession for fear they will become competitive with each other. It is still uncommon to find black sociologists married to other sociologists or any other similar matchup. Probably a more common pairing is that of the older male professor and young female graduate student. While she is in the same discipline, her student status renders her less of an immediate threat to his ego.

ON THE CURB

Assuming the failure to meet people at any of the aforementioned places, it is suggested that people simply become receptive to meeting potential mates in the course of their normal activities. As a 30-year-old female writer commented, "The best way to start a friendship is when you're bike riding or jogging. At least you have some other pretext for meeting, other than hungrily looking for someone." Surely, it expands one's options if one strikes up conversations with people in the grocery store, laundromat, on the bus, and other places where being there is not suspect. Yet this is an option that was generally unacceptable to black women only a few years ago and a difficult one to handle for black men. A 31-year-old female educator expressed her reservations:

I have always met men under structured conditions. The man I am with now I met through a friend. If I meet a man in an unstructured setting like in the street, I will arrange a date, that is, a group situation with some of my friends. That way I feel safer. I'm not comfortable with having to deal with a strange man alone.

Not all women have a fear of meeting men in a spontaneous encounter. Sometimes it is contingent upon the man and the circumstances. A 34-year-old female social worker reported her experience:

Once, when I had missed my connecting flight at an airport, I had to talk to a black ticket agent about catching a flight the next morning. Really, I didn't want to talk to a black guy because I was pretty mad about being bumped off my flight. Well, the airline agreed to put me up at a nearby hotel. He asked if he could drop by later, when he got off work, and join me for a drink in the hotel lounge. He looked like a very nice guy and I agreed. We talked in the bar until it closed and we then went to my room and continued talking until the next morning. It seemed safe enough because I sensed he was not the type of man to get out of hand. Besides, I knew what he did and where he worked.

Although the spontaneous meeting can be fruitful, it does entail some risk. Women, for instance, cannot screen out the pretenders when they meet under unstructured conditions. Nor can they control for status compatibility when they meet men in certain situations. There is in addition the risk, albeit small, of physical harm from a man whose identity is not known. For men the dangers are somewhat different. If they decide to approach women in the so-called natural situation, they are subject to a greater probability of rejection. Some women are unreceptive because they are not available or interested. Many women refuse because they believe it improper or risky to meet men this way. One woman expressed her feelings about meeting men when jogging:

As far as I'm concerned they're hassles. When I'm running there's only one thing I want to do and that is run. If I wanted to meet people, I'd go to a singles bar. But it's awfully hard to convince these people that I'm not playing hard-to-get or aloof. I really mean it. When I'm sweaty, out of breath, and red-faced, the last thing I want to do is meet someone when I'm in that condition.[10]

Thus, the advantages of the spontaneous encounter have to be balanced against the risks of meeting strangers, whose motives can only be confirmed by their actions.

PLAYING IT SAFE

The old standby of many singles is the arranged meeting. Usually mutual friends or relatives bring two people together for the purpose of introducing them to each other. Since both people are known to the arranger, there is some independent validation of the parties' character and motives. While such an arrangement works for some people, there are numerous cases where such meetings are unproductive. A 39-year-old male college professor gave this explanation:

My cousin and a few female friends are staunch matchmakers. For some reason the women I've met through them never worked out very well. In fact, I rarely saw the women again after one date. One thing that commonly happens is that their standards of beauty radically differ from mine. While I'm not stuck on a woman being superfine, I couldn't believe some of the women they selected for me to meet. One was about a hundred pounds overweight. Then, the atmosphere can be very coercive. Since you know the purpose for which you're there, it can be very awkward when you're supposed to like each other. There's an unnatural pressure to seek some basis for finding some common interest when you know this is a matchup. When I meet a woman in other ways, I can check her out, and if she's not cool, just go on to somebody else.

Women are more likely to prefer the arranged meeting because they assume their friends, especially women, would not introduce them to a playboy or other undesirable type. One disadvantage of such an arranged meeting is that women and sometimes men who meet in this manner are labelled as desperate. This sort of meeting can bring on embarrassment when a woman meets a man for the purpose of forming some kind of relationship, and he never follows up on the initial meeting. Hence, there is a more direct feeling of rejection. Still, for many women it is a last resort when other methods fail. As a 30-year-old female program evaluator reported, "I prefer to meet men through others. That way it cuts down on the sickies and those without good intentions. Discos are a new avenue for meeting people but I am reluctant to date anyone I meet there. I find it's better to enjoy the outing and not expect too much."

Meeting people on the job or through work contacts has always been a common and productive way to find a mate. Unfortunately, it has not been that viable for many of our black singles. Assuming they want a member of the same race, many blacks find it difficult to meet anyone in a work setting. The higher their position, the lower the likelihood they will work with other blacks. Hence, a black nurse rarely meets a black doctor or a black airline stewardess will not often encounter a black pilot. Many singles do not meet or date people who work with them, but find a potential mate through their co-workers. This alternative, again, is not that available to black singles. Even their same-sex co-workers, in all probability, are white, and they lead separate social lives. Those in positions dealing with the public may have the opportunity to meet potential mates. A black airline stewardess may meet high status black men among her passengers. The same may be true for salespersons, nurses, newspaper reporters, and business people. Some of these meetings may be too brief to be of much use, and an assertive personality is needed to arrange future contacts.

Given the presence of eligible men or women in the same job environment, dating them is fraught with danger. One example illustrates what can happen when one dates on the job. A male medical administrator had an affair with one of the staff doctors. She was also having an affair with another male doctor who worked in the same clinic. In turn this male doctor was engaged to one of the staff nurses while simultaneously having a sexual liaison with one of the clinic's secretaries. Subsequently the male administrator commenced an affair with another one of the secretaries in the office. Eventually, the affairs were all revealed and a combination of jealousy and embarrassment caused the male administrator and the two secretaries to lose their jobs.

Most on-the-job affairs are not so entangled and do not result in such disastrous consequences. More likely they result in the awkward situation of facing a former lover five times a week and some tensions in work relationships. People have been known to quit their jobs rather than endure some of the tensions. The problem is abated somewhat when the work associates are coequal, thus lessening the possibility of unfair recriminations. One woman, a 31-year-old nurse commented, "I dated a man once on the job and will never do it again. After the affair ended, working with him every day was so unpleasant that I dreaded going to work. We found it hard to even maintain eye contact with each other. I eventually resigned for other reasons but he certainly hastened my departure.''

GO FOR BROKE

When all else fails a common tactic among some whites is to utilize the personals ad or dating service. Few blacks seeking a mate within the race have utilized this method. One reason, of course, is that few if any black-oriented magazines will accept such ads, and there are no black dating services. One very reputable black magazine published a personal ad once from a black woman, but never ran another one. A well-known black leader in the San Francisco Bay area has advocated the institution of a personals classified section in a leading black journal. "Such a service," he says, "would allow members of our community a means of getting in touch with suitable persons who meet their selection criteria. It would be a positive service to black people who don't relate well to, or don't like to seek new relationships with new people within the context of singles bars." At this point, the only thing that comes close to personal ads for blacks is *Ebony* Magazine's most eligible bachelors and bachelorettes feature. Women who want to meet men, and vice versa, write in and ask to be featured in the magazine. Many of them subsequently are selected and receive letters from men and women who want to meet them.

A black man advertised in one of the predominantly white newspapers for a woman. His ad read:

Liberated, well-educated, black gentleman, Aquarius, unmarried, mellow, 41, handsome. Enjoys reading, music, sports, relaxation, sharing. Desires to establish a non-traditional, warm, honest relationship with an intelligent, compatible, attractive woman (25-40) of any race who likes herself and is financially/emotionally independent.

According to him, none of the women (ten in all) met his criteria. All were white, and most were past the age of forty. He exclaims, "After this experience I know that a man who wants to meet well-adjusted women would fare better if he went through clubs and mutual friends. Through the classifieds he is almost certain to meet women who can only be regarded as losers.'' Any well-adjusted black woman who places such an ad would face an even worse situation. Most black men would assume that a black woman who placed such an ad, no matter what she said, was desperate and wanted a sexual partner. This tendency to label people who resort to such methods makes it a very futile and unproductive device to secure a mate.

A couple of rarely used but innovative techniques have been suggested or tried. One group of white feminists has expressed a desire to establish a data bank service on boyfriends. By collecting enough dossiers on men, they would be able to inform any woman interested in a particular man about specific complaints registered against him by former girl friends. Their thesis is that every woman formerly involved with him knows something about him that should be passed on to his next "victim."[11] Another method developed by a black woman in San Francisco seeks to understand the potential and quality of personal relationships through astrology. Known as Alim's Associates, she uses astrological charts to tell a person what his or her problems are in finding a mate. Through the interpretation of the planet's movements, a person's inner conflicts are explored, and the type of person to seek out and the kind of energies at play are determined. While the merits of such a method may be questioned, many of our singles are ready to put their faith in the stars.

SUMMARY

It is in the process of seeking socially acceptable avenues of meeting a mate that blacks are disadvantaged by their status as a racial minority in the general society and as an elite minority in the black community. Middle-class whites are favored by the fact that it is their society, and the majority of people encountered in their world will be other middle-class whites. Because they control our social institutions, they can structure them to meet their needs. Middle-class blacks, on the other hand, have yet to develop many institutions designed to cope with the increasing numbers of singles in their midst. Hence, they have to cope with the intractable problem of meeting eligible black singles in a comfortable setting as well as the imbalanced sex ratio and the difficulty of sustaining a harmonious relationship.

Blacks can and do meet all the time. The problem arises in where they meet and whom. For many reasons blacks seek status similarity in potential mates. While the black community contains a number of arenas in which to congregate, these facilities by and large are inhabited by and cater to the needs of lower-income blacks. Middle-class blacks, by virtue of their much smaller numbers and recent arrival, have yet to fashion many institutions and facilities of their own. Their small numbers can lead to a sort of social incest when the same middle-class singles continue to meet in the same place over and over again. Thus, we find that places where singles meet shift very often. After these places are in existence for a period of time, black singles realize they are not meeting anybody new and move on.

Not only can blacks not control very well the status of singles they meet, but the motivations of people in certain settings are questionable. This is particularly true of men who do not have a compelling need to participate in social life in order to meet eligible women. One could reasonably question the intent of men who are found too often on the party circuit, in singles bars, and discos. These are not the type of men who are interested in finding a wife and settling into a permanent relationship. Yet there are some black women who continually meet and get involved with men encountered in these settings. Ultimately they encounter failure after failure because it is built into the setting where they choose to select and form their relationships. Even men of decent and noble intentions abandon them when meeting women in these settings. Women become victims of a labelling process which stigmatizes them as lonely, desperate, and sexually vulnerable prey.

No matter where singles meet, they are subject to the operative effects of the sex ratio. Since there are so many more single women than men, the eligible male does not have to roam the parties, singles bars, and discos in order to find stable female companionship. Hence, the men found in those settings are often the ones who want or require transient and surface relationships. The men who require them are typically married to somebody else and find those settings conducive to maintaining anonymity and clandestine liaisons. Still, despite the imbalanced sex ratio, there are black men who are looking for sensitive and intelligent women, and who find it difficult to meet them. Many earnest men and women seldom encounter each other because after a number of negative experiences they may cease going to the places which constitute the singles scene. Some, after painful relationships in the past, have dropped out of the dating game altogether, especially if they have had children. Thus, until new and socially acceptable avenues are developed to bring them together, the problem of where to meet eligible partners will continue to pose one of the big challenges to black singles.

NOTES

1. Stanley G. Robertson, Do you remember when?, *The Los Angeles Sentinel*, 5 July 1979, p. A6.

2. Charles V. Hamilton, *The Black Preacher in America* (New York: William Morrow, 1972), pp. 208-216.

3. Bea Pixa, How the singles make connections, *The San Francisco Examiner*, 16 June 1976, p. 22.

4. Alan Bayer, College impact on marriage, *Journal of Marriage and the Family* 34 (November 1972): 600-610.

5. Dorothy William, Foxtrappe: A new lifestyle—or just a throwback to the old playboy era, *The Washington Post*, 18 January 1976, p. D12.

6. Ruth Stein, The truth about S.F. single bars, *The San Francisco Chronicle*, 23 May 1978, p. 18.

7. Lewis Yablonsky, How infidelity can strengthen ailing marriages, *Detroit Free Press*, 15 February 1979, p. 5C.

8. Bernard Berk, Face saving at the singles dance, *Social Problems* 24 (June 1977): 530-544.

9. Vernon C. Thompson, Jack and Jill chapters: the top of the hill for black professionals, *The Washington Post*, 5 October 1978, p. 6.

10. Sarah Pastel, Sex and the runner, *The American Runner*, December 1978, p. 49.

11. Bob Greene, Used chauvinist husbands, beware, *The San Francisco Chronicle*, 9 April 1977, p. 30.

The Dating Game 3

It is the process of dating that most markedly distinguishes single people from married people. The difference is not absolute, since many married individuals (particularly males) participate in the dating game, but their relationships are ones of discrete liaisons rather than the structured ritual involved in the dating situation. One often hears that people do not "date" anymore. However, there is some question as to what has taken its place. As one woman reported to us: "I have friends who consider the word date or the situation known as dating passé. They haven't really come up with new words for activities they are involved in which are essentially identical to dating."

One thing is certain—that the process whereby the sexes formed relationships has substantially changed in recent years. Dating began as part of the courtship process in the 1920s when the concept of romantic love became popular among middle-class whites. Prior to that time marriages were arranged as a result of negotiations between two families or groups. Once individuals were ostensibly given free choice in the selection of a mate, dating became the method whereby unmarried men and women mutually explored each other's strengths and weaknesses as potential spouses.[1] In most cases dating partners were young and met each other in their respective communities. As a result, most Americans married persons who lived within six miles of them.[2]

Nowadays dating or whatever we choose to call it is an entirely different matter. For some singles it is the most valuable aspect of their lives and provides them with an active social life, new experiences, a variety of new and interesting people to meet, and freedom to sexually experiment. To others it ranks as the most undesirable element in singlehood. However one responds to the dating situation, the one predictable element in it is its unpredictability. Once it ceased to be part of a structured courtship system, it became literally a social anarchy. The people in today's dating game are not necessarily young people who grew up together and who are searching for compatible mates. They form a diverse group in terms of age, values, background, motives, and experiences. As a result dating has a different character and dynamics than some ten years ago. Individuals caught up in the dating game must develop skills and resilience to cope with its chameleonic structure.

Dating was rarely a structured process for blacks. Lewis describes it as a catch-as-catch-can matter among the blacks he studied in the rural South.[3] Even in urban areas and among the middle class, dating in public places was restricted due to racial segregation in the South and lack of recreational outlets in Northern black communities. Most blacks met their future mates in school, the neighborhood, or at house parties. With the increasing mobility of middle-class blacks, those sources of potential mates are no longer as available. Moreover, they now meet members of the opposite sex as individuals whereas in the past they were part of a larger social unit. This has certain implications for those who participate in the dating games. It means that people are more subject to image management techniques, since they have little independent verification of a dating partner's character in settings which are new to them both. Also, the controls on negative or antisocial behavior in dating situations are lessened when the social sanctions that can be exercised by relatives or friends are absent.

While such problems are not unique to blacks, they are heightened by what Carolyn Greene calls the silent war between black men and women.[4] This consists of the distrust, negative conceptions, and hostility that characterize many relationships between the two sexes. It is a silent war because there is often no overt articulation of these feelings; but they intrude in intersexual relationships in very unobtrusive, but significant ways. On the overt level it is exemplified by the saying, "a nigger ain't shit," and the kinds of defense or avoidance mechanisms blacks use when dealing with each other. Originally these silent hostilities arose out of a collective self-hatred that blacks had because they accepted the inferiority label assigned to them by the dominant society. While there are still remnants of self-hatred, it is also possible that experiences in the dating game serve to reinforce these feelings. Conversely, having negative preconceptions serves as a self-fulfilling prophecy.

The silent war notwithstanding, dating can be fraught with anxiety-raising tensions. For men, who still generally have to take the initiative in asking for dates, it means having to cope with rejection. As one man complained, "Some women think men get used to being rejected because they experience it so often as a normal part of life as a male. But no matter how many times I had to face it, being turned down for a date was never pleasant for me." The problem of rejection is not made easier by women who see flirting as an art or weapon. Some men use cues such as an inviting smile or sustained eye contact as invitations to make further advances. Women who use that kind of body language without the necessary meaning attached to them are seen as setting up men for rejection. Under the anomic conditions of the new dating game, few of the old rules have validity for everybody. One result is the complaint by some women that "men don't like to flirt nowadays. They just ask directly for sex."

At the same time women face more and more the problem of rejection themselves. Since many females have become more aggressive in their relations with men, they, too, must cope with being turned down—a feeling often exacerbated by the fact that they have deviated from their role function. Most unmarried women, however, are more likely to be plagued with the disadvantages of the traditionally passive role they play in heterosexual relations. That means selecting from the men who approach them instead of aggressively pursuing men of their liking. One woman lamented that "it's very difficult to meet men. I haven't gotten to the point where I'm aggressive enough to approach them. Black men are very conservative and traditional in their attitudes. It's difficult for them sometimes to deal with women who are aggressive."

Being an unmarried woman also means having to deal with the

unwanted attentions of some men. Sometimes the more undesirable the men are, the harder they pursue a woman. Black women in particular have to cope with men who may be only practicing their seductive techniques. There are some settings in which one or more black males may approach every woman who walks within their speaking range with full knowledge that they could and would not deal with every woman that could accept their invitation. One woman devised a technique to deal with this type of male. According to her, "When a woman is unmarried, she is approachable by anybody. I have to wear a wedding band to protect myself."

Not everybody is in the dating game in the same way. At one time or another they may have a serious involvement with one person that takes up most of their time and attention. With the short duration of many relationships, and the awareness by many that "nothing lasts forever," most people fit into what McCall calls the "permanent availability" model.[5] According to this model, everyone is always available to a member of the opposite sex, including those who are presently married. Due to the lack of legal or kin control, individuals go freely in and out of relationships, including marriage. However, being involved in a "serious" relationship and participating in the dating game simultaneously is qualitatively different from being an unattached individual. It affords one a greater selectivity in choosing dating partners, a more leisurely pace in developing the relationship, and the ability to negotiate for higher rewards. No matter how one (i.e. married, single or attached) may be in the dating game, it still requires the ability to cope with different situations and diverse personalities.

THE SILENT WAR

Among some of the more pronounced problems in the dating game are the irresponsibility and dishonesty of many black men. The irresponsibility charges range from borrowing money and not ever repaying it to the pervasive pattern of not showing up for dates. To add insult to injury, according to one woman, men will insult your intelligence by telling some ridiculous story about why they did not show up. Susan, a 28-year-old schoolteacher, tells of how she had a date with a Ph.D. candidate for an evening out at a very plush restaurant. She had made a special trip to the hairdresser and bought a new outfit in order to look her best. The scheduled time arrived and he had not. Two and a half hours later it was obvious he was not coming. The next day he called to say that he had intended to take a brief nap and overslept about eight hours.

Such stories are repeated by a number of black women with only the names, date, and location changed. In most instances the excuses given are fabrications. Chances are that most of the men find something or somebody better. The accumulation of such episodes helps to sustain the silent war between black men and women. A single black male psychiatrist asserts that "Black men are not allowed any responsibility in this country. Responsible people are dangerous so whites prime black men not to be responsible. We internalize all of this and act on them as if they were real —if not beneficial."

Much of this irresponsibility is confined to younger blacks and men. By younger I mean those under 30 years of age. Due to changes in child-rearing patterns (for example, more permissiveness) and the prolonged length of time black professionals must spend in school, many do not become independent and responsible for their own behavior until relatively advanced ages. Thus one notes that black singles in their twenties are often living in a carefree fashion. In some cases it is impossible to make structured dates within this age group. They have to be caught on the run. Dating may consist only of catching them at home at a propitious time, getting stoned together, and perhaps a sexual interlude. Singles over thirty are not exempt from irresponsible actions, but it is much rarer in that group.

Women of all ages do their share of defaulting on dating commitments. Unlike the men, they are more likely to call in advance, sometimes as late as 7:30 P.M. for an 8 P.M. date. Their reasons are also more understandable. Due to their training to be passive and congenial with men, many women are simply intimidated into accepting dates which they do not want. An attractive graduate student commented:

I had run out of excuses not to go out with this guy. After accepting I knew I couldn't go through with it. Yet I didn't want to hurt his feelings. At the last moment I just called and told him I couldn't make it due to an illness in the family. When he suggested another time, I said I just didn't know when I would be free again.

A number of the professional black men we interviewed commented on the tendency of black women to be no-shows for dates. One man told us, "It's gotten so bad that I won't agree to pick up a woman at her home anymore. She has to meet me at my place. And, I always have an alternate set of plans if she doesn't show."

Continuing this saga of the silent war, we find a number of complaints about the behavior of black males who do show up for dates —many of them related to insincerity and deceit. A common problem was the man who promised a woman a gala evening out on the town but instead headed straight for his abode. In some cases they are occasionally taken directly to a motel for purposes that are not easily disguised. Most likely, the men are married and that is yet another prevalent example of the dishonesty women encounter. The dating game is so full of pseudo-singles, that a female college instructor cites "having to compete and becoming involved with individuals who are married" as the greatest problem in being single.

Some black women are constantly on the lookout for pseudo-single men. One alert woman had her own rules for dealing with them. She said:

I believe honesty is always the best policy in the dating game. This way everyone knows where he or she stands and the individuals are able to deal from whatever level they wish. Some men will tell you they are married and give no further explanation as to why they are fooling around. Others try to pretend they are single but can't really fool you. Sometimes you can see the imprint on their ring finger where the ring was just removed. I have a policy of not giving any man my phone number without getting his. And, I ask very clearly for a home number—not an office.

Not all single women are turned off by married men. Some get involved with them and never bother to raise the question of their marital status, why they only can be called at their office or why they always go to her apartment after a date. It is an indirect way of saying, "I don't mind, but I don't want to know." There are other women who not only tolerate married men, but actually prefer them. One such woman revealed, "Yes, I have no hangups about someone being married. Sometimes it's good—they are wild." What she is saying is confirmed by other single women who believe that married men treat them better than single men. Of course, there is the obvious advantage of higher economic rewards from dating married men who must often offer women certain amenities since marriage or even regular companionship is ruled out.

There are even some women who date married men exclusively for advantages that accrue to such a liaison—one of them being their own fear of marriage or emotional involvement. A woman who had this policy told us, "I found it hard to avoid emotional involvement after seeing him for awhile. After extensive sexual relations my feelings were just out of control. But at least I was able to keep my perspective about what the relationship was all about and didn't entertain any false hopes. And that was more than I could expect from most single men who won't tell you where you stand in the relationship, friendship or whatever, or if you stand any place at any given point in time." Another woman admitted that she dated only married men in order to avoid sexual involvement. "The moment they asked me to put out, I brought up their marital status," she commented.

A problem that many professional blacks face, due to their small numbers, is the formation of dating and social cliques. This is a group of people who primarily work together and socialize with each other. Due to their limited numbers, similar interests, and social isolation, many blacks find themselves dating people who are all in the same social circle and know each other. A woman who moved from a southern city to Oakland observed, "I've seen more cliques here than in my hometown. That means a lot of incestuous relationships happen—seeing someone who is a friend of a friend—or seeing the same people time after time." The implications of dating in cliques can be serious. It makes image management considerably more difficult when your dating partner knows your former dating partner(s). Women can be labelled as an "easy lay" by other men they have dated. This makes it more difficult to resist the sexual advances of the next male they meet. For men, it makes playing around with several women simultaneously a lot harder when they are in the same social circle. Some men are not deterred by this situation. A psychologist informed us that it was not uncommon for him to go to a party and encounter four or five women that he was currently dating. For this reason he always went to parties alone.

The dating problems of the black singles studied are complicated for several reasons. They are members of an elite group, many of them at the top of the black social strata. For many of them success has not necessarily meant happiness in interpersonal relationships. In response to the question of what problems are unique to unmarried blacks, a female psychologist described her impression:

I can't really define it properly but I feel a sense of very basic alienation, separateness and an inability (or lack of motivation) to do anything to overcome the distance between self and others. I see it as unique because the people I deal with (well-paid professionals) often got there by being suspicious of others, hardworking—a kind of rugged individualism and goal-oriented isolation that is non-functional once they arrive. In other words, successful black professionals have had to acquire personality traits which may help a career but can be damaging to interpersonal relationships.

Perhaps the greatest obstacle—one that may supersede all others —is one that is unique to the group of black singles studied. All are over 25 years of age, and many have had a marriage or serious relationship in their background. Hence they are not in the dating game without experiences—many of them negative—or preconceptions about what they can expect from members of the opposite sex. The words of one male, a dental student, are illustrative, "Sometimes I meet a woman who just got out of a relationship that didn't leave too many scars and we are very mellow together. But mostly I have to deal with women who have been 'out there' a long time and have developed a certain cynicism and negativism toward men. They tend to be defensive or manipulative."

That this feeling is shared by many women about the characteristics of men they meet in the dating game is exemplified in the statement by a female nurse:

At this stage in my life cycle, and for the age group of men I'd date (27 to 32 years) most have had previous marriages or shacking experiences and/or children which can oftentimes affect the present relationship and their desire to become close with another woman. Overall, I would say that relationships between people are seriously complex. The single woman has to be flexible, cautious, wise, and alert to deal with herself and any relationship with a man.

IMAGE MANAGEMENT

The kind of caution about which she speaks is often reflected in the ways individuals cope with the dating game. Image management, while on the decline, is still used by a large number of singles. It is the presentation of self that conforms to the normative role expectations in the dating process that essentially conveys a positive image while concealing negative features. Members of the dating game may be always on good behavior, a situation which Bernard asserts leads to shock and disenchantment at the end of the romantic idealization period.[6]

While both members of the dating game may engage in image management, it is more often a refuge for women. This is particularly true of black women who must operate in a more competitive dating situation than white women. One of the central problems of an educated woman, black or white, is that she has to be aggressive and achievement-motivated to obtain job mobility, but passive to attract and hold a man. The skills it takes to achieve a high paying job are often those not wanted by most men in their wives—at least in the years when mates are selected. It is probably no accident that one of the most common complaints black men lodge against black women is that they are too aggressive or domineering. During the peak of the black nationalist period, many black women very consciously followed the "one-step-behind your man philosophy" of the movement.

Although in increasing disfavor, some black women still attempt to convey the impression of sexual conservatism, assuming that the less a woman indulged, the higher her bargaining price in the dating market. A social worker, for instance, reported that she had told all her potential lovers that her sexual experience had been confined to only two men. Such claims, however, lose some credibility when women come readily prepared with birth control pills or other contraceptive devices. This woman had actually been sexually involved with over a dozen men. At the age of 28, with extensive dating experience, she had found it difficult, even if she so desired, to avoid frequent sexual contact.

Very few women will claim virginal status nowadays. In fact none of the women we interviewed did so. For one reason, a woman who remains a virgin after the age of 25, while highly desirable to a traditional male, is also strongly suspect of having sexual hangups. A further sign of the times is the pseudo-sexually liberated female who actually suffers from serious mental blocks in the area of sex. As a symbol of their liberation many of these women give the impression that they are sexually as free as men when in reality they confine their sexual activity to one man at a time and furtively seek an exclusive relationship with one man.

Then there is another age-old image management technique that women use—that of being pursued by a number of different men who ardently desire them. One male took notice of all the different women he encountered that claimed to have boyfriends. In some cases this was only a way of politely telling him they were not interested. More often they would agree to date him, and he would get more involved with them only to find the boyfriends had mysteriously disappeared from sight and mind. Finally he concluded that boyfriends existed primarily to add to the value of a woman. It was a way of saying that "I don't want him to think I'm out here all alone because no other man wants me." Nowadays the image manager is more likely to claim that she is presently unattached due to her high standards for a man.

As a result of mostly negative experiences, individuals do develop methods for coping with the dating process that can best be described as defense mechanisms. Sometimes defensive behavior can be interpreted as insincere behavior. At the same time much of the behavior generated by the dating experience is insincere. In such cases it is commonly called "gaming." The Milners define gaming as "an attempt to secure money or personal gain by manipulating human emotions such as fear, greed, lust, or love."[7] While gaming may exist among all racial groups, it seems to have been elevated to the status of a fine art within certain segments of the black community.

Gaming is practiced by both sexes, but may be more common, in one sense, to the female members. In all fairness, females are probably more forced into game playing because of the powerless and often passive position they occupy. Moreover, as sellers in a buyers' market, they resort to guile and manipulation to make the odds more even. Men, particularly black ones, are placed in a position where they can make their desires or demands known, with the knowledge that if they cannot get what they want with one woman, there is always someone who will deliver. Other sociopsychological factors enter into the process, including the basic value conflict between men and women over sex versus commitment and fidelity versus sexual variety.

To play games is nothing particularly new. Within the black middle-class, however, it takes on a new dimension. First, there is the more sophisticated use of language, which makes game playing easier to do and to defend. Second, there is more at stake, not only in terms of the material rewards that come from successful gaming, but the middle-class values which require defending such values as sexual discretion, fidelity, marriage, and monogamy. In the context of the new dating game, where women cannot count on any of the above, they are more likely to resort to games.

Despite the heralded sexual revolution, most games are still played over the old issues of sex and money. Take, for instance, the case of Mona, an attractive, light-skinned woman and her female companions. Their guiding motto is "no romance without finance." Most of them grew up in cities such as Chicago and New York where they learned gaming at their mother's knee. Never did they realize the rewards could be so high. So far they have managed to get expensive jewels, cars, trips to the Bahamas, and even the rent paid on their apartments. Although their personal tastes run to writers, musicians, and poets, they find them a poor source of finance. Their main patrons are businessmen, doctors, lawyers, and other professionals.

Many of the opportunistic gamers have to settle for much less, especially if they are of a darker hue. But you get what you pay for! These women will settle for a nice evening out, and the reward for it is a nice smile at the end of the date. As one man complained, "Women expect a real nice time on the first date where she receives all and gives little other than conversation. I go out with a definite purpose—either sexually or mentally." Such goals can be obtained if a man is willing to pay the price. According to a businessman living in San Francisco, he has to travel a lot and never finds a shortage of women willing to accompany him on trips to the East Coast. Strangely enough, these same women will not go out on a date with him in San Francisco.

It is understandable that members of a group who have a recent history of relative economic deprivation may tend to place more emphasis on material success or security than on the intrinsic worth of an individual. Consequently, a sizable number of black women rank a man according to the type of car he drives, clothes he wears, and the residence in which he lives. Coinciding with the lessening chances of a secure relationship or marriage, some black women decide to milk the market for all it's worth. An extreme example, for instance, is the reported case of a professional woman in Washington, D.C. who asks for one hundred dollars up front before going out with a man. To wit, women develop a utilitarian view of dating and use it for whatever purposes it suits them.

Not all the gaming for material rewards is confined to women. Since a lot of black women have relatively high incomes, they are ripe game. A number of the black women complained of black men wanting financial assistance. In the Bay Area black men in the arts without steady sources of income are particularly on the lookout for women of means who can subsidize their artistic endeavors. Men in graduate school also look for women who can supplement their student stipends. Numerous cases abound where women have supported men while they obtained a graduate degree, only to be dropped after the graduation ceremony. In Washington, D.C., where black men are in large demand, there are examples of men requesting and often getting at least the payment of their car note.

A main criticism of black men is that they tend to play the field while trying to restrict their women to exclusive relationships. Even some men receiving monetary support from women are known to have several additional women on the side. A woman reported the gross humiliation she suffered when she loaned her man five hundred dollars to pay off a loan and later found out he used the money to pay for the abortion of another one of his women. Another woman who dropped out of the dating game reminisced that, "I no longer have to deal with the other woman problem. It seems that the men I was dating always had a number *one* woman and I was never it." At the same time these men can be very possessive of the women with whom they have the slightest involvement. An extreme example is the college counselor who lamented that, "One reason that I date as little as I do is, if a man spends any money on you, he expects your heart and soul."

In order to maintain the exclusive rights to a woman, men have to lie about their status as faithful lovers. Few are entirely successful, as they are uncloaked eventually by a phone call, a letter, or rumors that reach the ear of their woman. A major reason that many women feel exploited is not because they find out that there are other women, but because they discover that they are not the main woman. A large number of women are not unrealistic enough to expect absolute fidelity (and increasing numbers of women are also unfaithful) but do expect his major allegiance. The woman involved in a secondary relationship feels the greatest brunt of a man's multiple liaisons. She is the one who gets only a limited amount of his available time and who has to accept the excuses as to why he cannot take her out. Most of the professional men we interviewed had a primary relationship with one woman, but continued to be active in the dating game.

As might be expected, game playing can only be effective if done to people who are naive or willing to tolerate the game for reasons of their own. Women often tolerate the games men run because they find it easier to accept them than to be without a man. The reason men are willing to accept the games women play is more complex. Some of them reward women economically because they can afford it, and it assures them of attractive female companions which they might not otherwise be able to obtain. We encountered few men who admitted to "buying women." Those who did would be classified basically as undesirable men due to age, physical appearance, or personality deficits. Desirable men are either running their own games or refuse to play them. According to one highly-paid professional male:

Once I see that a woman is running a game, I simply tell her that I don't have time for it. I once set up a dinner date with a very attractive college professor who was attending a conference in town. She was very elusive and hard to pin down to a specific day and time. Finally, she agreed to have dinner with me early one evening at 5 P.M. When I asked why so early, she responded that she had to be back in her hotel by 7 P.M. I told her to forget it.

Middle-class norms of politeness and the use of code language (for example, "I'm too busy," or "I have a boyfriend") makes direct confrontation with game players infrequent. The lack of clearly defined mores for dating makes communication between the sexes difficult. Males interpret a woman's acceptance of an invitation to dinner as at *least* giving them the right to make sexual advances, whereas women take the position that it only provides them with the "pleasure" of their company. Both assumptions are based on anachronistic premises that (1) sex is always engaged in as a reward to the male partner and (2) women, regardless of their own income level, are the beneficiaries of dates and should not share the expenses. As long as these traditional values come into conflict with contemporary realities, the sexes will continue to play games with each other.

An example of one man who chose to transcend game playing in a very facetious way is illustrated in the note he sent to a woman who had accepted a date with him:

TO: C. J.
FROM: G. A.
RE: Date of July 28

Per our telephone conversation of July 24 you will visit my domicile on July 28 at 8 P.M. Said visit to be of indefinite duration for purposes presently undetermined. You will be unaccompanied, without a child or friend or other defensive weapons of a harmful nature. Normal rules of the dating game will be temporarily suspended for this engagement. No game playing allowed; intentions are to be clearly stated and unequivocal answers are to be given to direct questions. Cancellation after the date of July 27 will not be accepted except for reasons of an act of God or physical incapacity.

Only a man with keen insight into the games played in the dating process could have written such a note. He reports that although the intention of the note was satirical, the woman's response was a mild form of outrage. Despite its humorous character, she considered it an ultimatum. Even if serious, such a note strips the game players of many of their weapons. Such a response by women to direct statements by men account for the continuation of linguistic manipulation to achieve expected but undeclared ends in the dating game. American society socializes men and women into this kind of manipulative behavior by its labelling of men as "catches" and women as sexual "property."

CHANGING TIMES

More and more people are questioning the traditional dating assumptions with their structural procedures and rigid role definitions. In the black dating game we still have a combustible combination of traditional and counter-culture types. Hence, many of the changes that are coming about are not accepted by many blacks in the singles' world. The extensive interracial dating engaged in by many black singles has exposed a number of them to the alternative dating modalities.

One of the reasons that people say they do not "date" anymore is the decline in the structured arrangement to see each other in public places. That this is an increasing trend is not in doubt, but the reasons why vary from individual to individual. A female journalist explained her situation this way, "I rarely date as such. Men seem to prefer dropping by to going out when a woman is involved. Since I am attracted to playboys, many reserve going out for stalking prey. I guess they do expect a lot of contentment on the part of women that they keep on terribly light diets." Another woman reported her observations of all the black men paired with each other at a jazz concert while a number of the women were also in all-female groups. She commented sardonically, "The only time black women see them is when they want to come by your house and watch T.V."

These comments, repeated over and over, indicate that many black women are dissatisfied with the new dating or nondating trend. A poignant response by one woman symbolizes their dismay, "The men I dated only took me from their living room into the bedroom. Once a fellow took me out to dinner. I was elated—it really made me feel like I was somebody." The response of one black man indicates his belief that women should be more grateful for the little men do for them. He said, "Women want to take more than give. They have exploited my kindness. I invite them over for dinner and they won't even offer to set the table, wash the dishes or bring wine.''

Women who do get invited out for an evening's entertainment do not fare much better. We heard a number of complaints that men often expect women to meet them in the street rather than pick them up at the door. This above man's response to such charges was: ''What's wrong with these women? They're living in the nineteenth century. Most of them have cars and can meet you for a date. I'll never forget one date I had with a woman who lived in San Jose. We were going out to a show in San Francisco where I live. She insisted that I pick her up at her door. That meant a 200-mile round trip. By the time the evening was finished, I was too tired to try and 'get over.' Of course that was probably what she wanted.''

A discernible change in the dating process is the expectation that women share the expenses. Men report that they do not hesitate to ask women to go dutch treat on dates. Some women refer to such men as stingy or cheap. As one woman reported, ''I'm very traditional in that sense. I don't like paying on dates. If a man respects you as a woman he'll pay your way.'' Perhaps a more typical response is the woman who declares, ''When the relationship becomes more steady I don't mind sharing the expenses.'' A related complaint of many women is that men manage ways of spending as little money as possible on dates by taking them to free concerts in the park or to fast food stands like MacDonald's or Kentucky Fried Chicken.

While many black women have become more aggressive as a result of the competitive dating situation and their growing sense of independence, there are resentments that men are becoming too passive. A young female educator told us:

I've noticed that many (not all) black males are expecting more and more from women. Many expect the women to be the aggressor, expect them to phone them and to invite them out. They have been spoiled by the fact that there are more available women than men. Most women aren't accustomed to being on their own and men know how to manipulate women around their needs.

These changes may gradually come to be accepted by the majority of black women if for no other reason than they seem to be the wave of the future. The old dating patterns emerged out of a period where women were economic and sexual chattel, and the patronizing dating behavior of men was, although chauvinistic, at least relevant to that period of time. Women who are sexually and economically liberated will have to accept the idea that liberation is not a one-way street. They will also have to be liberated from the attitudes and customs of the past which they believe worked in their favor. Such a conversion will facilitate the necessary changes in men's behavior where they, too, will be freed of their belief that women are objects of sexual prey to be manipulated at a man's will. In the meantime, the dating experience will continue to be the process which binds us to our outmoded past.

NOTES

1. William Goode, The theoretical importance of love, *American Sociological Review* 24 (February 1959): 38-47.

2. John S. Ellsworth, The relationship of population density to residential propinquity as a factor in marriage selection, *American Sociological Review* 13 (August 1948): 444-448.

3. Hylan Lewis, *Blackways of Kent* (Chapel Hill: University of North Carolina Press), 1955, p. 92.

4. Carolyn Jetter Greene, personal communication.

5. Michel McCall, Courtship as a social exchange: some historical comparisons, in *Kinship and Family Organization* ed. Bernard Farber (New York: John Wiley and Sons, 1966).

6. Jessie Bernard, *The Future of Marriage* (New York: Bantam, 1973), p. 38.

7. Christina and Richard Milner, *Black Players* (Boston: Little, Brown and Co., 1972), p. 301.

Finding and
Keeping a Mate

4

Relationships between humans are, at best, riddled with tension and difficulty. Thus, it is understandable that relationships between the sexes on the most intimate level could prove to be problematic. While this has been true for centuries, the current conflict in male/female relationships seems to be unusually strong and sustained by other changes occurring in our society. In this age of industrialization, urbanization, and complex technology, the anchors of stable relationships are eroded and weakened by the new requirements of individuals' needs in the family. Historically mate selection and family stability were insured by the arrangement of marriages by family and kinship groups. Those same primary groups maintained the stability of families through social sanctions against persons who did not conform to the norms applied to the regulation of marital and family life. Men, women, and children had explicitly defined roles in that epoch, and deviations, at least overt ones, were not tolerated.[1]

The twentieth century witnessed the gradual emancipation of individuals from societal mores regarding their conduct within and outside the family. Even the functions of the family were redefined. The family shifted from an institution designed to serve the needs of the society to a unit where one could find harmonious companionship.[2] While this could be perceived as a healthy step toward the increase of individual freedom, it created a situation where the rules were ambiguous and the goals nebulous. Moreover, it is folly to believe that people can free themselves from their culture when culture always imposes some restraints on individual freedom. People are products of their culture, and free mate choice continues to be made within a circumscribed context. Ostensibly, mates are selected at random on the basis of emotional and sexual attraction. In reality the principle of homogamy dominates our selection of mates. That is, individuals still tend to marry persons similar in age, status, religion, and racial background. As Davis noted some years ago, "A cardinal principle of every stratified social order is that the majority of those marrying shall marry equals."[3]

This raises some salient questions for the mate selection process of our middle-class black singles. While society dictates the marriage of equals, a widespread exception has been the practice of men marrying down. This practice has been defended as necessary to maintain some fluidity in the social structure.[4] However, the problem our middle-class cohort confronts is a ratio of two women for every one male in the ranks of eligible bourgeoisie. Moreover, marital endogamy is a problem of recent origin since the practice of women marrying down was very common and acceptable in the black community. In one study of black college-educated women twenty-five years ago, it was revealed that over 50 percent of them were married to men employed at a lower socioeconomic level than they were.[5] Yet that seems to be a coping style of the past. Most of our single women wanted a mate of comparable status, and it is the interplay of this desire for homogamy with the low number of black men in the eligible pool that sets the scenario for our analysis of the mate selection process.

At the bottom of the problems in black male/female relationships are changes in the larger society. The sociodynamics of Euro-American culture has penetrated deeply into the middle-class sector of the black community. Today's black bourgeoisie are largely creations of the black movement in the 1960s. They are the most acculturated of the black masses in this nation's history. One clue to their depth of acculturation is the fact that most will have received their higher education in predominantly white colleges. Over 75 percent of all black college students are presently enrolled in nonblack colleges. The reverse was true fifteen years ago.[6] It is in these white-dominated institutions (in terms of values and population) that they acquire new values as well as an education.

White society, of course, does not transmit values that encourage people to remain single. The family is still officially a sacrosanct institution to our opinion leaders. However, social conditions and the mass media have cultivated attitudes which are not consonant with finding a compatible mate or staying with one for long. The changes in the economic structure, for instance, have pitted men and women against each other for social values that are becoming increasingly scarce. Tensions in the job marketplace are often reflected as tensions in interpersonal relationships. Economic change, whether for better or for worse, can influence romantic involvement. This parallels Durkheim's observation that psychic disequilibrium increases during periods of economic change, regardless of its direction—either a boom or depression. Beyond a certain level changes in expectations are psychologically disorienting.[7]

IMAGES AND STEREOTYPES

Among the problems encountered in finding a mate are the values of individualism and materialism. This translates into a self-centered philosophy and an emphasis on the acquisition of material possessions. These values coexist with others to sustain the mythology that singlehood as a way of life is the best of all worlds. One problem is the image conveyed by the mass media. A cursory review of radio, television, movies, magazines, and books will reveal an exaltation of the free-floating single. Magazines such as *Playboy* and *Cosmopolitan* contain mostly articles about living a solitary but pleasurable and sexually fulfilling life. The radio brings us songs which convey the impression that there is nothing wrong with drugs, infidelity, and broken marriages. With few exceptions television and movies play up the single individual, not couples or families. Blacks, of course, are also exposed to this underscoring of the single way of life. Furthermore, the black family image in the mass media is almost nonexistent or negatively portrayed.

Television's portrayal of black families has been so negative that protests from black leaders and organizations have reached a new crescendo. In some cases new programs featuring blacks were cancelled after the protests. While individual television series come and go, those that depicted blacks usually featured fractured families. Only in a few cases were black families intact. Most were headed by one parent whose children were incorrigible. When black men and women interacted, they were typically screaming at each other. The image of black women suffered the worst. The majority of black women depicted, even in commercials, were overweight and domineering, thus reinforcing the matriarchy image.

Movies did even worse by blacks. Almost all the men were depicted as macho-styled playboys and the women as semiprostitutes. Due to the protests and a dwindling audience, the 'blaxploitation' films have largely disappeared from movie houses. Still, blacks must contend with the recent trend in black music that romanticizes extramarital affairs and transient relationships. Such songs as "Weekend Lover," "Me and Mrs. Jones," "Ring My Bell," "Hot Stuff," all contribute to the "do your own thing, if it's pleasurable" philosophy. The concern about these types of songs reached the point where Reverend Jesse Jackson attempted to organize protests against radio stations that continued to play that genre of music. Even black-oriented literature has failed to depict tender, loving, relationships among men and women. Currently the most popular books on blacks are written by women. In one analysis of stories by and about black women, Mary Helen Washington concluded, "Many stories black women have written about love and marriage suggest that relationships between black men and black women are often deadlocked. The literature of black women strongly implies that in the future the black woman will more and more choose to be alone."[8]

These images, unfortunately, have their counterpart in folk beliefs that black men and women have about each other. When we asked our subjects to describe what problems, if any, are unique to unmarried blacks seeking a mate, the most frequently given responses were the shortage of black males and the negative stereotypes held by men and women. While many black men and women have a positive relationship, there are large numbers who are wary and suspicious of each other's motives and actions. The stereotypes are many and varied, and contribute to a litany of complaints the sexes have against each other. One complaint is that black women are hostile. According to a 28-year-old male musician:

> What do you say when a brother or group of brothers say "What's happening baby" or "you're looking good?" I've repeated these questions to sisters on the street where there was no one but us and over 90 to 100 percent of the time I don't even get a response. I mean if a sister can't even take a comment or even a hello, how can a black man ever get to know her? It doesn't take much to say thank you or anything else. Also, it's a two way street. I mean how many sisters tell a brother "You're looking good or you smell nice."

Many black women, due to past negative experiences with men, are cautious in their response to some but not all black men. This defensiveness can be manifested in the public encounters described above and interpreted as hostility. Few black women respond in such a manner when introduced by a mutual friend or in other settings. Ironically, the black male's perception of her hostility, and his rejection, hardens his own attitudes toward black women. Still, it is not only black men who harbor the stereotypes. A 34-year-old female personnel specialist told us:

> The average black male is egotistical and wants to be pampered and catered to, thus avoiding lavishing the proper attention on a lady. The black man is selfish and strictly for himself and simply does not want to give. They want the woman to foot the bills and think nothing of asking a woman to buy dinner and/or pay for a motel. Who needs that?

A paradox in the ritual of complaints is that the sexes are often making the same complaints about each other. A 29-year-old businessman reported:

> I consider myself very open in terms of "women's lib." Indeed, I prefer a strong, independent black woman. Many sisters today, however, are so into themselves that they don't know how to please a man. Financial independence, I feel, has a great deal to do with this. A smooth, confident, woman knows how to handle success. Most professional black women I know are so conceited they're no good to anyone, least of all a man. These same women expect a man to wine and dine them and will do little for the man in return.

Obviously, some of the grievances are related to the sexes not fulfilling the expectations of each other. While it is difficult to make sense of some of the complaints, they appear to stem from the fact that the individuals are often not matched up well with members of the opposite sex, that is, those with similar sex role expectations. Many tend to generalize a few experiences with a male/female to all men and women. Some of the criticisms derive from the recent changes in sex role expectations. A 32-year-old female librarian commented:

> Black men are extremely insecure and have no true sense of self. They are so easily threatened, which makes it difficult for aggressive or independent women. Black men are very dominating, always wanting to take charge. They are very chauvinistic, not willing to take the role of the sole provider. They want black women to be traditional but they are unable to maintain the male role.

Indicative of the stereotypes arising from their new class level and acculturation is the criticism of a 41-year-old male community planner:

> It's hard to find a black woman with the same background, priorities, and mental flexibility. Black women are very rigid socially. For example, they feel uncomfortable in a nice restaurant, especially with white people. Most black women came from families in the South and may never have had a healthy relationship with a man. Some black women aren't used to a man who gives them an option. They want to be kicked in the ass. In groups blacks don't relate as human beings. They discuss each other in negative terms—rarely (saying) positive things. This reinforces negative stereotypes.

There were numerous other stereotypes cited, ranging from black men feeling inferior, being too dependent on women, preoccupied with sex, or obsessed with white women. The women were characterized as opportunistic, materialistic, unsophisticated, superficial, and sexually inhibited. In sum, their faults covered the range of human flaws. During our interviews with the subjects most of them were extrapunitive. That is, they externalized the blame for their failure to form a permanent relationship on to the system or the opposite sex. Of course, scapegoating is one of the functions of stereotypes. What actually appears to be the case is that, in the process of bargaining for a relationship, many persons do not seek an equal exchange of values. Instead they attempt to gain a profit by concentrating on the satisfaction of their own needs, not their partners. And stereotyping is only one weapon in this negotiating system.

A MATTER OF QUALITY

When it comes to finding a mate, the biggest barriers are the standards erected by our black singles. Not only are the standards incredibly high, making their achievement unlikely, but they are in many cases nebulous and frivolous. A number of our subjects admitted they had given little thought to what qualities they desired in a mate. They knew what they did not desire in one, not what they wanted. Within the array of qualities desired were many that appeared to have little relevance to the maintenance of a successful relationship. Among those qualities were nonsmokers, men over six feet tall, or a person without an arrest record. These escalating mate standards of blacks, especially women, were attributed to the influence of the mass media. A 28-year-old female criminologist added:

Given the orientation of media in this country I am sure that dating and marriage cannot even begin to approximate some of the life styles on television and in the movies. Considering the realities of conditions in the black community, it seems that one could become quite depressed and frustrated in dating if one thinks that dating, "finding a mate," and so forth, is like it appears on television and movies—boy meets girl, falls in love, and so forth. With the sex ratio like it is, you are not even assured of meeting a man that is not already taken, either married or committed to a relationship.

The imbalanced sex ratio is not the only factor that precludes a wide variety of choice in mate selection. Blacks have never been a monolithic group but the diversity among them is currently greater than ever. Thus, finding someone with common interests and values is more difficult than in the past. A 30-year-old male lawyer addressed that problem:

Black people are unique in that their interests run a broad spectrum. Consequently, it is hard to find the ideal partner for marriage that most other races look for. They are not a homogeneous group. Most other ethnic groups share more on the whole. They range from Southern and Northern blacks, urban and rural, nationalistic to integrationist, religious to atheists, etc. It makes it difficult for them to really relate to one another. Someone who meets your intellectual needs can't meet the emotional, etc.

Finding all the desirable traits in one person is an unlikely possibility at best. Among black women it is complicated by the extreme shortage of black males. Many, however, continue to hold out for the perfect mate. In response to our question about what qualities she desired in a mate, a 31-year-old female social worker told us:

Just everything. I would like someone that I find physically attractive, which includes being taller than I, and not overweight with good personal hygiene. He should be successful and it should be translated into economic terms. I like a man who can express himself verbally and has thoughts about a variety of ideas. I look for someone who has a certain degree of emotional stability, which includes a good sense of what he wants; tenacity, planning. He should see a value in sharing; be nonhostile and optimistic. The quality of empathy is of utmost importance. I would like a man who can be supportive and confident of my abilities, who does not feel necessarily competitive with them. One who basically likes and trusts women; likes and trusts himself. I would like a man who can give as well as receive emotional nurturance.

While those are eminently desirable traits, they are a tall order and a combination rarely found in one man. At the time of this writing, she had not found him and was contemplating giving birth and raising a child independently. Her ability to achieve her goals, in part, depends on what she can bring to a relationship. Men have their own agenda for selecting a mate. These are the requirements of a 31-year-old male accountant:

I am looking for a woman who is sensitive, loving, and warm. A woman who is smart but not an intellectual; and throw in a little wit. I want a woman who can laugh and who is strong and willing to fight for her desires, call it independent. I want a beautiful woman with a glowing smile and a love of life, children and nature. I want my woman to be my best friend, my partner, someone who I could trust totally. I would like a woman who is aggressive, yet not dominant, a woman who is passionate and tender. Most of all, I want a woman who will inspire me to be the best me. I would like a mate who I feel deserves my worship.

What these lofty standards suggest is that singles desire somebody who is pleasing to them in the precise way they want them, whatever their mood or needs may be at the time. The standards are not only high but are capricious and contradictory. In a list of *twenty* traits desired in a mate, one woman wanted him to be both adventurous and level-headed. A 34-year-old female psychologist spoke to this dilemma:

> Men seem to want to change the very things they pretend to be attracted to in the first place, for example, wanting to make an aggressive, outgoing, competent woman more docile and conservative. A man once told me that I should be more like Angela Davis, yet he was very threatened by me at my level of professional functioning.

The fact that people tend to constantly look for somebody "better than" themselves may be indicative of their low level of self-esteem and the desire for security through a better endowed partner. Or by seeking the perfect mate, which proves to be an elusive goal, they avoid making a commitment to any one person on a permanent basis. Whatever the reason, the standards desired in a mate and what they eventually achieve may be very different. People often marry persons who have none of their standards for mates. Many women continue to marry one of the men who approaches them first. They do not, in most cases, aggressively pursue a mate of their choice from a wide universe. When Chavis and Lyles asked formerly married black women why they had chosen their husbands, they listed (1) personality (for example, kind person, had charm, nice guy, paid me lots of attention), (2) everyone else had gotten married, (3) I was pregnant, (4) he was stable.[9] In some instances it boils down to the basic feeling that he was interested in her, treated her "nice" and was available. Men can be equally arbitrary in their selection of wives. Often it is the woman who looked decent, had a pleasant personality, seemed to care about him, and wanted to get married. Sometimes he had achieved his work goals and believed it was time to settle down and raise a family. The woman he was currently involved with would be his future wife. In other words the process of mate selection may be a matter of subjective readiness to marry and the available opportunity structure.

HIGH AND LOWER CASTES

In every society certain categories of people are ranked as more desirable and prestigious than others. The criteria of desirability will vary from culture to culture and even within cultures. Although few of our subjects mentioned physical factors or socioeconomic status as an important variable in their standards for a mate, it is a decisive force in the mate selection process. La Frances Rose, a black female sociologist, has asserted that:

I would maintain that the initial attraction is a physical one—not physical in the sense that one's initial impression is that "I sure would like to go to bed with him/her," although in some cases this may indeed be true. But I am speaking of a physical attraction which social scientists presently cannot nor have they sought to measure. Whatever the criteria used, there seems to be certain types of people who are attracted to each other before any words are spoken.[10]

The allure of physical attraction continues to be more important in women. While sociologists cannot measure or define the physical attraction of individuals, for women it is frequently their physical beauty. Standards of beauty can vary in individuals, but it is possible to reach a consensus on those women who are considered extremely beautiful. These women may be referred to, in the popular vernacular, as foxes. Certainly, self-conceptions of beauty can run counter to cultural standards. When we asked the women (and men) in our sample to describe themselves in terms of physical attractiveness, with few exceptions, they gave a self-definition of attractiveness. Many, in reality, are attractive but do not fall in the category of the foxes.

Most foxes are mulattoes, with long hair and Caucasian features. Despite the pride in blackness movement, the women who most closely approximate their white counterparts are the most desirable to middle-class black men. The fair-skinned black woman combines the accessibility and safety of black women with the appearance of the white woman. Numerous studies have demonstrated that the higher status black male tends to be physically darker than his wife.[11] Psychologist Juanita Papillion contends that "many black men either want a relationship with a white woman or with a black woman who looks like a white woman."[12] Some black men claim that it is not the skin color of fair-skinned women that attracts them but the "fact that they are more feminine" and have pleasant personalities. Another psychologist, Ruth Beard, says, "In fact, many of them are, because their femininity has worked for them. However, darker women who have perhaps been rejected or ignored in their early life develop a demeanor that results from disappointment and anger."[13]

If fair skin or physical beauty was the only requirement for a desirable mate, we would expect few who meet that standard to remain unmarried due to difficulty in finding a mate. Such is not the case for several reasons. One of them is that men are not as inclined to settle for beauty alone. As one honest, 31-year-old male executive revealed:

I want someone with a good sense of humor, about five feet four inches, light skinned, long hair, nice body and cute face. But I really could settle for less physically if she has a nice personality and likes sex. I'm at a sexual stage in my life and that is a big factor in the relationship. But in the end a meaningful relationship has to be based on personality. So I would like someone that can listen openmindedly to opposing views, have a funny side, and not nag.

What beauty can do theoretically for a woman is provide a better opportunity structure for meeting men. The foxes that we interviewed did not seem to lack for male attention or dates compared to the less attractive women. A problem of sorts arises from the men they attract and the men they want. Most men of average means are reluctant to approach a fox for fear of being rejected. This leaves beautiful women with those men who are very assertive, egotistical, themselves very handsome, or desirable in some way. If she plays a passive role, the man may be assertive or egotistical. He may want a beautiful woman to show that he is totally in control of his situation and has "gotten over." As a New York businessman has noted, "The only place where a black man can experience real power, the only time he can be totally in control of the situation, is with a black woman, but we (black men) tend to abuse that."[14]

It is possible that beautiful women have much more difficulty in their relationships with men. Not only may they be abused by their frequent encounters with the assertive, egotistical, black male, they are victimized by their own unrealistic standards for a mate. Because they have a high value in the marriage market, they aim for the most desirable men available. One student of their situation, a 34-year-old female psychologist, has observed:

> A lot of high income/beautiful women remain unmarried because they have unrealistic standards which they won't compromise. They want a man with power, reputation, and money and won't settle for less. Often the same man they find so attractive is everybody else's center of attention. He is the "slick brother" who has a lot of women. Some of these men are unconquerable, and women wind up in a cliffhanger relationship. Family and peer pressure may force them to deal only with men that have a high status, money, and visibility.

The more stable but less desirable black male may avoid the beautiful woman because of the stereotypes about her. A number of negative images are attached to beautiful women, including the ones of dilettante, egotist, shallow personality, and low intelligence. There is some validity to the stereotypes. Exceptionally attractive people of both sexes may fail to develop their full potential because there is little need to do so. The eminent psychologist Karl Jung once commented, "To me a particularly beautiful woman is a source of terror. As a rule a beautiful woman is a terrible disappointment. Beautiful bodies and beautiful personalities rarely go together."[15] Whether that is true or not, men continue to pursue them as mates. Partly they do so because an attractive woman elevates their own social image. A man who has a beautiful woman is perceived as more intelligent, exciting, and successful than a man with a less attractive partner.[16]

There is little to gain by stating that beauty is a poor basis for forming a relationship. It is a time-honored criterion for selecting a mate and will probably not diminish as an influential factor. Given their shortage in the marriage market, many black men tend to select the most desirable (that is, attractive) woman available. This situation led a 37-year-old female sociologist to suggest that:

There are two classes of women among the middle-class black population. There are those with an abundance of dates and attention and whose company is sought even though they're not viewed as "good" marriage material by the men who date them. The second class consists of those women who have little or no attention from males. And though not always, they tend to be less attractive (or know less about making themselves attractive). The second group sometimes feels hostile to men because they have little contact with them or do not have men respond positively to their flirtations. The first group only develops negative views when they want to get married (or enter into a serious relationship) and the men they see don't want that.

Men, too, are ranked according to physical traits. The most desirable males are those who are tall and dress well. In most cases this must be combined with a high level of education and income. When women only want a sexual partner, they may select a man who has style. Translated, a good style is represented by the man who is tall, dresses well, has dancing ability, and knows how ro rap. The man who knows how to rap (that is, talk with facility) may transcend the other criteria. When marriage is involved, women look for the other qualities. But a hard-working, stable, male may be less desirable, even for marriage, than the man with style and status if he is uninteresting and dull. A male's skin color is largely irrelevant to the majority of black women. When skin color is considered, the light-skinned black male is regarded as more untrustworthy than darker-skinned men. While money is important to black women seeking a mate, it is ranked below educational and occupational parity. Many black men in blue collar jobs earn higher salaries than male college graduates but are not acceptable. As one woman told us, "I need somebody I can talk to, not just a guy who brings home a sizable paycheck."

Men are not as bound by the woman's standards for a mate. In the main they may circumvent her criteria by mere aggressiveness in their pursuit. Women, too, may be assertive in pursuing a man, or at least manipulate the situation in order to be "caught." The difference is that women more quickly retreat if they encounter an initial rejection while men persist in their quest of a woman. Women are also cast into a devalued status by virtue of their age. In part this is because beauty may be linked to younger ages. It creates a dilemma for black women, however, when men in their thirties seek out women in their twenties. While women in their thirties will accept men in their forties, the number of eligible black men in that age range is severely limited.

In sum, it appears that singles rate themselves and others on the basis of their degrees, clothes, cars, positions, and physical attractiveness. Despite their avowal that they want certain sociopsychological traits in a mate, the initial elements that attract our singles are those most observable on the surface. It is not that the declared attributes are not desired, but they must be contained in a person who has other qualities that are objectively manifested. Whereas men without high incomes or style and women who are not beautiful may be compatible partners, our singles often will not take the time to know them. In the main the mates black singles will pursue will be men with style, education, and a high income and women who are very attractive. The end result is that the quest for a perfect mate will continue.

COMMITMENT VERSUS FREEDOM

A central problem in finding and keeping a mate is the issue of commitment. The seventies has been characterized as a decade where freedom became more important than commitment. A feeling of transiency has permeated many interpersonal relationships. As one person commented, "With each introduction there is the almost automatic preparation for termination." A similar observation was expressed by another black single, "It just seems like any relationship you enter nowadays will only last about six months. You just get to the point where you think what's the sense of putting much energy into any relationship you get into." One 32-year-old male psychologist attributed it to the social system. He said, "It's external pressures that disrupt people's lives. They have an effect on their relationships, from economic pressures to working in hostile environments. They make people angry and alienated. All people in urban societies experience this, but it seems worse for black folks.''

While partly true, there may be other forces at work. Some of them emerge in early childhood. The willingness to make a commitment to another person may derive from feelings of security fostered in the family. Women, for instance, who grow up in biparental homes, with close relationships to their fathers, may be more inclined to commit themselves to permanent relationships. However, many black women are taught very early in life that black men are not dependable and to be prepared to fend for themselves. Black writer Alice Walker has been quoted as saying, ''Most women in the age range from 25 to 35 were told at some point in their adolescence either by their mother, their aunt, or grandmother, to get an education for two reasons: Either so you won't have to depend on a black man or so you can give him a hand in his struggle to survive.''[17]

On the other hand, black men may be subject to a different set of forces. Certainly the glamorized image of black playboys and superstuds does nothing to encourage commitment in black men. The excess number of black women in the eligible pool and the concentration of so many educated, attractive, women and their implicit sexual and emotional demands may overwhelm them. With so many women to choose from, it becomes more difficult for black men to form committed relationships. One 30-year-old male counselor commented:

My problem is the inability or need to make a decision. There are too many smart and pretty women. I'm immature and irresponsible. I have a fear of being overwhelmed by the responsibility of having to share something that you aren't certain about. At times I have the feeling of being abandoned at some point. I've never met a woman I'd like to spend the rest of my life with. I've never discovered commitment or how to make it to a woman.

Women, too, have motives for avoiding commitment which relate to the desire to avoid any kind of responsibility. A 27-year-old female engineer declared:

I love being single, since I was tied down to school so long. It feels good now to be free to be promiscuous, in addition to feeling I have no commitments to anyone but myself. Just as long as I have a male to date sometimes, it's o.k. I know I'm in demand in my profession and that anything I desire or feel the incentive to do, I can, and I will be accepted as the double minority. In short, I want to be somebody in my profession, and I'm willing and going to make it and I want to make it.

Some women have a fear of making a commitment and suffering the fate of many black women—being rejected and winding up as a divorcee with children to support. This is especially true of those women who come from broken homes. A 25-year-old graduate student remarked:

Like almost every other woman, I would one day like to get married, possibly when I'm finished with my graduate studies. It's sort of scary, the thought of being attached to someone all my life (not that I can't get out of it). Just the divorce rate makes me wonder sometimes if it's all worth it. I hope, though, that if I do get married it will turn out for the better.

Occasionally it is not a desire to avoid commitment but the timing. Men and some women may pursue a professional career in the early stages of their life and later devote themselves to marriage and family concerns. An oft-cited case was that of the individual who wants a commitment from his/her partner and is rejected but in turn rejects a partner when he/she wants a commitment. This is frequently stated by women as "the men I wanted to marry didn't want to marry me and the ones who wanted to marry me, I didn't want to marry." A 32-year-old male accountant summed up this view:

It seems that black men often encounter two extreme types of women. One type is the woman who totally enjoys her freedom or is totally dedicated to her career and has no intentions of getting married in the foreseeable future. The other type is the woman who tends to interject the idea of marriage very early in the relationship, which puts a lot of pressure upon the male, who may not be willing to commit himself so soon. As far as my experience is concerned, I have met very few women who can talk about marriage seriously and openly without adopting one of these attitudes.

Looking for the right person is sometimes a defense against commitment and getting hurt. What people are looking for is often what they sense they lack in themselves. While the desire to avoid commitment is common among both sexes, it seems to endure longer in males. One woman, a 29-year-old college instructor, found this out the hard way:

I have, in the past, had very positive experiences with black men, and it is only now that I'm realizing why. Before I was never interested in becoming too serious and making a commitment. Now that I find I'd like to change my style, I find the black men I meet are not able to commit themselves to a permanent relationship.

Among the other factors shaping attitudes toward commitment are past experiences with the opposite sex. If a person has a previous history of good experiences with a companion, trusted and tried over time, those experiences help make commitment to a future relationship possible. When past relationships have resulted in rejection, humiliation, and pain, that individual ponders whether the risk is worth the reward. Black men, in particular, have a fear of being vulnerable in a relationship. Leaving themselves vulnerable to be hurt or taken advantage of are two things black men fear most—both in their relationships in the world and with women. A history of rejection in a past relationship makes them very tentative about future commitments.

Vulnerability is closely associated with commitment. Whoever is the most committed to a relationship has the least power in it. Whenever there is an objective conflict, it is the most committed partner who generally gives in.[18] Due to the black male's desire to maintain control of his situation, and his image of masculinity, refusal to make a commitment is one way of achieving the power balance in a relationship. As his emotional involvement with a woman increases, his feelings of insecurity may be heightened. Generally the person who has the most emotional involvement is more subject to fear of losing his partner. Frequently feelings of jealousy erupt as a result of separation anxiety. It is at this point that some black men make marriage proposals in order to insure her fidelity and loyalty. Or, as often happens, he may withdraw from the relationship altogether.

Freedom versus commitment may not be a real dichotomy. In essence there is no freedom without commitment. Those who are afraid to make commitments are locked into a mental prison of their own making. Commitment provides one with the freedom to share one's life with another and to work toward dreams and goals. Marriage does not have to be an institution in which all individuality and autonomy are suppressed. Problems and responsibilities will always be a part of it. But so will the vital sharing experiences and joint pursuit of goals upon which societies depend. When commitment is not made, the bond of intimacy cannot be sustained. The universal need for security requires a commitment to another person at some point in our life. It is not a question of whether to make a commitment or not—but when.

LOVE AND JEALOUSY

Throughout this study notably absent was any mention of love as a factor in choosing a mate nor was that emotion very evident in any of our questionnaire responses. It could be that these singles felt they wanted a relationship with some emotional basis but that the existence of a strong love feeling should be secondary to other attributes. Possibly a concern with love is endemic to the young. In a separate sampling of attitudes among young black college students ages 18 to 22, love emerged as a more dominant force in their mate selection criteria. Many of our older black singles had past experiences in which love was present. The breakup of those relationships could have created a cautious approach to the notion of love. Our guess is that some of them used euphemisms for love such as caring, affectionate relationship, and emotional involvement. Love may be regarded as an outmoded term to describe the emotional intensity extant in their interpersonal relationships.

Possibly the fear of intimacy and commitment makes love a dangerous emotion. Because of the fear of failure and rejection, love is avoided since it raises the spectre of powerlessness in a human relationship. Hence, one does not fall in love anymore, one gets involved and subsequently disengages. Once a person has fallen in love several times, he or she may attempt to manage his/her feelings in order to be cushioned against the expected termination of a relationship. Conventional wisdom has it that women are more inclined to fall in love than men. A 34-year-old female executive affirmed this belief:

> Black men are insecure. I think parents have raised black men to be this way. They feel inferior at times and are afraid to do things because they don't know enough about themselves and don't want to take the risk to learn. Black men are afraid to love, afraid to give of their emotions more than their white counterpart. Their parents have brought them up to be inhibited.

Although that is a strong folk belief, and women are certainly more socialized to fall in love with a potential mate, the available research (mostly on whites) indicates that men demonstrate a quicker tendency to fall in love and experience more emotional trauma after the disruption of a love relationship.[19] The limited research on black attitudes toward love, primarily confined to those under the age of 25, shows black males to be more oriented toward romance and love than their white male counterparts.[20] Students of the subject have claimed that women tend to be more careful about who they fall in love with than men. The reasoning behind this assumption is that love is associated with marriage. And a woman is choosing more than a lover but, also, a standard of living since her future status will be determined by her husband's status.[21] Such an assumption may not hold up for our black singles because love, to a large extent, has been divorced from marriage. Moreover, our group of college-educated single women are not that dependent on a male's status in defining their own socioeconomic level.

Love can be more practically managed when one realizes that it does not last very long. The average period of duration is six to thirty months. The same can be said of a romantic liaison.[22] One researcher discovered the median durability of a romantic entanglement to be about fifteen months.[23] It seems that love and romantic relationships have become just one more commodity in a materialist society. If you do not like it, return it within two years. Moreover, romantic love as presently defined is another facet of the culture of narcissism. Generally, people define it as being loved, not loving. In our study few individuals mentioned their capacity to love. One exception was a 29-year-old female nurse:

I am not bitter. I can give love freely. I have the ability to make people view themselves positively and lovingly. I make people feel good about themselves. I am able to make myself feel good about myself. I have a sense of humor which is a great asset in this world. I also have an inner strength because that helps me face the ordeals life throws my way.

Love can give rise to jealousy. As relationships become more emotionally intense, people are inclined to be possessive and anxious about their partner's fidelity. The motivations for jealousy can have a number of origins. Among men it can be a form of control, a way of demonstrating their dominance of their partner. Black women often complained about the tendency of men to restrict them to monogamy while they had a number of sexual liaisons. According to a 37-year-old female medical technician:

> Black men get into possessiveness rather early in a relationship. I know women are usually accused of doing this but men are equally bad, if not worse, offenders. Men often act as if your life started today, and act very offended if you have some "loose ends" from the past that can't be resolved overnight.

All jealousy is not a function of irrational fear, insecurity, or a power struggle in the relationship. A number of changing social forces contribute to the persistence of jealousy in human relationships. Since people are permanently available, this means they can and do exit relationships when they find somebody better.[24] Black women must cope with the intense competition for a desirable male because their numbers are so few in the dating pool. Many adopt an attitude of resignation about male infidelity and only ask that he not make it public. Conversely, many black women are in male-dominated occupations where they come into constant contact with other men who may be available for a sexual fling if not a relationship. Because some of our singles are physically mobile, they may form long-distance relationships with a person. The distance and time between their visits lend themselves to outside affairs by one or both of the partners. Overall, the loosening of the sexual mores and the weakened commitment individuals make to a relationship makes multiple sexual relationships more of a probability, and jealousy is a predictable outcome.

THE PROFESSIONAL WOMAN'S DILEMMA

A relatively recent and common problem cited by our black female singles is that of alleged male "sexism" or the failure to treat women as equals in a relationship. This is an unusual complaint coming from a group where the women have been labelled as matriarchs. Certainly it is a strange problem when one considers that black women have long been in the labor force and have had a higher educational level than black men for years. Unlike in the white population, historically black women have been full working partners in the family. Hence, it is rather surprising to hear a 32-year-old female social worker say, "From a black woman's perspective it appears that some of our men overlook concepts of equalitarianism and humanism in women. I highly respect black men and would appreciate similar regard first as a *person*." It is charged that not only do black men refuse to treat professional black women as equals, but also exclude them from the pool of eligible mates. One woman asserted that the bigger and better they become, the less attractive career women are to men. According to Katherine Nash, "Anything a man accomplishes enhances his sexual desirability. For women success is still a deterrent—for many men she becomes less desirable."[25]

If black male sexist attitudes exist, it is likely due to the acquisition of majority group values about the role of women being subordinate. Also, some black men have attained a very high position in their profession and no longer need a working wife to help achieve a desired standard of living. These men may want their wives to play the traditional role of women in the family. A 34-year-old female anthropologist summed up the professional woman's dilemma this way:

It is difficult to find a person that one is truly compatible with, and that's especially true for a highly educated woman whose expectations often differ from those of most women and are not always consistent with the *eligible pool* (similar status) of men who seem to have some preference for "traditional" women. I believe that most men in the eligible pool mostly want physically attractive women who take for granted traditional role definitions and the deference they imply.

Certainly some black men view women as considerably less than full equals to them. One extreme comment by a black male was, "I am unable to consider a woman as anything other than a sex object. I cannot conceive of any other role for a woman in my life." More representative of the black male "sexist" perspective is that of a 41-year-old government employee:

I'm looking for a person who is ambitious, who enjoys the simple basic things of life, who values her health, and works to stay healthy. I want a person who has respect for herself, her family and mate, a person who is not working herself and will become involved in her mate's work. She should encourage me and manage what I provide. Most of all she should love family closeness and want and love children.

When they encounter such men, black women are forced into making a career-versus-mate decision. We hear constantly of women who decide not to go to graduate school because they will never find a husband if they are "overeducated." One woman who wanted to be a medical doctor pursued that ambition but blended it with her desire to be a "regular" wife. She decided to become a pathologist because they work more regular hours than other physicians. Still, her marriage broke up when her husband abandoned her for another woman. In the past women received their feeling of security from a marriage. Increasingly they are obtaining that same security from a professional career. A 31-year-old female psychologist remarks:

I did not marry because I was not ready to assume the responsibilities unique to the dynamics of marriage. My history in the last twelve years has been that of choosing, or being forced to choose, preparing myself academically for my career (completing undergraduate and graduate school) or marriage. I wanted first to achieve a secure financial situation as a means of negotiating on issues with a man if necessary.

This notion of negotiating with a man on the nature of their relationship is perceived as a threat by many black men. Black women are cognizant of that fear. A 28-year-old female army officer noted:

I think black men and women, especially those who are struggling for upward mobility, find themselves competing with each other instead of assisting each other. I have found black men have fragile egos and find it very difficult to deal with a proud, confident, black woman. In this respect, it is hard to maintain a lasting relationship with a man.

Few black males admit to being threatened by very successful black women. At least they deny that it is her success that makes her unacceptable as a mate. A 31-year-old male medical student retorted:

Another problem appears to be that many successful black women, while bemoaning the lack of educated brothers, literally can't relate to brothers who are successful. Some of them believe that all black men are less competent than they, regardless of their educational level. They are accustomed to knowing everything and making all the decisions. Many of them are very self-centered and think the world revolves around them and their interests. In talking to them it's hard to get a word in edgewise. I don't care about how much education a woman has, how much money she makes. I just don't want to compete with people on the job and come home and compete with my wife.

Indicative of those black women who assume an air of intellectual superiority over black men is this 33-year-old female lawyer:

There is great difficulty in finding someone to relate to on an intellectual level. Most of the time the woman is intellectually superior. Therefore, there is no blending of the minds unless a couple is in school together or is interested in the same subject. For some reason, black men don't seem to be interested in anything but sports and sex. You can't get them to go to a play, the opera, or anything outside of the two areas I mentioned. For a successful relationship there must be oneness of mind, body, and soul.

In contrast to what some women believe about men wanting to be leaders in male/female relationships, others claim that men are too dependent. One woman confirms this opinion: "I still think that a lot of single women would like men to take the lead, professionally and socially, if they are competent to do so. Unfortunately, a lot of them want to lead but don't have the ability." A 29-year-old female graduate student responded that:

> Most importantly I want and need a man I can depend on and not have him always depending on me. I have gotten tired of men pushing all the problems on my shoulders and not handling them themselves. They want you to take care of business that relates to the world. I saw a student for awhile. He would always put his phone in someone else's name—always a woman's. He never paid his bill—so he'd have me call to ask for extensions on the bill. I'd have to be the woman. I'm not afraid to talk to anyone about business issues—he was.

One complication in this whole issue of female equality versus male dominance is the possibility that, while advocating parity in a relationship, many women want men to be strong, sometimes dominant. Such ambivalence is manifested in the view of this 34-year-old female administrator:

> One problem is being somewhat feminist in my thinking, relatively independent in life-style, and relatively successful professionally, and seeking a man who can accept me as I am, who is not threatened, and yet able to recognize my underlying vulnerable side. It is difficult to reconcile my feelings as a black feminist with my genuine appreciation of men. Also, a side of me likes a bit of sexism, and I often do things to appeal to sexism. I find that many men become threatened when they see you living a relatively liberated life-style, partly because they wonder what they can offer you. They seem to be uncomfortable with offering themselves. Yet, that's what I really need—emotional support.

Merging a career with marriage has never been easy. In the past career women simply remained single because they realized the constraints that a marriage placed on career opportunities and mobility. With the increased numbers of women in top professional jobs, it appears that men will have to make some adjustments to their wives' job demands just as women have done for men in the past. This is particularly a problem in the black community. Not only do more black women have professional careers but there are indications that the majority of black professionals will be women as we enter the twenty-first century. Presently many black men are attempting to screen them out of the mate selection process. Due to the excess number of women available, they have been relatively successful in their effort. In the future the pressure of their numbers will require a different resolution of this issue.

KEEPING A MATE

Whereas finding a mate is problematic, keeping one seems an even more difficult task for our black singles. Throughout their singles career, most will form a serious attachment to a member of the opposite sex. These serious relationships will develop to the point where marriage may be discussed but dropped as a possibility for lack of interest on one or the other's part. Although they may have been in conflict over differences in values and attitudes, or his/her behavior, in many cases it is nothing more than a lack of commitment to a permanent union. And it is the tenacity of commitment that serves as the cement of most marriages. In her research on what constitutes a happy marriage, Arlene Skolnick found that factors such as conventionality, religious participation, and freedom from conflict have little influence on marital happiness. The most important factors, she discovered, were a strong commitment and an affectionate and enjoyable personal relationship between the husband and wife.[26]

It is the absence of a strong commitment to a relationship, at least on the part of one partner, that plagues our black singles. Even when strong conflict has not been present, individuals have been known to exit relationships, often for the most trivial reason. We have heard of cases where one incident of a minor nature has brought about the termination of a relationship. For example, a woman reported to us a story about how she became angry when her boyfriend cancelled out on going to a Nancy Wilson concert the morning of the performance and wanted her to prepare dinner instead. She refused to do so, and they did not speak for a week. When they finally engaged in a dialogue, they were unable to have a meeting of the minds and decided to break up. The question of faultfinding here is less important than the lack of tenacity in both partners.

Another problem that besets our black singles who enter into relationships, defined as serious, is the tendency to become intensely involved at the initial stages of its formation. It is common for some couples to spend every leisure moment with their new partner, thereby overloading the relationship by the intensity of interaction. Somehow the romantic involvement is seen as a panacea for all their other woes in life. Many courtships cannot withstand the burden of constant togetherness, and one of the partners may try to retreat into a private sanctuary. Such a withdrawal may be interpreted as a loss of interest or love by the other partner who may act out his/her resentment or feelings of insecurity. The most common pattern of withdrawal is usually an act of men. While the need for some space to reflect, or pursue other interests is understandable, a single person may be rather capricious in their desires. As one man told us, "I think it would be hard for me to carry on a good consistent relationship with a woman who'd be my wife or whatever. It's awful because you want them, you may love them, but you want it at your own time and your own space. It's difficult."

Relationships can be fragile because single individuals can be unclear about what traits are most desirable. For instance, it is often assumed that complementarity in interests and behavior is the best basis of compatibility and harmony. But individuals may be best served by a diversity of traits. An extroverted, assertive, person can be more in tune with an introverted, passive, partner. They may not have the same conflict over competition in talking to each other or socializing with other people. However, it is not the opposition of traits that will bind people together but the possession of traits that are admired in the other partner. When people are supercilious about their own personality and interests, they can fail to appreciate the variations in a romantic partner. Those who stay together frequently develop an appreciation of the differences in their mate.

Homogamy in education and income may be exaggerated as a factor in marital happiness. Even people who have graduated from college may have a narrow sphere of interests. And that sphere of interest may be more linked to gender than educational level. Not all college graduates are well versed in international events, classical music, and great literature. Many husbands and wives, especially those with children, do not spend that much time talking together. What seems to be of greater importance is their enjoyment and appreciation of each other's personality. While women who marry down seem to have a higher ratio of marital breakup, it is probably more a function of attitudes either the man or woman brings to the situation. The man may feel insecure because of his education or economic inferiority. Or the woman may demonstrate an arrogance of power due to her higher educational and economic level. Neither discrepancy need be the basis of interpersonal conflict.

Failure to communicate may be an important factor in losing a mate, but communication is overrated as a facilitating technique. The reason is that discussion of an issue in conflict is not communication. Too often couples do not listen to each other's concerns and do not try to address them. They simply take turns in listing complaints about the other's behavior. This could be part of a bargaining process whereby one partner will not rectify his/her attitude or behavior until the other one alters his/hers. Such beefing sessions can result in nothing more than a stalemate. Again, the couple may have different perceptions of the same conflictual event. She may be very upset by something he considers very normal or minor behavior. Sometimes one partner may be oversensitive to the meanings of the other's behavior. Other times the partner may be insensitive to his/her mate's feelings. These are the sort of issues that have to be worked out and frequently are not addressed very well in the couple's dialogue.

Overall, keeping a mate is a function of the degree of commitment and the acceptance of each other's differences. Unfortunately, relationships tend to be ordered along power distribution rather than reconciliation of diversity in traits and interests. People are more inclined to seek perfection in a mate than learn to tolerate, even appreciate, their variations. Since few people are perfect and even fewer are precisely matched for desired traits, the problems of a quest for a mate and the inability to sustain a relationship, will remain with us for some time to come.

SUMMARY

As we have seen, finding and keeping a mate is complicated by a number of sociopsychological factors as well as structural restraints. Social structure and individual attitudes interface to make male/female relationships ephemeral rather than permanent. The imbalance in the sex ratio will continue to deny large numbers of professional black women a comparable mate. There are only a limited number of ways to deal with that irreversible fact of life. At the same time there does exist a pool of professional black males, who are available to this group of women, yet the tension between them builds barriers to communicating and mating. This is a complex problem and there is no easy solution. While there are some black men who are threatened by the successful black woman, further investigation reveals other underlying forces. Men are torn between the need for security and the desire for freedom, the quest for a special person to call their own, and the temptation of sexual variety. They see marriage as a way of establishing roots but are seduced by the enticement of all the attractive, possibly "better," women in their midst.

Given his advantages as a male in a sexist society, and his high prestige, a quality in short supply in the black community, there is little incentive for some black men to undertake the actions needed to meet the needs of women. The women who feel that their emotional needs are not being met begin to recoil and adopt their own agenda based on a conception of their self-interest. Some recognition must be made of the changing relations between men and women. The old exchange of feminine sexual appeal for male financial support is in a declining state. Women are increasingly able to define their own status and are economically independent. What they seek now is the satisfaction of emotional needs, not an economic cushion. While men must confront this new reality, women must realize that emotional needs can be taken care of by men in all social classes. Although a similar education and income can mean greater compatibility in values and interests, it is no guarantee of said compatibility nor personal happiness. As some of our subjects' comments suggest, common needs, interests, and values are more a function of gender than class.

We should not be deluded by the ostensible reluctance of many black singles to enter the conjugal state. When people have not been able to develop a lasting permanent relationship with members of the opposite sex, they have to play it off and make the best of whatever it is they have at the moment. As one woman told us,

"I see the experience of being black, single, and female basically as a positive one, because that is what I am, and I view life positively —and with faith." However, while the industrial and urban revolution has made singlehood more viable as a way of life, it has also made the need for belonging more imperative. The tensions of work and the impersonality of the city have created a need to escape the depersonalization by retreating into some sort of an intimate sanctum. This is especially imperative for blacks in the middle class, who have their personhood tested daily by a racist society and who must often work and live in isolation. In our modern society individuals are required to depend on each other for permanence and stability. That is a function previously served by a large familial and social network.

It is the fear that even marriage no longer provides that permanence and stability that causes people to enter and exit their relationships quickly. It is the fear of failure that comes from failure. Until our black singles develop a tenacity to work at relationships as they did their schooling and jobs, we will continue to see this vicious cycle repeated again and again. Marriage and the family continue to be the most important buffer for blacks against racism and depersonalization. When we look at the strongest predictors of happiness in America, they are inevitably social factors such as marriage, family, friends, and children. Across the board, married people tend to be happier than unmarrieds. The best confirmation of this fact is that most people who divorce eventually remarry. Before anyone can find happiness in a marriage, they have to form a strong basis for marriage. It is that task that continues to perplex our black singles.

NOTES

1. Arthur W. Calhoun, *A Social History of the American Family* (New York: Barnes and Noble, 1960).

2. Ernest W. Burgess and Harvey J. Locke, *The Family: From Institution to Companionship* (New York: American Book Company, 1953).

3. Kingsley Davis, Intermarriage in caste societies, in *The Family: Its Structure and Functions*, ed. R. Coser (New York: St. Martin's Press, 1964), p. 106.

4. Winston Ehrman, *Premarital Dating Behavior* (New York: Henry Holt, 1959).

5. Jean Noble, *The Negro Woman College Graduate* (New York: Columbia University Press, 1956), p. 108.

6. Herman A. Young and Brenda H. McAnulty, Traditional black colleges: the role, social benefits and costs, *Western Journal of Black Studies* 2 (Fall 1978): 170.

7. Emile Durkheim, *Suicide: A Study in Sociology* (Glencoe, Illinois: The Free Press, 1951, original edition 1897).

8. Mary Helen Washington, *Black-eyed Susans: Classic Stories by and about Black Women* (Garden City, New York: Anchor Press, 1975), p. xxviii.

9. William M. Chavis and Gladys Lyles, Divorce among educated black women, *Journal of the National Medical Association* 67 (March 1975): 134.

10. La Frances Rodgers Rose, Relationships between black males and females—toward a definition, in *Women and Their Health: Research Implications for a New Era*, ed. V. Olesen (Washington, D.C.: U.S. Department of Health, Education, and Welfare, 1975), p. 64.

11. Thomas Pettigrew et al., Color gradations and attitudes among middle-income negroes, *American Sociological Review* 31 (June 1966): 365-374; Jeffrey Jacques, *The Concepts of Self-esteem, Color, Social Status and Mate Selection in a Predominantly Black Community*, Ph.D. Dissertation, Florida State University, 1974.

12. Shades of black, *The Oakland Tribune*, 13 May 1979, pp. 17-18.

13. Ibid.

14. Sheila Banks, Success and beauty: A blessing or curse. *Ebony*, September 1978, p. 41.

15. *San Francisco Chronicle*, 4 August 1979, p. 31.

16. Ellen Bersheid and Elaine Walster, Beauty and the beast. *Psychology Today*, March 1972, pp. 42-47.

17. Black marriages—victims of the affluent rat race, *San Francisco Examiner*, 25 April 1976, pp. 1, 24.

18. Willard Waller, *The Family* (New York: Dryden, 1938).

19. Ellen Walster and G. William Walster, *A New Look at Love* (Reading, Mass.: Addison-Wesley, 1978), pp. 49-50.

20. Carlfred B. Broderick, Social heterosexual development among urban negroes and whites, *Journal of Marriage and the Family* 27 (May 1965): 200-203; David L. Larson et al., Social factors in the frequency of romantic involvement among adolescents, *Adolescence* 11 (Spring 1976): 7-12.

21. Zick Rubin, The love research, *Human Behavior*, February 1977, pp. 56-59.

22. Walster and Walster, *A New Look at Love*, pp. 108-126.

23. F. B. Meeker and Carl La Fung, *Broken hearts: dissolution of romantic relationships* (A paper presented at the Western Psychological Association Meeting, San Francisco, California, April 1978).

24. Bernard Farber, *Family: Organization and Interaction* (San Francisco: Chandler, 1964).

25. *Jet Magazine*, 12 October 1976, p. 24.

26. Rx for a happy marriage, *The San Francisco Sunday Examiner and Chronicle, This World*, 2 April 1978, p. 35.

Who's Got the Sexual Revolution?   5

Despite the advent of the so-called sexual revolution, the area of human sexuality remains subject to a number of misunderstandings. Theory and research on the matter are often guided by the moral precepts of the social scientists rather than an objective sorting out of the conflicting attitudes and behavior in the sexual arena. If we add the additional variables of gender, race, and class, the complexities of human sexuality are even more difficult to capture in traditional social science categories. Previous research on black sexuality, in particular, has been value-laden. Conclusions have ranged from blacks being endowed with hotter sexual passions to an exaggerated puritanism characterizing their sexual education and behavior. While the prevailing societal stereotype depicts blacks as morally loose, the liberalization of white sexual expression has made most of these invidious racial comparisons moot.[1]

Our concern here is with the sexual behavior of middle-class, unmarried, black women. Historically this group has been subject to a different sexual history than their lower-class counterpart. Because blacks were so stigmatized by their different form of sexual expression, the middle class response was to assume an even more rigid moral code than the majority rule. Black males of the middle class preferred that their wives remained at home to avoid sexual advances. Virginity at marriage was often expected. According to Walters, the most extreme expression of middle-class morality was exhibited on the black college campus. Curfew hours for incoming-freshmen coeds was as early as

6 P.M. Some colleges had rules prohibiting two students of the opposite sex from meeting each other without the presence and permission of the Dean of Women or a teacher. Members of the opposite sex could be dispatched home for walking together in broad daylight.[2]

Among members of the upwardly-mobile lower class, prudence in sexual activity was often a pragmatic adaptation to the requirements of achieving a higher education. Women who engaged in premarital coitus could become pregnant, drop out, or be dismissed from college, and remain in the lower class. Thus, it was best to abstáin. Those who did not and became pregnant sought abortions to cover up their moral lapses.[3] While middle-class black women have generally been more sexually conservative than their lower-class sisters, the available—albeit limited—research consistently shows them to engage in premarital sex earlier, more frequently, and with more partners than comparable white women.[4] They are less likely to have casual sexual experiences, and the slight differences between them and middle-class white females are probably more a function of the black male's high level of sexual liberality than any other factor.

Not only has the sexual revolution liberalized sexual attitudes and behavior among black and white women, but the increasing trend of women to remain unmarried much past the normative age has had a dramatic effect on their sexual patterns. This is particularly true for college-educated black women. Since they are the one segment of American society most likely to remain unmarried past the age of thirty,[5] they continue to date or interact with men. Hence, sexual factors must be dealt with in untraditional ways. As we shall see, few have chosen total abstinence, but not many have become completely liberated from the conservative sexual values of the past. The complexity of their response is what we seek to unravel in the present study.

CHANGES

During their college years, most of our female subjects adhered to a rather conservative sexual code for the reasons described above. Many of them remained virgins until after graduation or confined their sexual experiences to a man with whom they had a committed relationship. A typical example was a 32-year-old social worker who commented, "My point of comparison would be college—ten years ago. Since then, when I was a young adult living in a college dorm, there have been some very major changes. Probably sexual expectations are the biggest change; since back then we were still in the 'virgin' syndrome." The changes she speaks of have, indeed, been most significant as attested to by a 35-year-old female educator who lost her virginity at the age of 22. She declares that, "A sexual relationship is a very normal part of an ongoing dating relationship. It may be an early part of the relationship or may develop over a period of sustained nonsexual contact."

Prolonged singlehood has imposed a more liberal acceptance of nonmarital sexual activity on the overwhelming majority of our subjects. Whether they wanted to be participants in the sexual revolution or not, the conditions of single life have required a significant alteration of their heretofore conservative sexual values. Only a small number of our sample held to a traditional stance on nonmarital coitus. That small group also exhibited a high degree of religiosity. A 30-year-old female teacher staunchly declares that, "No, I don't think that one should have sex with a person that they're dating, not even if they're engaged. Sex was intended for married couples only."

That few of our subjects share such a categorical attitude toward nonmarital sexual activity is partly due to changes in general societal attitudes toward that behavior. The women's movement helped by legitimizing the right of women to participate in and enjoy sex on an equal basis with men. Yet, the sexual revolution, as it is popularly called, was much more in conformity with male than female values. As Hite has noted, "the sexual revolution is a male production, its principles still concentrated on male values."[6] That many black women are not totally comfortable with the new sexual morality is expressed in the complaint of a 27-year-old female program manager, "Sexual expectations of black men sometimes make it difficult for single women to want to date them. The women would rather have relationships develop along other lines than just sexual."

Being an unattached single woman and wanting to date means

having to deal with the sexual expectations of men. Due to their different socialization, most men view dating as an instrumental (that is, goal-oriented) activity. What they do on the date is not as important as the aftermath. If the outcome is a sexual experience, the evening is a success. For women the date is more of an expressive goal; to enjoy the activity and the companionship. The particular dilemma this places single black women in was expressed well by a 32-year-old female graduate student:

> It's understood—that if you don't plan on going to bed with him, don't expect more than one date. So enjoy yourself. You feel that maybe you lose out on a lot because you may never see that person again. So, I'm getting to the point where it's almost not worth going out just to be going out—unless you are really attracted to the man.

That males expect instant sexual gratification is quite obvious in our interview data. A typical male view was held by a 38-year-old male college professor, "I think you should seek to sleep with any lady that you can, under any conditions you can. I think physical consideration should be a consideration in all sex matters. I don't like having to take a trip to the doctors to get the old penicillin shot." An equally candid response was that of a 27-year-old male insurance representative, "I don't have to date any woman for money, conversation or fun. And I don't waste a lot of time on any that don't want to give it up." A more pensive position is that of a 40-year-old male political scientist: "Your first interest in a woman is sexual, so that you tend to discover what else (some would say everything else) there is to her in the course of the relationship originally stimulated by sexual attraction."

Not all the males in our sample were that aggressive in pursuing sexual relations on dates. Some were equally as conservative as the women. A 41-year-old male private detective told us, "I find that most girls expect to be asked to go to bed on their first date. And they usually will comply. This usually will not happen with me because I will not allow this to be brought up in conversation." Other men, while not as conservative, were still discriminating in their sexual pursuits. A thoughtful 27-year-old male insurance adjustor believed:

Sex is so all encompassing in the relationship, people think about when it is going to happen, how and what it is going to be like. You never get to know the person until after it's done. I think it is stressful to the relationship. You don't know what the person's emotional makeup is. You overlook negative points while trying to seduce the person. Black males and females never share ideas or ideals until the sex is out of the way. I think sex should be a secondary consideration in a relationship because it can be taught. You can't teach a person personality.

In some cases our single women did not object to the sexual relationship, but the means used in pursuing it. A number of them commented on the tendency of men to be very direct in stating their sexual desires. Many women preferred more ritual or flirtation in the process of obtaining sexual access. Another common desire of these women was that there should be a mutual understanding of the meaning of a sexual relationship. Many black men, they complained, are unwilling to discuss sex in an intimate way with their partner. A 39-year-old female newspaper reporter says, "The black man still feels sex is a closed subject. They have got a lot of hangups to overcome." Given greater communication on the part of the male, chances are that there would still be conflict since the male would likely define the sexual relationship as being recreational rather than creating an emotional bond. An old male adage is that a certain amount of deception is necessary in sexual seduction. Attempting to elicit agreement in advance from a potential sexual partner is, in essence, asking her to take responsibility for what happens. All things being equal, a man is more likely to encounter a negative response.

SEXUAL ROLES AND PRACTICES

From all accounts most of our subjects continued to play traditional sexual roles. Males were expected to initiate sexual relationships and women to exercise a negative control. Women, of course, gave out receptive cues to encourage male sexual advances. Nowadays a large number of women are given to espousing liberal sexual beliefs, which may or may not be translated into concrete acts. Some women claimed they would be more sexually aggressive if a male made no sexual advances after a couple of dates. In most cases the male moved first. A number of women were variable in their sexual responses. A 34-year-old female college professor reported:

Men don't realize that women go up and down emotionally. We're turned on one minute, the next minute we're turned off by little or nothing. This is part of a woman's makeup. As for sex, I have no real set rules for myself, except that the "vibes" should be right. Sometimes I have sexual relations with someone I've just met, other times, someone I've known and dated for a long time may not turn me on physically. One time I was in bed with a man and smelled a strong foot odor. This completely turned me off but I went through the act anyway.

Not only have some black women assumed a more aggressive sexual posture, but they believe men have forced them to. A 38-year-old female researcher pointed out, "I've noticed that many (not all) black males are expecting more and more from women. Many expect the woman to be the aggressor, to phone them, invite them out, and even go so far as to expect them to initiate sexual relations. Yet, if the woman should suddenly become the initiator of sex, most feel threatened." There seems to be some gender disagreement on this issue. A number of black men feel that black women are not as sexually aggressive as they could be. One black man, a 42-year-old urban planner, dissents and claims, "Black women are sexually aggressive. They participate equally in love-making; they may initiate a new position or be more willing to make love; they have less hangups about sexual role playing."

One of the restraints on female sexual aggressiveness is the co-existence of the new ideology of sexual liberation with the old double standard of sexual conduct. A new study on male sexuality found a large number of men are greatly disturbed about women having sex without emotional commitment.[7] In at least one study black men were discovered to hold a double standard more often than white men.[8] Very few of our female subjects spoke to this issue, perhaps due to ignorance of its existence or lack of concern about it. One woman, a 28-year-old college professor, did note that, "In Atlanta to be seriously considered as a mate, one has to avoid a reputation for promiscuity. So I consider the potential for the relationship as well as who the person is in the total scheme of things (how visible the relationship is likely to be in the society in which I operate).'' The rather large majority of our women who have had sexual experiences has served to undercut any male insistence on female sexual ''purity.'' Yet, they can still screen out the very permissive female in favor of a woman with limited sexual experience.

There are, of course, women who appear to engage in nonmarital sexual relations for the same reasons of physical pleasure as men. Some men have difficulty believing that any women can reduce the sexual act to nothing but a physical one. Such a man was a 27-year-old social worker who declared, ''Baby, sex is my living. Once I lay a chick she's mine.'' That men cannot believe women are capable of separating sex from emotional involvement is puzzling to a number of females in our sample. According to a 30-year-old female school teacher:

The men I have sex with are very self-conscious. They have feelings I just don't have. I mean, they'll really be getting into the groove when I just lie back and let them do their thing without feeling anything for them. Men don't seem to understand where I am coming from. They seem to think that I have sex with them because I love them. But, really, the only reason I have sex with them is pure and simple: For the pleasure I get from it all.

That women can receive physical pleasure from sexual contact is not to be doubted. Whether large numbers of our single black women are capable of sustained sexual contact with one person without emotional involvement is open to question. Surely there are other cultures where female sexual expression does not differ markedly from that of the male.[9] Yet most of our single female subjects were socialized into conservative sexual values only ten years ago. And for black women in particular, the stigma of being ''morally loose'' carries with it a special historical and social meaning. The realities of prolonged singlehood has imposed upon many of them a liberal sexual behavior for which they have not internalized the appropriate values. Much of the contemporary rhetoric of black female sexual liberation we hear may best be explained by their need to avoid cognitive dissonance. When there is incompatibility between an act and a belief system, the individual must reduce the dissonance by altering her behavior or beliefs.[10] Consequently, black women, who of necessity are sexually active, develop liberal views about their sexuality.

Such psychological compartmentalization has its limitations. Within their liberal sexual activity, most black women are bargaining for a stable relationship. And they are doing so with a group of black men who have a high level of noncommitment. A perceptive analysis of this situation was given by a 39-year-old male writer:

> You can sleep with someone faster in the seventies than in the fifties and early sixties. I think the whole sexual culture is faster in that respect. But there's a curious contradiction because at the same time that there is all this sexual hedonism most women seem to be looking for someone to settle down with, for a non-one night stand, are looking, that is to say, for their man.

One more example of the changing sexual scene is the variety of sexual practices in which our singles engage. Acts which were once taboo among blacks have become common place. Probably the greatest change has been in the practice of oral and anal sex. A 38-year-old female nurse hints at this, "They do sometimes ask for different kinds of sex from the normal or what I'd consider normal and sometimes it's all right, different, but a good feeling." It would appear that many of these new sexual techniques are initiated by the men. A 38-year-old female researcher notes, "Those who are or have been involved with white women all expect oral sex." The use of oral sex does not occur in all sexual contacts. Many women regard it as a more intimate form of sexual interaction and reserve it only for "serious" sexual partners. And according to the one study on the subject, a black woman is almost twice as likely to perform fellatio on a male as he is to engage in cunnilingus on her.[11]

The onset of female sexual liberation has increased the pressure on traditional black women to exhibit their enjoyment. For women the concentration on having an orgasm puts anxious thought where erotic emotions should be. Men expect women not only to have sex with them, but to achieve an orgasm as well. A woman's failure to do so is translated into a failure for the male. Many a male has withdrawn from a woman who has not given him this visible affirmation of his masculinity. For women the pressure to act satisfied often results in deception or destroys spontaneous enjoyment when their sexual identity is measured by a series of successful physical acts. And many black women complain that the men do not adequately stimulate them to orgasm. A 36-year-old female high school counselor said "I think a lot of black men don't realize the importance of foreplay before lovemaking. Either they don't know that it takes time for the woman to get ready or they don't care or they don't have the patience. The woman is simply an object for their pleasure. If she doesn't have an orgasm, then he is unhappy."

SEXUAL STRATEGIES

When single black women become accustomed to relatively frequent sexual activity, they may begin to accept the existence of sexual needs. In the main, however, they generally face one of two problems: how to avoid sex with men that are not of sexual interest to them or how to gratify sexual urges when they are not actively involved in an ongoing relationship. The former problem has existed for a number of years, but is exacerbated by the tendency of men to expect an instantaneous sexual response on the first date. One response to male sexual demands is to drop out of the dating game. A 40-year-old businesswoman said:

I don't want to have sex with anyone casually and didn't feel very good about it when I did. I have essentially eliminated dating to take the pressure off for having sex with a man because he took me out. I wish there could be more relationships with men that did not have sexual overtones, ones where he does not feel required to make the overture and I don't feel required to comply.

Women who continue to date must develop some techniques of sexual avoidance. Those with frail personalities are particularly prone to male sexual aggressiveness. Hence, they often avoid situations where sexual advances can be made. One ruse is to avoid going to the male's domicile. Here a concept of territoriality is set into motion. A woman controls the interaction in her residence, the man has control in his milieu. Abstaining from any physical contact (for example, kissing, petting) helps avoid further sexual advances and male outrage at being misled. Some women of firm conviction and strong personality use a verbal approach. A 29-year-old female college administrator reported, "There is a likelihood that I'll be asked to go to bed with someone the first time I've gone out with him, but oftentimes I can take care of that expectation beforehand by telling the person that I prefer to take things slowly until I know where things are going. I think this tends to alter the expectation that if I agree to go out with you, I'll also agree to go to bed with you."

Patterns of sexual avoidance are not unique to women. Because many single black women are sexually aggressive, some discriminating men also must devise ways to eschew coitus. Of course, some men are merely threatened by any sign of female sexual interest. If they do not have control over initiating the sexual relationship, many assume they will not have control over what happens in the course of it. More to the point, they fear being judged on their sexual performance and found wanting. One such recalcitrant male, a 31-year-old artist, stated, "Sometimes to avoid it (sex) I'll leave or ask her to leave. Sometimes the relationship continues and sometimes it doesn't—sometimes it converts to either a casual, friendly, or professional relationship. When they feel rejected, our relationship discontinues or the issues linger for a time as a strain in relations."

The other problem, and a rather common one, was the issue of sexual deprivation. A rather large number admitted to experiencing this problem. Surprisingly, many of the formerly-married women claimed to experience less sexual deprivation than when living with a husband. But for many of the free-floating single women, those not involved in an ongoing relationship, the satisfaction of sexual urges presented them with a curious dilemma. Many did not want to engage in casual sexual adventures or found their dating partners sexually unattractive. One woman, a 34-year-old nurse, reported, "I don't often feel sexually deprived, but it is thus far a problem without a solution for me. I don't like sex only for gratification of my physical needs, so I don't seek a partner for only that purpose." According to some of our subjects, they were likely to resort to subliminating their sexual needs into a frenzied outburst of work or leisure activity. A significant proportion of them stated they turned to autoerotic stimulation. According to a 26-year-old female social worker, "Sexual deprivation is much more difficult as I am very uncomfortable with one night stands. Masturbation helps the sex drive but not the feelings of affection. I masturbate occasionally rather than one nighters."

Many of our single women dealt more directly with the issue. They simply called up a male who would satisfy their sexual needs. A 36-year-old female psychologist declared, "I have rarely felt sexually deprived as sex is not hard to come by. I have arrangements with a few male friends that permit occasional sexual contact." These men are generally former lovers or males whom the women regard as unsuitable for a long-term alliance. This 29-year-old female teacher says, "When I feel needy for sex, then I call my old standby. He has served that function for three or four years. He's a guy whom I like and respect and he likes and respects me, but we cannot make it on any long term basis. When we are seriously involved with other people, we don't get together at all."

It is worthwhile noting that these emergency calls for sexual relief occur on a very subtle level. Many of the men we interviewed claimed not to know of women calling them to meet sexual needs. A 35-year-old female sociologist explained how she operated:

Whenever I feel sexually deprived I can usually arrange to receive some satisfaction. I haven't gotten to the point where I'm aggressive enough to approach a man directly for sex. What I customarily do is call one up and say what I want to do is go to a movie, out to dinner, or something. Most of the men I've slept with before, and I know that if I am in their company, they will try to go to bed with me. But I say that I want to go to a movie when I actually want the sex.

Many of these expressions of sexual deprivation are actually the need for male affection and closeness. This illustrates the multiple function of sexual contact for many women. Much of the pleasure black women associate with sexual contact is the feeling of being close to another human being. In fact, it is often difficult for them to divorce the emotional impact of the fusion of bodies from the physical sensation. Some were aware of this emotional and physical link. A 28-year-old female graduate student admitted, "There have been periods when I felt a need for sex, but it has been close male companionship I wanted—rather than sex. At times when I'm lonely and just need a man to hold me, it's easy for me to engage sexually and feel better afterwards."

Strangely, few of the men in our sample claimed to experience sexual deprivation. With the excessive number of women available to them, many of them lonely or with a liberal sexual ideology, few men experienced any difficulty in meeting their sexual needs. A typical comment was that of a 34-year-old businessman, "In this epoch of sexual libertarianism, there is no need to be sexually deprived." One man, a well-known athlete, claimed that it was not necessary for him to go outside his apartment to seek sexual gratification. He simply called one woman on an extensive list he kept and invited her over for a drink. Most times, he said, they accepted the invitation. However, an unusual response was that of a 35-year-old male college professor:

Sexual deprivation is likely to exist, and relief is often not available because of other complications. Mostly I find that women deal with sex in two ways. Some will engage in it once or twice, then withdraw before they become emotionally involved. Those you deal with sexually over a longer period of time want some commitment, which in most cases I'm not willing to make. It makes it hard being a single male. Either I spend all my time securing sex from a lot of different women or find a meaningful relationship with one steady person. So far I haven't done either.

THE FUNCTIONS OF SEX

Since time immemorial sex has served a variety of functions. It has rarely been just a physiological function of the human body. The same is true in the world of black singles. While it is true that few of our single women could use the enticement of sex as an inducement to marriage, most realized its potent potential in a relationship. A relationship without sexual congress nowadays is ipso facto not a relationship. At the same time sexual contact does not a relationship make. As a 31-year-old female sociologist responded to our question, "Have you noticed any change in what men expect or do on dates nowadays?" "Nope, in the sense that in my mother's day there was a saying, 'a hard dick has no conscience.' Yes, in the sense that there is more honesty about sex but more confusion over what is a relationship."

One purpose that sex does serve, particularly for women, is to set up obligations and claims for time, attention, material rewards, and commitment. A person with whom there is no sexual contact is by that fact alone a friend. Whatever a friend does is at his or her personal discretion and based on feelings of generosity and goodwill. A sexual lover, on the other hand, is subject to a different set of expectations. When sexual contact occurs, it is often an act for which some exchange is taking place. It may be an implied agreement which neither partner affirms. Yet the consequences of failing to live up to the implied contract are, in many cases, very concrete. Mainly it entails the withdrawal of sexual services. Generally it is women for whom sexual access is the more valuable commodity. Due to the lingering effect of the past and the double sexual standard, it is the woman who is defined as sacrificing respectability and marriage chances in exchange for whatever a male can or is willing to offer.

In the present context it is still female sexual access that is most difficult to obtain. And women in the main still exercise a negative control over sexual conduct. At the same time, with the imbalanced sex ratio extant, sexual acquiescence guarantees a woman nothing. A number of women complained that many men will not even take them outside of their respective domiciles or bring them gifts. As one woman bitterly stated, "All they want to do is come over to your place, sit, smoke, watch TV, and have sex." Women who do not accept this male "dating" style soon find out that men have other women, very lonely ones, to turn to. What they find out is that sexual pliability gives them the *opportunity* to press claims and obligations, given a satisfactory sexual performance and reasonable physical attractiveness on their part. While some women find platonic male friends more reliable and generous, they are not easy to locate nor to retain. In the words of a 32-year-old female educator, "A single woman automatically rules out the possibility of having male friends. The sexual component must be dealt with. If I would rather be friends, it sometimes limits my interaction with males.''

Over a long period of sexual involvement, women can lay claim to a male's time or attention. In essence a certain amount of accountability is expected. She claims the first priority on his time, except for his work, and may even demand the appearance of being the exclusive woman in his life. In time her demands may escalate into a required commitment for cohabitation or even marriage. All this is rarely possible without the normative sexual relations. This, of course, is not the sole nor even most important reason women engage in sexual relations. In the present context, however, it is certainly a most compelling one. Given a conservative sexual code, or lack of interest, women must still submit to the contemporary sexual mandate if they are to have any chance at a stable or permanent relationship.

Despite the conventional wisdom that men engage in sex for physical pleasure only, they, too, have their hidden agenda. Unlike in the past, few of our single males were oriented toward sexual conquests to obtain status among their male peers. The availability of women has tended to undermine sexual conquest as much of an achievement. There are, of course, men who still pursue the sport of chasing women for prestige among their peers. Such was the case of a 27-year-old male dentist, ''I spend my time going to bars and clubs with the fellows. Chasing women is like a sport. I compete with other men for women. Most of my male friends are buddies and running partners that I can share sexual experiences with.''

A common tactic of men is to use sex as a control over women. A 31-year-old female social worker spoke to this issue:

> What bothers me is that the men I've met have not been satisfied with having sex but they want to control your mind as well. Some of them have believed that just because I went to bed with them, they have the right to dictate my life-style. They want to control my movements, change my clothes and hair, and alter my values. I find that many men become threatened when they see you living a liberated lifestyle; partly because they wonder what they can offer you.

It is not uncommon for men to withdraw sexual services as a way of denying affection to women. As long as a man gives and takes away sex when he wants, he is asserting a form of control over a woman who may otherwise be psychologically and economically independent.

In the early stages of a dating relationship, women may use sex or the enticement of it for material rewards. At the lowest level this may only involve an evening's entertainment. For many women this has a symbolic meaning; that they are not being sexually exploited without getting something in exchange. One woman, a 29-year-old teacher, explained that she automatically refused to engage in sex with a man that refused to take her out. She didn't care where they went or how much money he spent, only that they went someplace and some money was spent. A 26-year-old female secretary summed up the problem well, "Most women expect for a man to spend some money on them before they will have sex; most men expect sex before they spend money."

In the contemporary dating game, where a woman's income may equal or exceed a male's, there is much bargaining over who pays for what and the outcome that can be expected. Some professional black women are willing to share the expenses of a date, but only with a "steady" partner. Others reciprocate indirectly by inviting the male over for dinner. There are men who consider the ultimate victory as romance without finance. A 29-year-old female researcher gave us this example:

One of my professional colleagues, who had been interested in becoming involved with me, suggested that I invite him to my place for dinner as a way in which we could discuss some business and have social interaction. I questioned this arrangement in my mind but decided not to raise any issues for professional reasons. Over dinner he told me that he could not see taking a woman out, spending twenty-five dollars for dinner and entertainment and not have a sexual experience that night. He said the "cost" of dating was too expensive for him not to receive a "reward." I immediately asked how he perceived our "date" and what he expected that evening. He said "nothing" since I had bought the food and cooked—we were "equal."

Sex does have a different meaning for men and women as well as the meaning bargaining imposes on interaction. Hence, a woman may be willing to engage in coitus in exchange for dinner, dancing, and fun, plus the *possibility* of permanence.[12] When permanence seems a remote possibility, women are very firm about having the evening's entertainment. There are, however, other and more benign functions of sexual relations for them. Sex may provide a substitute for other deficits in their life; a sense of belonging, a sense of identity and unity, and a way of giving pleasure to a male.[13] On the other hand, the meaning of sex has become more ambiguous for men. The sexual availability of women has stripped the sexual conquest of much of its thrill and prestige. The growing independence of women has weakened sex as a form of emotional control. As a result more and more men are converging their sexual values with those of women, viewing it as an all-encompassing set of feelings and reactions that make up the total person.

ADAPTATIONS TO THE NEW REALITY

As we have seen, sex is the cutting edge of the singles experience. For single men and women who remain in the unmarried category for long periods of time, it, along with loneliness, will continue to be the bane of their existence. Consequently, they will devise coping modalities which suit them at various stages of their psycho-sexual development. And these adaptations will often change in response to their circumstances and needs. The question of sex continues to be more problematic for women than for men. Women find the changing sexual norms more difficult to adapt to since it is they, and not men, who are subject to all sorts of constraints on free sexual expression. How they will remain unmarried for years and cope with the ever-present sexual demands of men, while maintaining a mental equilibrium, is a constant and almost insolvable dilemma.

The most obvious and sensible response for women is to be highly selective in their choice of sexual partners. And a number of our female subjects operate on that principle. For some of them it works with some men and not with others. Men who ask for instantaneous sex may be argumentative and even violent in their pursuit of a payoff for the evening's entertainment. Such male responses are rarely that pleasant for the reluctant woman. A number of them simply give in to male demands. One woman, a 32-year-old social worker, reports, "Nowadays I won't have sex with men that don't respond to me emotionally. Once I felt that I had to go to bed with them just to keep them around. And it just seemed easier to give in than fight or take a chance on losing them." Continuing to date and being discriminating in sexual matters is easier for some women than others. Those who maintain a manner of aloofness and strength can often intimidate men from making sexual requests. Very attractive women may demand much deference during dating, including an outright ban on sexual advances and discussion.

What has happened to a number of our single women is an early period of relative sexual permissiveness and a relapse into total sexual abstinence. This may or may not preclude any dating activity. Sometimes it is a temporary phase in their life. A 37-year-old female lawyer told us:

My periods of abstinence are generally between relationships. I usually get involved in activity that is very relaxing. The more relaxed I am, the more fluid I become and able to flow into social contacts. My interest in sex goes in cycles—during the period of transition you may not be as horny. The transition periods are times for inventory. Sometimes they last for a year or two.

The woman who engaged in very permissive sexual activity may have the most dramatic reversal of her behavior. A woman, 33-years-old, and unemployed, says, "It was like the more sex I had to make me feel wanted—more like a woman, capable of being loved —the more alienated and unloved I felt. I have nothing against premarital sex, but sex is only meaningful after a nonsexual intimacy has been achieved."

Asexuality or celibacy seems to be a tendency that is increasing among single black women. After more than a decade of social pressures propelling women into having coitus, a number of them discovered they were having more sex than they wanted. For many of them the issue is no more complex than the contradiction between the conservative sexual values imbued in them and the contemporary demand that they be sexually liberated. As a result they may act in a very liberal manner, but they don't necessarily like it. Consequently many have a reaction in the opposite direction. The results, however, may be counterproductive. Sex can and does enhance a relationship with a male. The new celibacy can make it difficult to have a totally integrated relationship with a man. Moreover, it coexists with a fear of commitment among many single black women. Their negative experiences of the past have created in many of them a fear of risk and a desire to avoid the pain which they had to endure. For others that same fear is expressed in their involvement in a series of casual sexual relationships. The more men they sexually deal with, the less they get into with each one.

One alternative for some black women, their numbers unknown, is homosexuality or bisexuality. How many have adopted these alternatives and for what reasons is not easy to determine. Unlike men, few lesbian black women have come out of the closet. There is reason to believe that some of the lesbians have been attracted to that life-style because of past disappointments with men. Others may be more physically and emotionally attracted to the same sex. The women who are bisexual (and their numbers may be higher than commonly believed) often are so because of the shortage of men. A number of them are initially enticed into bisexuality through group sex activity, which may only involve having coitus in the same room with another couple. The few lesbians we heard about declared their same sex relationship to be an immeasurable improvement over their heterosexual relations. They received more attention, affection, respect, and a greater sense of security. While there were problems with a lesbian lover, they were not the same or as mentally taxing as with men.

SUMMARY

There is no clear-cut picture of black female sexuality that emerges from our study. One reason is that the black female response to the liberal sexual ideology was very uneven. They chose to adapt in a variety of ways; conformity and rebellion or a mixture of both. One thing is clear: sexual liberalism signaled to men that one could pursue all the sex possible. Women who tried to use the traditional excuses for nonindulgence found they lacked credibility and that men had a number of alternatives. The bargaining power of sexual access was weakened by its sheer availability. The value of sex only existed as long as it was dear. When men found it in great abundance, their willingness to pay homage dissipated, as many found that its availability even undermined their own use of it.

At the same time many women found that sexual pleasure was theirs for the asking. No longer did they have to restrain their sexual urges until a marital union took place. Some women delighted in this turn of events, probably the majority were pained by it. The real issue is not one of sexual pleasure or abstinence, but the universal human need for belonging and security. To a large extent sexual freedom gave women neither of these things. The biggest change that occurred was that many men reduced all women to sexual objects. Marriage, at least symbolically, gave women a status which was respected and occasionally revered. But, to use them as sexual objects, was to demean them as human beings and as women. Conterminous with women's long tenure in the single state is the need to handle the question of sex and all its ramifications. This is not a simple problem and there are no easy answers.

NOTES

1. Robert Staples, The myth of black sexual superiority: a re-examination, *The Black Scholar* 9 (April 1978): 16-23.

2. Raymond Walters, *The New Negro on Campus* (Princeton, New Jersey: Princeton University Press, 1975).

3. Paul Gebhard, Wardell Pomeroy, Clyde Martin, and Cornelia Christenson, *Pregnancy, Birth and Abortion* (New York: Harper and Row, 1958).

4. Alan Bell, Black sexuality: fact and fancy, in *The Black Family: Essays and Studies*, ed. R. Staples (Belmont, California: Wadsworth, 1978), 77-80; Harold T. Christensen and Leonor B. Johnson, Premarital sex and the southern black: a comparative view, *Journal of Marriage and the Family* 40 (November 1978): 721-732; Ira Reiss, Premarital sexual permissiveness among negroes and whites, *American Sociological Review* 25 (October 1964): 688-698.

5. Alan Bayer, College impact on marriage, *Journal of Marriage and the Family* 34 (November 1972): 600-610.

6. Sheri Hite, *The Hite Report* (New York: MacMillan, 1976), p. 449.

7. Anthony Pietropinto and Jacqueline Simenauer, *Beyond the Male Myth* (New York: Quadrangle, 1977).

8. Christensen and Johnson, Premarital sex.

9. Robert Staples, Male-female sexual variations: a function of biology or culture, *Journal of Sex Research* 9 (February 1973): 11-20.

10. Leon Festinger, *A Theory of Cognitive Dissonance* (New York: Harper and Row, 1957).

11. Morton Hunt, *Sexual Behavior in the 1970's* (Chicago: Playboy Press, 1974).

12. Ralph Turner, *Family Interaction* (New York: John Wiley and Sons, 1970).

13. Joyce Ladner, *Tomorrow's Tomorrow: The Black Woman* (Garden City, New York: Doubleday, 1971).

Friends or Lovers:
The Difference
It Makes   6

If individuals are to remain single for any length of time, it is no understatement that friendship is the lifeblood of their existence. Whether it is an adequate substitute for a satisfying marriage may not be beyond cavil but its necessity is. Some would even contend that the importance of friendship supersedes the importance of marriage. In a classic study of friendship, Robert Brain asserts that we come into the world programmed to need love—but not to marry.[1] Because the need to love is basic to the individual, it is only through special relationships such as friends that this need can be satisfied over a long period of time. Having friends give us a feeling of somebodiness that spouses often cannot provide. A spouse may stay with you out of feelings of duty, custom, law, or fear. The endurance of a friendship, however, is reaffirmation of our worth as a human being with certain redeeming qualities.

Friendships are as old as the world itself. Aristotle once divided friendships into two categories, ones based on utility and the others based on pleasure. In the former, individuals gain some kind of benefits from the relationships. They are not loved in and of themselves but for some rewards derived from their relationship. People in utilitarian friendships may be of opposite temperaments, possess different values, and may not even like each other. On the other hand, pleasure friendships exist when people are agreeable to us. They are people we enjoy in social intercourse.[2] Historically friendships have followed a different trajectory than what exists today. We started out with same-sex friends in our formative years and retained them until the age of marriage. Our friendships were then formed in a community of married couples along with members of the extended family. Whatever cross-sex friendships existed were derivative of the marital relationship; they were generally friends of a spouse.

While those friendship arrangements have changed for married couples in contemporary American society, they certainly differ in the world of black singles. Even the close friendship of family members is denied them as their mobility has removed blood relatives from close contact and frequent communication. Hence, in order to satisfy that deep human need, establishing networks that transform friends into family is necessary. How those friendships operate for adult singles is a very complex question. A primary problem is operationally defining the friendship role. One reason for the confusion is that marriage is defined as a formal relationship, undergirded by legal and ritual sanctions, while friendship is regarded as an informal one. A pair of researchers attempted a formal definition of friendship as a primary relationship between two individuals unrelated by kinship. They argued that a primary friendship consists of a sharing of a wide range of activities and a positive feeling which is expressed by mutual concern and the felt freedom to make demands on each other.[3]

However, friendship has a much wider definition for many people. Many individuals regard as friends those who are blood relatives, people they have known a long time, individuals with whom they have frequent communication, a person that they can trust, and so forth. Accepting a self-definition of the friendship role is fraught with danger. Our black singles tended to use the term friend for a variety of relationships ranging from a person who they met once to an individual with whom they were cohabitating. The problem of accurately defining the friendship role was particularly acute when discussing the role of cross-sex friends. Eventually, we concentrated on those people they defined as "close friends" and classified them in terms of the frequency of association and communication outside a work setting.

THE BASIS OF FRIENDSHIP ROLES

Race. While there were widespread exceptions, most blacks have as their close friends other blacks. Similar life experiences, values, and attitudes account for racial homogeneity in friendships. There are some practical considerations in this racial bias. Because even middle-class blacks constitute a closed community, the social activities in which an interracial friend can participate are restricted. Most collective social activities are racially exclusive and the non-black participant is rare. Strangely, this is not as true among whites, but blacks are accustomed to being a numerical minority in white settings while the reverse situation is uncommon. There are, of course, numerous exceptions. Multiracial social affairs are more common on the West Coast than in the South and East. Anyone involved in an interracial romantic relationship is more likely to participate in or arrange multiracial social affairs.

Work. The setting in which people form close relationships is often at work. Obviously, the frequent opportunities for contact should enhance a coworker's chance of becoming a close friend. Coworker friends see each other more than average in white collar occupations and this gives them ample opportunity to plan off-work activities.[4] While this is generally true of our black singles, there are numerous cases where it is not. And the reason why is related to the aforementioned basis for friendship: race. Many black singles work in a predominantly white setting and have few, if any, blacks to choose as friends. Additionally, the tensions related to working together may lead some people to choose a friend not associated with or causing those tensions.

Residence. Neighbors also have frequent opportunities to become close friends. Yet living in close proximity is not a strong basis for friendship among many of our black singles. This, again, may vary by region. Many black singles on the West Coast are diffused into different sections of a city. Their neighbors are more likely to be white and not close friends. In the East and South, blacks live in closer proximity to each other and may choose friends on that basis. Due to a perceived need for privacy, some black singles may deliberately avoid close relationships with a person living nearby.

Region. Because many of our blacks are migrants to their city of residence, they may choose to associate with people from the same city, state, or region of the country. This does not appear to be an important criterion for friendship selection. People from the same region may just have similar life experiences and values that bring them together. In some cases they may have moved to another city due to the presence of people from their home state. In previous years the superiority complex of Northern blacks forced Southerners to band together. Such regional snobbery has diminished in recent years.

School. The sharing of four years of high school or college can serve to foster an emotional bond between individuals. This is especially true of blacks who meet in a new city. The various alumni associations operate to bring them together in various social functions. Blacks from Southern black colleges may have belonged to the same fraternity or sorority. Of course, the same school experience generally means that they are at a similar class level. Most middle-class blacks have middle-class friends, although not to the same extent as whites. There is more class fluidity in their associations since most are recent arrivals from the lower class.

Age. Age is a strong basis for friendship among black singles, although the range may be fairly wide. Because singles go through various stages in their single careers, people may seek out those who are in similar stages. A woman who is single and 25 years old may have radically different attitudes than a woman who is a childless divorcee of 37. Different levels of maturity can signify a value difference which may preclude a close friendship. Yet some young singles may use older singles as role models and fountains of wisdom.

Similar Values and Interests. Values and interests are a powerful basis for friendship choice among unmarried black adults. Generally people choose as friends those who are closest in values and interests to them. A similar value system forms the basis of a close friendship. A person who is materialistic may be in constant conflict with an individual who is spiritual in nature. Having some similar interests is essential if friends are to participate in activities together. However, it does not have to be a precondition of a friendship. Some people become friends when one of them attempts to acquire some of the interests of the other. Many people become afficionados of classical music, tennis, skiing, and so forth through the efforts of a friend who enlightened them on the subject or activity.

While people may require value and interest similarities, they do not necessarily desire, or want, similarity in other traits. Hence, it is not uncommon to see friendship matches between attractive and ugly women, tall and short men, and extroverted and introverted personalities. In some cases these traits may be deemed irrelevant to a friendship choice. Conversely, opposites have much to offer each other in a friendship. An aggressive personality may prefer passive friends with whom there is less competition for time and attention. The same may be true when friends are paired on traits that differ in prestige. An attractive woman may have her self-esteem heightened by associating with an ugly one, while the less attractive woman may revel in reflected glory by her association with a beautiful one. The same may be true of tall and short men. In some cases the opposite trait friends may be trading off equally positive traits or values.

While friendships are crucial to most of our black singles, there are a minority who are without any close friends. And they may not have any friends for the same reason they are unmarried: a fear of intimacy. If friendship is synonomous with emotional support, there are people who eschew the closeness that implies. A friendship, however defined, can have the same characteristic of a marriage or romantic relationship. It can involve an invasion of private space, the need for some kind of reciprocity, and demands for time and emotional support. However important friendships may be, they are considerably more fragile than marriages. Until the recent decline in marital stability, some people got married because friendships were not that enduring. While friendships may be a valuable ally in the single experience, they are subject to a number of fluctuations over time. New friends, however, are more easily acquired than new spouses or lovers. Moreover, as Stein suggests, there are people who fear involvement with friends more than anything else. That is one reason they become overinvolved with a mate.[5]

SAME-SEX FRIENDS: FEMALE

Anyone who has visited places where blacks congregate knows the importance of same-sex friends to black women. Everywhere you go there are pairs and groups of black women, at parties, concerts, lectures, restaurants, and so forth. These female pairings are so common that many men and some women refer to them derisively as female gangs. Yet they help to stave off loneliness and the total destruction of a single woman's self-esteem by meeting the needs for companionship that men are not available for, or refuse to meet. A 40-year-old female employment interviewer told us:

> Because there are more women than men, you become running buddies. They fill in space and are someone to share activities with. They are mentally life saving. If I didn't have other women to relate to, I think maybe I'd crack. Older women especially are good to share companionship with. Socially, we spend time together at dinner, one another's house—take short social trips together, playing cards, records, sharing one another's experiences.

While most women had some same-sex friends, they did not always relish going out with them to public activities. A few of them, for instance, thought being with a group of women in public visibly exposed the fact that they had no man to take them out. A 28-year-old female college counselor noted:

> I usually don't run around with a lot of women because I don't like herds. I would rather be with one man than with a bunch of women. Besides, many of them aren't really going out with you just to enjoy your company, they're looking for men. And if they find one while they are out with you, then they just might leave you sitting there.

Although females might consort with women friends in order to meet men, pairs of women are often a deterrent to those same men they want to meet. Only the most bold of men will approach a woman who is in a group. The guileful male seductor knows his chances of a quick sexual fling are slim if he must entice a woman away from her friends.

Women friends do play roles other than social companions. Some of our female subjects relied heavily on their women friends for emotional support. According to a 30-year-old female psychologist, "My girl friends are around me for companionship, to talk over problems, hopes, dreams, a sounding board, a shoulder to cry on. They listen to my thoughts and ideas concerning community or personal problems. They provide a positive image of self even when you are experiencing failure.'' The emotional support that same-sex friends provide often has to do with male problems. A number of women reported the important role of female friends after a romantic relationship had ended. The availability of women friends allows single women to take a hiatus from men while they reflect on what went wrong.

The use of female friends as counselors for male problems does have its drawbacks. There is the natural tendency of women friends to reinforce the female friend's subjective definition of a failed relationship as victim versus villain. One woman, a 36-year-old social worker, recognized this in her statement:

My women friends keep me off the bridge. For the most part they are the people who help me to keep laughing about the things I cannot change. I use them less and less for talking things through because their points of view are often too similar to mine to add much, and their empathy too great to be objective.

Usually there are two different interpretations of why a romantic relationship ends—the male and female's. A female friend only hears one interpretation and may be quick to counsel her complainant to withdraw from the relationship. One woman, who had a fear of commitment, created a network of female friends who encouraged her to sever relationships with her boyfriend. She informed her friends how terrible her boyfriend was and then went to them for encouragement in her attempt to withdraw from the relationship.

There are inherent dangers in using a female friend as a counselor for male problems. Often the female friend has a vested interest in seeing the relationship fail. While this may conflict with a genuine desire to see her happy, the same-sex friend realizes that how much of a friend's time and companionship she gets is a sum-zero equation. One woman, a 28-year-old nurse, put it well, "Mostly my female friends are important to me when I don't have a man. When I'm not involved with a man, I spend 90 percent of my free time with my women friends. When I'm involved with a man, I spend maybe 10 percent of my time with my female friends.''

A number of our female subjects confirmed the fact that the availability of female friends for companionship was contingent on a man's presence or absence in their life. A 36-year-old female educator observed, "It's kind of demoralizing when your friend finds a man and you don't have one. I had two good female friends, and both of them got involved at the same time. When I called them, I felt like I was intruding and they just weren't available to do things with anymore." Additionally, there are an increasing number of women who have become very bitter toward all men. With such women there is no such thing as female culpability for what goes wrong in a heterosexual relationship. They will be supportive of whatever a female friend does in such a relationship. Even when it is obvious that the same-sex friend is at fault, they rationalize that "men deserve it for what they've done to us all these years."

Some women try to preserve their female friendships after a romantic relationship commences. A 28-year-old feminist reported, "My women friends are very important and have been very consistent in my life. They are supportive of me and I of them. Our activities are important, and I am protective of time with women friends. I try and not let men destroy that." One novel approach, that of a 32-year-old schoolteacher, was, "My female friends and I do everything together. We are really very close. When one of us is involved with a man, we all share time with him. We party, drink wine, play cards together. Even if my friends don't have a steady man, we always know plenty of men to invite along." While such an approach would seem to reconcile the potential conflict between boyfriends and girl friends, it is not workable in most situations. The nature of heterosexual relationships is oriented toward privacy and exclusivity. When friends enter the picture, they are more likely to be the male's friends.

Some women avoid female friends when involved with a man because they see them as potential competitors. Enough stories abound of a girl friend who enticed away a boyfriend to lend credence to that fear. This fear is exacerbated when the girl friend is markedly more attractive or personable. While there are informal rules about not making seductive gestures toward the mate of a friend, there are numerous violations by both men and women.

One woman reported the story of a girl friend who stayed with her while looking for a job. While she was at work, her boyfriend began to make more and more visits during the time she was gone. Before much time had passed her girl friend had found a job and a boyfriend—hers.

Such possibilities make many married women something less than receptive to having single female friends. This, of course, does not prevent the formation of friendships between married and single women. There is a special value to such friendships for unmarried women. According to a 34-year-old female political scientist:

I always keep a few married friends who have children. They provide a positive model of the family for me. Sometimes I go over and play with their children. Occasionally I keep the children for them while they're gone. They also tend to be more stable than my single female friends. Generally, I can find them at home on weekends while my single friends are out partying someplace. I often ask them (or study) how they make their marriage work, even over the rough edges.

Married friends have their limitation in terms of emotional support. They are rarely having the same type of experiences to share or understand with a single girl friend. This is particularly true when they were married a long time ago, before dating practices changed.

When women find so much gratification in their female friendships, it can condition them for a sexual relationship as well. Only a few of our female subjects mentioned that their female friends were sexual partners. We suspect the number to be much higher, especially for bisexual relations. Women whose lives are so interlocked and satisfying often develop sexual feelings for each other. As a 35-year-old female public school administrator asserted, "I do believe sexuality can come anywhere where there's love. I am not opposed to people of the same sex sharing a sexual experience. I believe that people should have control over their own bodies and the decisions they make without big mother government peering over their shoulders."

Finally, there are women who do not care to have any female

friends at all. While few of our subjects stated it in such terms, a large number of them preferred male friends. The reason most commonly given was that men made more interesting friends. A typical response was that of a 28-year-old dance instructor, "There are one or two women I will go out with or invite over when there's no man available. Mainly because of a personal preference, I don't sit and chat with women. Too many women's conversations become gossip, games, and nosiness." Probably an underlying factor here is the historically low value placed on friendships with women due to the strong idea that women are of less worth than men. Most of our single women seemed to have transcended this notion and found that in a world fraught with uncertain and unstable heterosexual relationships, friendship is basically an act of will and commitment, and fundamentally, it does not matter much what the gender of the person is.

SAME SEX FRIENDS: MALE

Male friendships were once regarded by Aristotle as the most perfect of friendships. Indeed, it was only masculine friendships that he considered, with a brief allusion to the possibility of friendship between husband and wife. The average woman in ancient Greece was regarded as too ignorant to be capable of deep friendship with anyone.[6] The present state of male friendships is far from what Aristotle intended. According to other research studies and our own, single males have fewer meaningful friendships with either sex than most women. A couple of reasons for the differences are clear. Women are more likely to be socialized into a nurturant role that compliments the friendship role. Men maintain a certain emotional distance from other men due to the fear of being labeled homosexual or weak.[7]

What friendships men have are often of a different nature than same-sex relationships among women. Whereas women see their girl friends as being emotionally supportive and someone in whom they can confide, men are more likely to view a same-sex friend as a source of help and someone to do things with. The consequences of such emotional distancing is that when problems arise, men are less likely to turn to male friends for personal support. A 34-year-old male psychologist summed up the problem, "Men try to avoid loneliness by absorbing themselves in their work. Their male friends aren't as supportive because they only share activities together. Women have a relationship where they can relate and share confidences with each other, men can't just say to each other, 'I want to come over and talk to you because I'm feeling low.'"

Many men are abandoning the strong, unemotional image of their gender. Feelings are beginning to be shared with friends of both sexes. A 29-year-old male businessman reported, "I have several good male friends who are important to me. It is important just knowing they're my friends. These are people I sometimes share my innermost feelings with." For men who find it difficult to talk to other men, they may find it easier to talk with female friends. As a 26-year-old male sales representative noted, "There are just some things you don't want to talk to someone of the same sex about. With women I share more deeply on the emotional level than with men. They are more open, and I feel freer to open up with them than with men."

What many men share with each other is the pursuit of women. In the younger years (25 to 30) men are often preoccupied with sexual conquests and spend much of their time furthering that goal. Frequently they work in tandem with other men. A few men reported this as the major activity they shared with male friends. In response to our question, "What role do friends of the same sex play in your life?" a 27-year-old male insurance representative responded:

We play the ladies together. They are buddies and partners that you can share sexual experiences with. We go out and drink and get high together. We talk about what women we can possibly get into. When one of us has screwed a chick, we pass the word around so that the others can shoot on her. Sometimes we get her to find other women for us among her friends.

Masculine friendships are subject to the same dynamics as female ones. Men are less available to their friends when involved with a woman. Unlike many women, they may continue to associate often with their male friends. The female partner may be resentful and suspicious of such continued associations. A female lawyer, 37, commented:

> He spends a lot of his time talking on the phone with his male friends when I could use that time with him. And they're always talking in code or whispers which makes me wonder what's going on. As long as he still has the same friends, I'll have a low level of trust in him. I know they were doing some heavy running of women before I came along.

Men are inclined to keep their feelings within in order to conform to the masculine image. Yet many of them suffer from loneliness more than women. Men find that many of their friends are too busy "running" women to provide them with much companionship. But they have been socialized to believe the stereotype that men are the adequate ones—self-sufficient, aggressive, managing. When they cannot pull it off, the effects of loneliness may be disastrous. Despite the changes in this attitude it continues to be more acceptable for single women to have close female friends than it is for men to relate to men. A male's own inner defense against running any risk of being thought to be homosexually inclined adds to the distancing from members of his gender. Such a fear contains the seeds of his own destruction.

OPPOSITE SEX FRIENDS: FEMALE

Women having close male friends is a very recent phenomena. In the past most cross-sex friends were linked through marriage. Since marriage was, and is, defined as a sharing relationship, exclusive friendships were not allowed, not at least for women. Hence, the male friend of a husband was also the friend of the wife. Circa the 1970s we find large numbers of single black women reporting that they have male friends. The reverse situation—males with female friends—is certainly less common. In confirmation of our own findings, a group of researchers at San Francisco State University discovered that single men tend to have other men for closest friends and confidants while single women almost always have persons of the opposite sex as their closest friends and confidants.[8] Although many of our respondents' closest friends were other women, the number of women who reported most of their friends were men far exceeded the number of men whose friends were mainly women.

There is an obvious discrepancy here that begs a reconciliation.[9] It appears that the possession of cross-sex friends is considerably more important to women than to men. For women a male friendship represents their acceptance as an equal and worthwhile partner and companion. When women are unattached, a male friend is sometimes an affirmation of their ability to mean something to a man, a way of achieving feelings of security and being protected when a love relationship is not available. In a curious way many male friends are subliminal lovers by fulfilling all of a woman's needs except sexual ones.

Whereas we demarcate the lover from the friend role, a number of women in our sample did not. Previously, individuals involved in a love relationship were not likely to define it as a friendship. For various reasons they now classify almost all relationships with men (except those with husbands) as friendships. Many believe that a male lover must be a friend first and foremost. According to a 28-year-old female sociologist, "I prefer to sleep with men whom I can talk to after we have a sexual relation—so my male friends are almost always my lovers." The majority of our female respondents defined sexual relations as part of their cross-sex friendship patterns. In part this is a way of convincing themselves that they were not mere sexual objects but had an intergrated heterosexual relationship.

Our conception of friendship, however, was consistent with the general meaning of the phrase and implied the absence of overt sexual expression. We were concerned about how, and in what form, cross-sex friendships were maintained in such a sexualized society. The answer we found, after close examination, was that they generally did not exist. One of the most honest responses to the question of what role opposite sex friends play in your life came from a 32-year-old female psychologist, "Very little. Apparently, you must be intimate to truly relate. To put it briefly, sex keeps becoming an issue because I like to keep friendships "pure." So, except for gay men, I'm running out of opposite sex friends rapidly. Seems nobody wants to be my friend, as I define it."

Hence, women may have male friends on a short term basis until the issue of sex is raised. Many women adapt to this situation by combining the sexual and the friendship role. One woman, a 34-year-old social worker, responded differently. She claimed, "Most men don't want to be genuine friends with a woman. I have very few friends of the opposite sex—usually they are or end up as lovers. I would really like to have more male friendships—just plain good friendships. But most men won't stay friends long without sex. So I just rotate my male friends." Another woman, a 31-year-old schoolteacher rotated her male friends as lovers and friends. She said, "Several of my close male friends are exlovers; and some slide back and forward—from friends to lovers to friends. Most of these men are casual lovers, who can be easily dismissed if a serious relationship with another man comes along."

Some women insist on keeping cross-sex friendships platonic because they believe sex can be a destructive force. As Brain has argued, "friendships are inherently more likely to endure and maintain satisfaction than sexual relationships with their pressure of passion. Sexuality is never one of the essential bonds of friendship and can even be an obstacle."[10] The experiences of a number of women confirm this outcome from combining sex and friendship. A 33-year-old female teacher commented, "I keep trying to combine sex and friendship—but not with phenomenal success. Men often get into possessiveness rather early. I am currently waging a battle with demon jealousy and wondering if there is such an emotion as love or only those of property and possession—and pride. It's at least easier to fool yourself that you can 'love' your friends unjealously—though I suppose even that becomes problematic."

Avoiding sex with friends also serves the function of maintaining a relationship at a less emotional level. Some men are labeled as friends because women cannot regard them as serious prospects for a permanent alliance. Eschewing sex is one way of avoiding the escalation of a relationship to a higher level of emotional intensity. For men sex may have no demonstrable effect on their emotions.

Many women find it difficult to maintain an emotional distance from men they are sexually involved with. A 38-year-old female educator spoke to this issue, "I don't sleep with my male friends because I've found that the danger exists of getting emotionally involved and marrying an inappropriate partner. That happened in my first marriage. So I don't sleep with anyone who doesn't meet my criteria for a permanent mate."

When we examined cross-sex friendships for women, we found certain discernible patterns. First, the definition of the relationship as friendship is generally unilateral. One partner, usually the woman, wanted to be friends while the other one wanted to be lovers. Problems do arise when the label of friendship is imposed on the relationship by one party. Unless given a compelling reason for being rejected as a lover, he or she may be dissatisfied or suffer an ego deflation due to being deemed as unsuitable for more than a friendship. Second, such unilaterally defined cross-sex friendships tend to be short-lived. Men may initially accept the definition with the hope that a woman will succumb to their pleas/demands for intimacy. When intimacy is not forthcoming (and it often is), they sever the relationship. Third, cross-sex relationships have certain structural characteristics. Generally, the men in these relationships can be classified into the following types.

Undesirables. A large proportion of the men defined as friends by women are in that category due to their undesirability as a lover. The most common reason given was that there was no sexual attraction. Few women could define for us what it was that they were sexually attracted to; most said it was intuitive or intangible. When we could pin down concrete traits, undesirable men were typically (1) too fat, (2) too old, (3) too uneducated, (4) physically unattractive, or (5) too different in terms of values.

Ineligible. These are men that might be acceptable as lovers were it not for certain statuses they hold. Some of them, however, are acceptable to some women and not to others. The most ineligible of them all are gay men. Many of the best friends that our single women had were exclusive homosexuals. The pressure for sex was not there, and they were often available to share activities in which the two had a common interest. Married men, for obvious reasons, were often excluded as candidates for a serious relationship although friendships with them could end up as casual affairs. A few of our female singles had white males as friends. They may have been desirable but were ineligible due to the social pressures exerted against interracial relationships. Other ineligible men were those who had girl friends who were friends, and men in the same profession or residential building.

Potential Lovers. Many single women maintain friendships with men who are presently engaged in primary relationships elsewhere, but who are potential lovers. Friendships with these men represent some sort of insurance for the future in case the current love relationship does not work out satisfactorily or is disrupted. Sometimes labeling a man as a friend is a way of gaining time to assess the viability of a more serious arrangement. This may involve controlling the setting in which one interacts. Thus, there may be telephone conversations, meetings at parties, having lunch, and so forth. But the male is denied access to a physical environment where he can make sexual advances.

Former Lovers. These men are very similar to same-sex friends. Once a couple has worked through the emotional and sexual elements of their relationship, they may then form a positive friendship that is devoid of the underlying tensions that characterizes other cross-sex friendships. Some of the best cross-sex friendships are facilitated by the elimination of the sexual and emotional factors. However, it is not always easy to bridge the transition from lover to friend. When it is attempted too soon after the love relationship ends, the friendship may revert to the earlier love relationship. Sex is the critical force in determining the future of a love relationship. When women and some men withdraw sexual access, they are also defusing the emotional intensity of their relationship. As previously stated, some men vacillate between the lover and friend role. Usually it is sporadic, and for some women that distinguishes between a friend and lover. Becoming a friend after the love relationship ends may be contingent on the ability of both partners to forgive and forget. As a 32-year-old female lawyer told us, "Sleeping with an old boyfriend is often unsatisfactory. If I have reached a point where I am not seeing him anymore, something has happened to change my attitude and, therefore, my feelings towards him."

Under the right circumstances, any of the men in the aforementioned categories may be transformed into a lover by a woman who will acquiesce to sexual relations. And this happens with regularity in the world of black singles. When women are "seriously" involved in a love relationship with another male, that male often finds it difficult to accept the existence of such friendships. Jealousy of a woman's male friends is a commonly reported response by our single women. One reason may be the encroachment of the male friend on time, attention, and experiences usually reserved for lovers or mates. In some cases the lover may be keenly aware of the tendency of some women, and not a few men, to disguise sexual infidelity as "just a friendship." A 34-year-old male health planner gave us one example:

She and I worked together on the same job. We were both sexually turned on by each other, but she lived with another guy. I first screwed her when we went off to a conference together and continued doing it about once or twice a month, often when she was pissed off at her boyfriend or he wasn't taking care of business. When I met the dude, I was just introduced as a friend and colleague. He and I used to rap all the time when I visited their house. Once he and I even held a joint birthday party at his place.

Perhaps our society would be healthier if the friendship role was not as fluid as it seems to be in the case of cross-sex friendships for single females. Yet it is reasonable to expect that men and women socialized to relate to each other on an emotional or sexual basis would find it difficult to maintain platonic friendships with each other over a sustained period of time. In each instance we are relating to a role that brings out certain predictable responses in us. Men and women are conditioned to view each other in sexual and emotional terms. Bringing them together under the definition of friendship does not eliminate sexual components such as desire and fantasy. Because women have been programmed to suppress their sexual responses, it is easier for them to maintain the myth of friendship in a context where nothing else seems possible or desirable. For many of them, cross-sex friendships are part of a labeling process. It establishes limits on sexual contact while retaining their ability to press claims for a man's time, services, and companionship. In such situations they enact all the normative aspects of their role relationship except the sexual one. When cross-sex friends go out together, the male may still bear the cost of the entertainment and provide the expected acts of chivalry and other amenities. Until sex roles are truly transformed into genuine friendship roles, women can continue to expect cross-sex friendships to be rare and problematic.

OPPOSITE SEX FRIENDS: MALE

The men in our sample were generally not involved in close cross-sex friendships. Those who initially claimed female friendships upon closer examination admitted that the women they regarded as "friends" were actually acquaintances or associates. Often their relationship with them was limited to work contacts, telephone conversations, and socializing together at parties, conferences, and meetings. When they had a more extensive interaction, it was only for utilitarian purposes. A 26-year-old male medical student gave a typical response.

They are sex objects. I don't have that many female companions to be bothered with. Some females have literally got me a job as to make money for the both of us. Once I had a financial crisis and she made a loan without a pending date for the payback. Another woman who had some knowledge in real estate intervened in negotiations for the purchase of income property. She steered me in the right direction.

Some men can be very devious in their relationships with women. Those who have extensive contact with women friends can afford a nonsexual relationship with many of them after doing a cost-benefit analysis. Much of the time most men would devote to same-sex friends, they devote to cross-sex friends instead. But there is a method to their deviation from the norm. A 29-year-old male store manager reported,

I have platonic relations with several females. They are women who can turn me on to what's happening—telling me about parties, etc. Of late I've been seeking them out for referrals to their female friends. This beats a lot of bar hopping in hopes of finding sexual companionship. I find that by avoiding sex with a few of my female friends they'll turn me on to a lot more women that I can get over with.

Hence, we find that some men will accept a woman's definition of friendship if there are other rewards forthcoming. Occasionally the only difference between men who become friends and those who do not is their amount of patience. Most males want their sexual gratification upon demand while a few are willing to wait. In both cases the men have no commitment to the woman beyond a mere desire for sexual congress. One man, a 36-year-old urban planner, operated this way. He would hold extensive telephone conversations with women, invite them over for dinner, and build up their trust. After a few months or sometimes weeks had passed, he would make a sexual advance. In 95 percent of his attempts he met with success, a much higher success ratio than men who asked for immediate gratification. After the sexual relationship ended, so did the friendship.

Of course, there are some black men who maintain platonic friendships with women because they do not desire sex, or they fear it. For some men sex is fraught with so much anxiety, anger, and negative emotion that they find it a better adaptation not to risk it. One such man, a 35-year-old social worker, commented, "My female friends play platonic roles—there is no sexual contact. They are emotionally draining and demanding. They require protection and cuddling. Once one is involved with a woman, she is not so easy to shed. I don't like castrating type women. I prefer women who are comfortable being women." A 33-year-old female college professor analyzed why some men become friends rather than lovers. She said, "These men were defined as friends because they didn't make any sexual overtures. Later—when they felt safer or closer—overtures were made. Many black men are afraid of black women sexually. Sex with a black woman validates a black man— that makes it threatening. Some black men are afraid of intellectual black women. They don't know how to handle them—so they become friends."

As was true of some single black women, the men classify some women as friends because they were undesirable or ineligible. However, men are not as consistent with their exclusion of certain women as sexual partners. There is an informal code among men that the girl friends and wives of their male friends are off limits. This code may be honored more in the breach than in its observance. It is frequently the female in question who exercises a negative control over sexual relations with the friend of a mate. A 28-year-old male accountant noted, "Usually the women who are friends are married or heavily involved in a relationship with someone else, who is also a friend. So, it would be up to her to take it a step further to the sexual level."

Married women are supposed to be the most ineligible of female friends. Yet, as Stein has noted, marriage provides no haven from the temptations of new sexual partners.[11] Many of the married women who have extramarital affairs engage in them with men who are classified as friends, usually hers, but sometimes the husband's. One man in our sample made a practice of cultivating friendships with married women. They would often tell him of problems with their marriage. He served a role as a counselor and safety valve at first. Eventually he would become sexually involved with them. Usually some crisis would occur in the woman's marital relationship where she would feel hurt or rejected. He would be a familiar person to turn to and having sexual relations with him would fill her need for belonging to somebody.

Undesirable women were often classified as friends by men. Sometimes they had abrasive or domineering personalities. Women they worked closely with were taboo. But generally they were women who were physically unattractive. Traditionally, "older women" were regarded as unattractive and would be put in the friendship category. This is beginning to change as many men start to realize the value of older women and what their greater maturity and sexual experience can bring to a relationship.[12] Just as unattractive women are involuntarily classified as friends, very pretty women may find it hard to keep men as friends. When a woman is sexually attractive she will receive more sexual advances from men than less attractive women. On the other hand, she may be more capable of imposing a friendship label on some men. These men will associate with her for the nonsexual rewards that derive from being around a beautiful woman. Researchers have found that a man seen with a beautiful woman is viewed as more intelligent, exciting, and successful than a man with an unattractive partner.[13]

A major problem for men and women in forming genuine cross-sex friendships is that men typically define sex as most important in a relationship while women give love the top ranking. For men sexual intimacy should be achieved early in a relationship while women believe love must evolve out of a nonsexual interaction. Many men find that after a period of sexual intimacy there is no basis for love and women discover the same. Yet men have achieved their goal, while the women have not. Few men are willing to delay sex, at least for long, to discover love. And very often they are not looking for love because they associate it with other negative attributes; accountability, responsibility, entrapment, and commitment. Because of the power balance in male-female relationships, women are forced to succumb to sexual demands before love enters the picture and must hope that it will grow out of the sexual intimacy.

There is a valid male perspective on the conflict between the friendship versus sexual intimacy question. Even a male who is seeking a meaningful relationship may be unable to find one. Yet he still has sexual desires, even if they are culturally created ones. That leaves him in the unenviable position of practicing sexual abstinence or having sexual relations with women to whom he has no emotional commitment. Unattached men find it particularly difficult to maintain cross-sex friendships unless they are kept under some kind of control. Given a situation where a platonic female friend and a man are spending a relaxed evening before the fire, drinking wine, and listening to soft music, one can feel a rush of affection for anyone who happens to be around at the time. Women are more conditioned to resist the sexual urges that may emerge—men are not. That suggests that men and women will continue to feel pressures for sexual intimacy when both may be best served by an enriched friendship.

SUMMARY

Like many other aspects of the singles world, friendships operate both as a support system and as a barrier to successful relationships with members of the opposite sex. Because friendships, especially same-sex ones, seem to be more reliable than other heterosexual relationships, many of our subjects clung to them as a buffer against the pain they encountered in male/female relationships. For a group that has endured failure after failure in its interpersonal relationships, friendships may appear to be the most practical response to their situation. But friends cannot fulfill the needs serviced by opposite sex mates. At best they serve as companions and sources of emotional support. To meet the human needs of affection, a sense of family, and the bearing and rearing of children, our singles will have to look elsewhere.

Finally, many of the friendships of our black singles proved to be quite fragile, often for the same reason as their male/female relationships were. That is, the harmonious integration of diverse traits and needs, within a close, interactional context, is difficult to achieve in our contemporary society. As we listened to many of our subjects discuss their past conflicts with same-sex roommates, and their eventual separation, it became apparent that those conflicts were a variation of problems they had experienced with opposite-sex mates. However, the formation and subsequent disruption of friendships do not bring about the same consequences as the more intense formation and disruption of romantic relationships. What our investigation of friendships does illustrate is that human relationships, of any kind, are complex. What may be needed is an understanding of how to best preserve individual autonomy and to maintain a sense of community among friends and lovers.

NOTES

1. Robert Brain, *Friends and Lovers* (New York: Basic Books, 1976).

2. Works of Aristotle, *Friendship*, Encyclopaedia Britannica, Vol. 2, 1952, p. 459.

3. Alan Booth and Elaine Hess, Cross-sex friendship, *Journal of Marriage and the Family* 36 (February 1974): 38-47.

4. Lois M. Verbrugge, Multiplexity in adult friendships (paper presented at the American Sociological Association Meeting, New York, August 1976).

5. Peter Stein, *Single* (Englewood Cliffs, New Jersey: Prentice-Hall, 1976), p. 71.

6. Aristotle, Loc. Cit.

7. Genevieve Knupfer et al., The mental health of the unmarried, *The American Journal of Psychiatry* 122 (Winter 1966): 841-851.

8. Ronald Moskowitz, Close look at S. F. bay life, *San Francisco Chronicle*, 20 December 1977, p. 4.

9. The discrepancy is heightened by the fact that women outnumber men. A reasonable outcome of the imbalanced sex ratio suggests that more men would have close female friends. But, that does not appear to be the case.

10. Robert Brain, Somebody else should be your own best friend, *Psychology Today*, October 1973, p. 120.

11. Peter Stein, *On Same Sex and Cross-Sex Friendships* (Paper presented at the Annual Me ..ing of the National Council on Family Relations, New York, October 1976.

12. Constantina Sofilios-Rothschild, *Love, Sex and Sex Roles* (Englewood Cliffs, New Jersey: Prentice-Hall, 1977), p. 98.

13. E. Berscheid and E. Walster, Physical attractiveness, in vol. 7, *Advances in Experimental Social Psychology*, ed. L. Berkowitz, (New York: Academic Press, 1974).

Crossing
the Color Line

7

LOVE IN BLACK AND WHITE

No other issue provokes such an emotional response as that of interracial dating and marriage. When we asked our black singles if they had ever dated a member of another race, two types of responses emerged. One group was so strongly opposed to it that they gave a strident "no" answer and underlined it. The other group had engaged in mixed dating and was quite defensive about it. Some of the latter group said it was a hostile, even stupid question and the question assumed there was something strange about people who dated across the color line. Whether it is strange or not, it is undeniable that interracial dating is a controversial activity in this country at this point in time. As one black woman wrote:

Male/female relationships without the racial element are a controversial topic, and race has historically been a volatile and emotional issue. With the two combined, what can you expect? It's just a fact that the scars of nearly 400 years of the worst human bondage known to contemporary man are not healed, and disapproval by many black and white people of interracial love affairs is one of the wounds.[1]

Miscegenation is certainly nothing new in this country. Its meaning and dynamics, however, have changed over the last 400 years since blacks entered this country. In the preslavery era black male and white female indentured servants often mated with each other. During the period of black bondage most mixed sexual unions took place between white men and female slaves, and often involved coercion by the white partner. A similar pattern of miscegenation occurred after slavery with white men/black women as the typical duo.[2] When blacks moved to larger cities outside the South, the black male/white female pairing became more common. As is commonly known, legal unions between the races were prohibited by law in many states until 1967. Legal prohibitions were not the only deterrent to such biracial unions. This country's history is replete with acts of terror and intimidation of interracial couples who violated the society's taboos on miscegenation. While blacks and whites came together in love and marriage over the years, it was generally at a high cost ranging from death to social ostracism.

Circa 1968 we witnessed the first significant increase in interracial dating. This was the year that blacks entered predominantly white college campuses in comparatively large numbers. Coterminous with this event was the sexual and psychological liberation of white women. While white society disapproved of all biracial dating, the strongest taboo was on the black male/white female bond. Hence, biracial dating increased in this group. The college campus became an ideal laboratory for experiments in interracial affairs. Young white women, who were not as racist as their parents, were liberated from parental and community control. Their student cohorts were more accepting or indifferent to their dating across racial lines. One study revealed that as many as 45 percent of the white female students had dated interracially.[3] There were, of course, regional differences. A national survey found that 20 percent of all Americans had dated outside their race. The South had the lowest incidence of biracial dating (10 percent), while the West and young people had the highest rate (one out of three).[4]

Those changes in interracial dating practices coincided with the civil rights movement and a greater white acceptance of blacks as racial equals. Moreover, in the university setting the blacks and whites who dated were peers. They had similar educational backgrounds, interests, and values. Along with increments in interracial unions came what appeared to be a change in public attitudes toward biracial couples. A 1975 poll indicated that only a minority of white Americans would not accept their child marrying outside his/her race.[5] This poll result could be misleading. As Poussaint has countered, "many people tend to give the liberal answer they think is proper or expected when asked about controversial issues such as interracial marriage. However, when confronted with the issue on a very personal level, their response is likely to be very much different."[6] Whether parents approve or not, it is clear that biracial matches have become part of the changing American scene. Mixed couples can be observed daily in the cities of the deep South and are commonplace in such liberal bastions as New York, Boston, and San Francisco. And parental approval is irrelevant to a number of black and white singles who have deviated from a number of society's other norms related to sexual orientation, sex roles, sexual behaviors, marriage, and the like.

Although black/white sexual and marital unions have not yet achieved widespread acceptance among whites and blacks, they have certainly become part of the single experience for our group of unmarried blacks, almost to the point where they have been stripped of any mystique for many of them. The typical pattern for our middle-class group was to have their first interracial experience in college. As many as 90 percent of the black males on certain college campuses have had interracial dating experiences while 30 percent of black females have dated out of their race.[7] The proportion of blacks who have dated interracially is often contingent on the type of college they attended. Those who went to predominantly black colleges had few such experiences while a student. Blacks who attended predominantly white colleges where few blacks were enrolled were more inclined and had greater opportunities to date outside their race. It seems that the size of a black student population on a predominantly white college campus affects the degree of biracial dating. The opportunity to find a black person with whom they are compatible is restricted when their numbers are small.

A few of the couples who dated interracially were eventually married. It is safe to assume that fewer interracial dating experiences result in marriage than intraracial associations for reasons that will be clear later in our discussion. Of the interracial marriages that occur in this country, most will come from the college-educated group of blacks and whites. During the period from 1960 to 1970 the pattern of interracial marriages changed. There was a

26 percent increase in such unions characterized by a shift in locale from the South to the North, a 62 percent increase in marriages involving a black man and a white woman, and a 9 percent decline in white men/black women unions. Biracial marriages had a higher rate of dissolution than unions between members of the same race.[8] While opponents of such alliances might take comfort in such a statistic, there is no evidence that anything inherent in an interracial marriage would automatically lead to conflict or divorce. A more probable cause is the normal conflict between spouses which are exacerbated by the social pressures that impinge on a biracial union. Moreover, mixed couples are more likely to have characteristics which lead to marital dissolution among all races and groups.

BLACK MEN/WHITE WOMEN

The black male/white female dyad has generally been the most controversial and common interracial duo for the last decade. How common it is was confirmed by our data. Approximately 85 percent of the men in our sample had at least one interracial experience. These experiences ranged from a one night fling to marriage. They usually began in college, although men who were over 35 years of age or had attended a predominantly black school were more likely to have met their white female partner through work contacts. A number of men had met their white partner through political or civil rights activity, others through organizations such as the Peace Corps and Vista. In contrast to theories about the inequality of status among biracial couples, almost all the men claimed that the white women were of equal status. In fact, according to a 39-year-old male psychologist, "in terms of family background, most of them were of a higher status. My father was a janitor. Their fathers were stockbrokers, medical doctors, and wealthy businessmen. I met all of them in school or through professional activity. They were all well educated. None of them would be considered poor white trash."

As to the motivations of black men for dating white women, they varied from male to male. Those men still involved in ongoing biracial dating tended to give answers such as "for compatibility or love." Men who had their interracial experiences behind them gave slightly different responses. A major reason for the initial encounter was the mystique attached to the hitherto unavailable white goddess. According to a 36-year-old male reporter:

I did it originally because of the mystique surrounding white women. They were all I ever saw in magazines, books, and movies. To me they represented the epitome of beauty and sensuality. The image portrayed was a cure for all my sexual ills as well as a release for all my sexual fantasies. Now I date them because of the same reasons I date any woman—for some sexual gratification, intellectual exchange, and to broaden my scope on women of all creeds and color.

Once they have penetrated the mystique of white women (and some men never do) the reasons for dating white females may be very similar to those for dating black women—but they may still be based on the assumption of racial differences in female behavior. Whether it is true or not, one of the presumed differences is that white women are more likely to be sexually permissive. A 29-year-old male businessman told us:

White women tend to be freer sexually, not only in terms of going to bed faster but in the kind of sexual activity in which they will engage. If you date a black woman you have to beg, plead, cajole, and threaten her all night to get a piece of leg. Whereas a white woman will deal with the issue right away—either she will say yes and help you take your clothes off or she'll say no and tell you why. A white woman will go down on you with relish where black women have to be pressured into giving you a blow job. Really, it's just less hassle with a white chick.

While the more liberal sexual behavior of white women vis-à-vis black women is confirmed by our other black male subjects, it is a racial distinction that is not absolute. Unlike the black women black men date, white women are rarely selected at random from the white population. The white women who are available to black men are probably less sexually inhibited than a typical white woman. In part they are generally more unconventional and liberal than most white women. They are rarely flag waving Republicans with very conservative social views. Much of the attraction between black men and white women is sexually based. Neither one of them, in many cases, considers the other eligible for marriage.

There are black men whose sole experience with white women

has been a sexual affair. A 35-year-old male teacher reported, "I have balled white women, but I've never taken them out to social functions. Usually they came over to my place and we'd get into a sexual thing. We never went out in public because I didn't have any need, nor could I afford, to be showboating a white woman." That many white women reciprocate that sentiment is expressed in a quote by a white woman in *City Magazine*, "It used to be that you could always depend on black men to fuck you and not want to get emotionally involved; in fact you'd only hear from them once every three weeks. But now they're getting paranoid that white women are ripping them off for their bodies."[9]

Interracial dating increased around the same time as the advent of the sexual revolution. It was the liberalization of sexual mores, especially for women, that made much of the biracial dating possible. Once sex became divorced from marriage, or the potential for it, white women were able to accept the idea of an interracial sexual liaison without worrying about the social consequences of a biracial marriage. As a result, we find that when women become more oriented toward traditional marriage possibilities, their sexual partners tend to belong to the same racial group. Of course, there are many white women who do not exclude black males as potential husbands. At the same time, as black men grow older the sexual variety becomes less important than finding a stable relationship. Many of them cease their involvement in biracial sexual flings; others are not racially exclusive in their choice of mates. It is becoming evident that the differences in sexual inhibitions between black and white women is narrowing. Hence, you have two different factors affecting many black men; women compete for his affection on the basis of factors unrelated to race; or he confines his search for a serious relationship to a homogeneous racial pool in order to avoid the complications attendant to a biracial union.

Another factor in the black male's selection of white women as dating partners is his disenchantment with or dislike for black women. Some of the black men who date white women do so to the total exclusion of black women. They actually stereotype all black women and all white women on the assumption that racial membership ipso facto carries with it negative and positive traits. The negative stereotypes of black women are that they are domineering, sexually inhibited, materialistic, and lacking in sophistication. A number of black women pointed out that the white women involved with black men tended to be ultrafeminine and blond. A few black men gave other reasons for their preference of white women as dating partners. One man, a 29-year-old executive said, "Non-black women I find are more friendly, frank, informative, and just plain more interesting to be with. The most noticeable thing is that the white and brown women I've dated shared the financial burden of a date more often than not."

One common and most valid reason for dating white women is that they are not as likely to expect a commitment from black men or to demand one. According to a 33-year-old male filmmaker:

Yes, I've dated white women. There seems to be boundless freedom, in terms of the relationships. Black women are okay because you're at home. They are not okay in terms of expectations. They have more of an idea of how and where you fit into their lives and vice-versa. It's a highly defined situation. With white women there is more flexibility in the relationship. If you don't see them one week, they don't complain. They allow you time for your work and other pursuits without getting jealous or demanding.

For many white women an interracial love affair is designed to round out their lives. It is similar to living in Europe for a year in order to enrich one's life and then returning home. Some black men report making a marriage proposal to a white woman and having it rejected. Conversely, white women in interracial situations have had a strong commitment to a serious relationship and experienced rejection at the hands of a black man. One 32-year-old male professor informed us:

I've dated two white women. One was my fiancee. On the whole the experience was good. They satisfied most of the expectations of what I desire in a mate. I couldn't marry them because of the racial variables in part and partly because they proved to be too demanding of my affections and attention. And because of their insecurity. Being white she needed double reassurance of my love—being a white woman and having committed herself to a black man.

There is no dichotomy between black and white women, interracial and intraracial unions. The similarities and differences constantly emerge in both groups and situations. Biracial unions continue to be controversial because they contain the same element as race relations in general: the notion of inferior and superior groups. This type of racial stratification is most obviously expressed in the selection of biracial mates. While there are exceptions, most black men do not initiate dating or marital relationships with white women. Only a minority of white women would be receptive to their attempts to establish intimate relationships. They become involved only with those white women who, through cues or context, are known to be interested in dating black men. To do otherwise would be to experience rejection of the worst kind. A black female sociologist analyzed this reversal of roles:

> The white female does not hold the view that the black male has a cultural right to initiate a relationship with her. . . . In a social order where white beliefs form fundamental explanations of how individuals should enact their color-sex positions and associated role expectations, black males do not, regardless of their economic status or intellectual capabilities, have the cultural prerogative to take the initiative.[10]

Since white women are not available at random, the question to be posed is who are the white women in biracial unions and how do interracial couples meet. Most of our black singles had their initial interracial date in college and met their white partner on the campus where she, too, was a student. In more recent years informed observers report a marked decline in biracial dating among black males. In part this must be attributed to a more conservative mood on college campuses. The political movements on campus are dormant, and there are generally fewer white female students in black studies and sociology classes. However, few of our black singles are still in school, and the place of contact has shifted to the work place. Moreover, the type of white woman they meet is often different than the one encountered in college. She may be apolitical, although generally liberal, and has little experience with men of other races. In cities such as New York, Washington, Boston, and San Francisco, there is often a shortage of white males. The white males available may be gay or uninterested in sex. Many single, career-oriented white women find black men more available and ready for a sexual fling.

In certain cities there are known interracial hangouts where white women can be found. Additionally, there appear to be various voluntary associations with a heavy concentration of white women and a few black males. Sometimes black women are unwittingly responsible for introducing a white female into a black setting where she will meet black men. The white woman in question may be a coworker who is invited to a black affair. The friends and coworkers of white women involved with black men are frequently eligible for a biracial date. A major difference in black/white encounters is that they are not as likely to occur in unstructured situations. While white men may meet white women in supermarkets, parks, bars, tennis courts, jogging, and so forth, that option is not as available to black men. This is particularly true in light of recent rape scares. In San Francisco, for instance, 75 percent of the *reported* rape victims are white women and 50 percent of the *arrested* rapists are black males. This makes many white women, even liberal ones, very leery of unsolicited approaches by black men.

Biracial unions are often disrupted for the same reasons as intraracial ones. That, however, does not mean there are no problems in the interracial dyad unrelated to race. Blacks and whites do come from different cultural backgrounds, and even a similar class location does not eliminate those racial variations. While not a major source of tension, the cultural differences were pointed out by a number of our respondents. A 33-year-old male engineer noted, "The experiences have been good. But you notice the differences in races culturally. You often have to explain the meaning of certain words or customs to them. Musically, their records are not as interesting. The music was good, but I didn't feel it deeply. There were cultural differences in the areas of cooking, speech, attitudes. The attitude is more visual. It's the different flavors of the same substance. It's not easy to describe." Sometimes these differences can be mutually enhancing in a biracial relationship. The black partner is generally more aware of white culture but may find new and gratifying interests in skiing, classical music, biking, and other activities that are not as common in his culture.

Occasionally there is no cultural interchange. In fact, the white partner may want to deny the significance of race or racism. She may, instead, stress that there are no racial differences and be totally oblivious to the unique character of her biracial relationship. This is not to be unexpected since many whites are not accustomed to thinking in racial terms. Since it is their society they only regard themselves as human, not white. The black partner is accustomed to race being the decisive factor in his life and is very sensitive to race-related behavior. A 35-year-old male artist commented, "One of the problems with whites is their lack of knowledge of what it is like to be rejected for something over which you have no control. You run into whites who feel they can take liberties—like asking racially oriented questions or making puns—not thinking that it would be a sensitive area. They don't recognize discrimination when it appears—like having to wait a long time in a restaurant before being served."

In contrast to the white women who deny the existence of race are those women who take on all the elements of black culture, including the sensitivity to racism. These women literally give up their white identity for a black one. A 39-year-old male educator reported: "I met this one white woman at a black place and didn't know at first that she was white. There seemed to be no racial differences because she had been around blacks all her life. She dated mostly black men. In fact, I find most of the white women whom I have dated have dated blacks before, and they have become black also." While imitation may be the highest form of flattery, there are some black men who avoid the black-acting white women. They may do so because they believe such imitation has a false ring to it or due to their need to negate their own racial identity. Although some white women may take on elements of black culture; speech, clothes, hairstyles, others date black males exclusively when their former interracial affair has produced a child who society labels as black. Some white women confine their dates to black men because they prefer their style or consider them better sexual partners than white males.

The problems in biracial unions may only differ in kind from other monorace couples or not be serious enough to cause the disruption of their relationship. A more serious problem, and the major one, is the external pressures on the biracial couple. Those pressures come primarily from two groups of people who are opposed to any mixing of the races; namely, black women and white men. The women resent the loss of one of their men and the implication that white women are superior to them; white men resent the alleged degradation of white womanhood. White men's opposition to black men/white women is generally acknowledged and has been expressed, historically, in their violent acts against black men who crossed the color line. While the opposition remains strong among them, interracial couples rarely face the violent intimidation of the past in most large cities of America.

Nowadays white antipathy toward biracial couples is expressed in more subtle ways such as stares, whispers, and avoidance of close contact with them. This is generally true only in large cities. If biracial couples should venture into what is called redneck territory, they may encounter some difficulty. A 38-year-old government employee told us of being attacked by a group of white men after he was observed camping in a rural area of California. The recent emergence of the white backlash has generated more open opposition to interracial couples among many whites. A black male newspaper reporter, 44, commented:

You'd be surprised how many people around Westwood are openly beginning to say nasty things about interracial couples. During the 1960s, nobody cared about interracial situations. There seemed to be a greater feeling of liberalism and change like we were really on the verge of a new world or something. Not today, however. Maybe it's the economy but I've heard more students telling Nigger jokes and white girls who date black guys being called Beulah by their friends. Maybe it's the competition for jobs, but ten years ago it sure wasn't like that.

Some of the opposition by white males to black male/white female alliances may be their fear of black sexual competition and the cultural stereotype of black males as superior lovers. One study demonstrated that even liberal white males harbor strong resentments against the black male/white female dyad.[11] Knowledge of these attitudes led a 35-year-old male social scientist to conclude:

I've dated many white women, and some of them have been really good people. Yet, I've always remained uncommitted for a possible permanent relationship. There's just too much race conflict. The Baake case and anti-busing demonstrations are only the tip of the iceberg. I have a hunch that black people are in for some rough times ahead. And I'd rather weather that storm with a sister that I know understands and is affected in the same way by those problems.

Racial conflict would mean increased stresses for biracial couples in the future. In the here and now a more troublesome source of tension is the often outraged opposition of black women. In contrast, some whites have looked very favorably upon blacks involved in biracial unions because they perceive them to be less hostile to whites in general. Black women, however, are greatly disturbed by the black male/white female affair for understandable, if greatly exaggerated reasons. While white women have been blamed for every ill that plagues the black community, the main charge against them is that they have taken away some of the most prestigious black men from black women. A 34-year-old female nurse comments:

> Being a black single woman is difficult. There are just not enough eligible men. Those who are available have not gotten over the white woman syndrome. The white woman has the best of both worlds: she has white and black men. Anytime she wants to, she can return home to the white man. And the black man will just seek out another white woman. I don't like being alone but it looks like I have no other choice.

What bothers many black women is their belief that they simply cannot compete with the white woman for black men. Because almost any white woman fits the society's standard of beauty better than most black women, she has an inherent advantage over them. A common charge by black women is that the white woman in biracial unions is physically unattractive. According to a 39-year-old female account executive, "You just want to scream when you see a white woman who is no way your equal marching off with a handsome bright black man. You know the relationship is based on her whiteness. He would never accept a black woman who looked like that." Whereas there may be some validity to this point of view, it is possible to explain it in other ways. Black men are selecting from the white women available to them. Among that group will be few truly beautiful women because they do not exist in great abundance among the white population. Very attractive white women are often able to bargain for a white mate with a much higher status than most black men are able to achieve. On the other hand the most attractive black women are available to those black men who hold a high status in their culture. Moreover, the white women in interracial relationships represent a variety of physical types.

Regardless, black women feel especially pained at what they perceive as the black male's rejection of them in favor of white women. And they have expressed their resentment in very explicit ways. One black male, a 32-year-old architect, reported:

At my college there were a few black girls dating white guys but mostly black dudes with white girls. This really made black girls jealous. It was not uncommon for the black guy to find honkey lover written on his car. One time a bunch of sisters cornered a white girl who was dating a brother in the ladies room and cut off all her hair. The black males on campus got along pretty well with the white students, but many of the girls believed in black separatism and acted very hostile toward whites.

There are some black women who refuse any association with a black male known to be an interracial dater. One example was this 36-year-old college counselor:

The choice of one's mate is each individual's own ball of wax. But to pretend that who you fuck/marry ain't political, smells to me. The implications extend further than the doors of one's bedroom. If I'm willing to pay the cost for my fucking, I can expect no less from black men. And believe you me, every time I pull my dress up I have to deal with the possibility that his dick might have last been in some pink pussy. If I know that, he won't go any further with me.

Black women also complain that black men involved with white women have made unfair comparisons of their behavior. A common assertion is that "if you were a white woman you wouldn't be acting this way." Others charge that black men who demand oral and anal sex learned about these practices from white women.

There are other penalties imposed on black men publicly associated with white women. A number of black leaders and scholars often have their accomplishments and biracial liaison spoken of in

the same breath, so strong is their identification as a person con-
sorting outside the race. One black male who heads a black-oriented organization told us, "I liked the white women I was involved
with but stopped because of the political consequences. White
women aren't as persistent about getting a commitment as black
women. But black women fit in better with my business interests."
A number of prominent black men we interviewed asked us not to
ever reveal that they dated white women. On a personal note, when
this writer gave a speech which did not set well with a black female
college audience, the disgruntled women circulated the rumor that I
was married to a white woman. At the time I was not even married,
and my former wife was not white. But that was one way of dis-
crediting what I said in the speech. As a 34-year-old female sales
representative declared, "When I meet a black male who I feel is
strong, and has demonstrated by his actions a concern for our
struggle, and I find he has a white wife, it still invalidates his
achievements for me."

Such vehement responses by black women force many black men
to be circumspect in their interracial affairs. While a few black
males have enough audacity to bring a white date to a predominantly black affair, most eschew such events. As a 28-year-old male
businessman said, "In dating white women I would avoid any large
gathering of blacks. I would rather be exposed to more whites than
blacks. I wouldn't want to be singled out among blacks as 'the
brother with the white woman'. Places that we'd go or things we'd
do would be out of the ordinary. We'd go to the woods or the
forest." Having to cut off ties with the black community can create
problems for the black male and his white partner. According to a
32-year-old male writer:

> The white relationships were okay but they increased my sense of isola-
> tion from black people. The social pressures were too difficult to contend
> with. I'd disappear on weekends. I'd spend them at parties. I wouldn't take
> her. I even gave some and didn't invite her. The social pressures made me
> feel guilty. It's more difficult today than ten years ago.

As a result of these pressures some black men have to alter their
life-style to accommodate their biracial relationship. In cities such

as New York, Boston, Berkeley, and San Francisco there are enough liberal white circles in which to circulate. That is not a viable option for some black men. One, a 30-year-old lawyer, told us: "I've never been relaxed in all-white situations, maybe because I was from the South. Going out with white people was the only safe thing to do. I did not like to be seen in public. I was paranoid. In private I could deal with it." Another recourse was to join the network of other interracial couples. A few black males reported that most of their associates were other biracial couples. These black/white couples were composed mostly of black men and white women. Although a number of our black males claimed to have many white female friends and intimates, few of them regarded any white males as close friends.

Not all the opposition to biracial dating comes from black women and white men. A few black males have joined in the crusade. Nathan Hare, a prominent black sociologist, has stated that white women were introduced into the black community to cause a rift between black men and women, hence disrupting the black struggle for liberation.[12] Another prominent black male social scientist has declared in an unpublished paper that all black men dating or married to white women should be expelled from the "community." The overwhelming majority of our black men had engaged, or were presently involved, in an interracial relationship. Those who had not, cited as their reason a basic mistrust of all whites. One such man, a 38-year-old college professor, asserted, "It's hard to tell if white women are genuine and whether or not to trust them. I don't believe that white women can give up whiteness for a human relationship."

For many of our black men, interracial dating was a time-contained and basically pleasant experience. There were many of them who claimed the primary motivation for their action was the unavailability of black women. This would be true for the black men who attended predominantly white colleges prior to 1968. Most of those schools had extremely small black enrollments (less than twenty) and the majority of them were black males, mostly athletes. As a result of penetrating the mystique surrounding white women, some found the interracial affair a pleasant one and continued such associations well into their adult life, and a few up to the present. In other cases they may have ceased all interracial dating because of the social pressures. Those involved in biracial dating because of a dislike for black women or who ceased such activities due to an antipathy toward white women are guilty of racial stereotyping. The positive and negative attributes of women of both races can be found in each one. The real problem is that in the present context biracial dating and marriage contain stone and mortar for the building of walls between people, sexes, and races alike.

BLACK WOMEN/WHITE MEN

Based on the aforementioned discussion, it would be reasonable to assume that black women have been largely absent from the interracial dating movement. That such is not the case may come as a surprise. Even more surprising is that many of the black women who are hostile to black male/white female relationships have an interracial relationship in their own history. This discrepancy between attitudes and actions can best be explained by the possibility that the black woman's hostility is motivated by a pragmatic fear of the white woman's encroachment on a low supply of eligible black men. Every black man that crosses the color line is one less black man available to black women. According to our data a substantial minority of black women (about 39 percent) have had interracial relationships ranging from a casual date to marriage. In confirmation of our findings is an earlier 1970 study by Willie and Levy which discovered that 29 percent of their black female college student subjects were engaged in interracial dating.[13]

While biracial dating is not unknown to black women, comparatively they are more opposed to such a practice for both men and women. Their antipathy for dating a white man is based on his historical subjugation of them, often for sexual purposes. Even in the present context, there is the suspicion that a white man is only interested in a black woman as a sexual object and will never elevate her to the more respectable status of wife. As a 29-year-old female librarian commented:

I do not see how blacks could ever really love white flesh, mentally or physically. From slavery till now, whites have continuously pounced on black people. We have been abused and misused so many, many times. We were thought to be less than dirt. Not even of our free will, but by white men's hands our bodies were used for work and sex. And now today, for some the past is all forgotten or should I say tossed aside for black and white flesh to get together.

As was true of our black male singles, many of the black women were introduced to biracial dating on a college campus. Some claimed that there were no black men available as their reason for biracial dating. Whereas black men generally outnumbered black women in the predominantly white university, many of those men were athletes whom black coeds considered their intellectual and cultural inferiors. Also, the college days were used as an experimental period by many people, who were liberated from parental control. A 30-year-old female social worker reported:

> I dated white men when I was in college but not in the last eight years. My interracial dating was part of my horizon-broadening phase. At that time I was heavy into the civil rights movement and a humanistic frame of mind—and considered it "class" to date white dudes. Curiosity, rather than genuine attraction, formed the basis for the brief encounters. That was eight years ago and my whole outlook on interracial dating has changed. I basically believe that blacks should marry blacks and the same goes for whites.

We should not be deluded into thinking that biracial dating is only a brief interlude in a black woman's college experience. Indeed, there has been a noticeable, albeit insignificant, increase in black woman/white male alliances in the last five years. Whether their biracial dating will have the same trajectory as black males remains to be seen. Almost ten years ago black sociologist Calvin Hernton predicted that, "in years or decades to come, more black women (no matter what they say now) will marry or associate intimately with white men than black men will marry or associate with white women."[14] Even earlier Hernton had written that, "every black woman at one time or another has experienced, in some dark crevice of her being, the illicit desire for a white man; especially those women who claim the contrary."[15] Considering all the historical and sociological ramifications of the relationship between blacks and whites in this country, that seems to be a reasonable hypothesis. Attraction toward men of other races has probably always existed among black women but was repressed. At the same time black men have actualized their fantasies about white women because the restraints were milder and the rewards greater.

When white men and black women come together, it is under qualitatively different circumstances than the black male/white female pairing. Again, it is the white partner who must make his interest in a biracial relationship known. Few black women initiated their dates with a white male. Unlike the black male, many black women were not sexually involved with their white partner. A white male who made a sexual approach to black women might be rejected immediately. A 34-year-old female researcher informed us, "I've gone out with white men. It appears that I fulfill a lot of safeguards and fantasies for them. But just like they don't want to talk about race, I don't discuss sex with them. I always felt uncomfortable and could never reach the point of extending the relationship to include sex."

Since the cultural image of black women is that of a sexual temptress, the relative absence of sex in their biracial liaisons seems strange. One explanation is given by a 33-year-old female professor, "Most of the men who asked me out were white. There were no available black men. White men tended to be slower sexually. I believe it's because they don't see highly educated black women as sexual objects. I found out that they will take care of a woman without expecting sex relations. One guy let me stay in his house during the summer, lent me his car." Of course, there were some black women who confined their relationship with a white man to a casual sexual affair in order to avoid public censure. According to a 33-year-old female lawyer, "I went out with a white man because I was away from home. We met on the street in Hawaii, and he asked me for a date. He was a lover, his body attracted me, I guess. He was the only white man I ever went out with. It was a summer romance. He went back to school, so did I. We called each other for awhile, then it tapered off."

Based on the primary reasons why the sexes are attracted to each other (for men sex appeal, women desire status), black women fared better in the selection of their interracial partners. Most of the whites they dated were of a fairly high status, partly because there are many more white males with education and wealth. Some of the black women made a special effort to inform us that their white partner was "well-off." A 33-year-old nurse said, "I've dated a caucasian. He was not the poorer caucasian and went way up in his profession. We were lovers. He treated me like a queen and gave me everything—wine, liquor, albums, jewelry. He catered to my needs and tried to make me happy, but I wasn't satisfied."

Another major difference in the biracial liaisons of the two race-sex groups is that black men are responding to qualities in the white female and black women are reacting to qualities in the black male. Not only is there a shortage of black men available to them, but the ones they encountered were regarded as less than desirable. A typical response was that of a 28-year-old female insurance representative:

> At first I was apprehensive about being seen with him but decided it was time to satisfy me and to hell with what other people thought. I also don't get the grief from him that I used to get from brothers: not showing up for dates, and not calling to say why, moodiness, expecting one to be understanding of their problems, never wanting to accept life the way it is, or always had the time for other's problems but never interested when I had a problem or just wanted to talk.

Among the qualities white men offer black women in greater abundance than black men are similar interests. A 32-year-old female librarian acknowledges, "I dated a white guy because I realized that he had many of the same interests I have. We both liked reading, the theatre, ballet, opera. How many black men are into that? The relationship was extremely harmonious and lasted longer than any of the others (which all involved blacks)." Another woman, a 31-year-old historian, has complained, "I have not met any black men who are not terrified of my intelligence and determination. I have found it easier to relate to 'liberated men' or men sincerely working on their sexism, and that does not include black men. I prefer black men, but . . . ."

While individual black women may meet white males who are more compatible than black men, the majority of them did not find lasting satisfaction in their interracial relationships either. As a 28-year-old female lawyer discovered:

Some things are just peculiar to men—not to racial groups. I experienced the equal amount of frustration and deceit with white men that I did with black men. In general I'd be less likely to enter into a serious relationship with a white, not because of his personal qualities, but because of the kinds of external pressures that come from a society stratified by race. Almost all of my close personal contacts are with blacks. Most of my interracial dating experiences occurred in graduate school.

The shortage and quality of black men available to them may force some black women to opt for a biracial relationship. Once in one they will find it to be at best a challenging experience.

The problems of the black female interracial dater are those of her black male counterpart and more. Black men face the greatest amount of hostility from black women, while they tend to be accepting, or at least tolerant, of biracial affairs among other males. In the case of a black woman similarly involved, she encounters ostracism from both sexes in her race. If the biracial couple follows traditional roles, she lives and interacts in his world; he does not enter hers. As typical of the black male, who is biracially involved, she must isolate herself from many segments of the black community. So reports a 29-year-old female sociologist, "I felt that sometimes he saw me as different from the masses of other black people. He would feel uncomfortable in a situation where there were only black people. He wasn't used to being around them. We went to movies and dinner. Sometimes we'd go out to the lake, take my sister's kids out to breakfast. We spent most of the time with his friends." One woman, a 32-year-old political aide, insists she would not be entirely excluded from her race, "I prefer to date men regardless of color. However, I would tell a white man that if it gets serious enough, he can't come into my world. There will be times when I will have to return to my world and he can't come along. He'll just have to understand that."

A black woman's isolation is considerably more exclusive than a black male's. Some of the males have brought their white partner into the black community. Indeed, some have preferred to keep her in black social circles as a way of attaining some kind of status. Those who do not remain in a black context retain ties to some part of the black community by joining a network of other black males with white partners. Other black males may go to black-oriented places alone. That option is not as available to black women. Biracial couples, where the male is white, are not as likely to be connected to an interracial network. The male in question will probably not relinquish his white associations for interracial ones. Chances are that the white community may be more tolerant of a white male with a black mate than the reverse. However, the black woman in such an arrangement may not find complete acceptance. A 27-year-old female reporter found this out, "There are times when I get tired of being in a white world, always being around his friends. I'm tired of hearing of black stories from his friends who are letting me know that I'm okay or that they have a black friend."

Although black men may be tolerant of black male/white female relationships, they can be quite hostile to the reverse biracial pairing. Their hostility is generally activated by the same forces as the black women's. Yet they are not personally threatened since there is an excessive number of black women from which to choose. Moreover, some of the black women would relinquish their white partner if they could find a "suitable" black male. The white males in such biracial alliances are often very threatened by black men. That accounts, in part, for their uneasiness in all black situations. Sometimes their fear is of physical violence on the part of black men. In other cases it is the sexual competition. Many white men are threatened by the image of black men as sexually superior. Some avoid sexual relations with black women for that reason. They worry that they cannot match the black male's sexual prowess, wondering how they can satisfy a black woman who is accustomed to the sexual competency of black men. Yet most of our single women denied any racial difference in sexual performance.

The women of her race are equally disapproving of a black woman's biracial relationship. As one black woman wrote:

The biggest game ever played is the myth of white supremacy, and a manifestation of it is the tendency to bestow nobility on white men or women in interracial relationships, characterizing them as somehow more loving and capable of appreciating their black partner. This view is just as racist and distorted as the belief that all black people are sexual geniuses. Sisters, don't lay your preference for white men at the door of some psycho-emotional malady black men are supposed to have. If these relationships are so fulfilling and you have no misgivings about your decision, then "live with it."

Such vehemence led one black woman, a 32-year-old college instructor, to conclude:

> I have dated members of another race. Although I found my companion of the opposite race compatible in most ways, the pressures from both racial groups proved too great. I hated the rejection my friends laid on me because of the relationship. All my friends are nationalistic—but he pursued me. The struggle to survive in such a racist society was enough of a problem, dealing with animosities from both groups was too much.

Despite those problems, the tendency of black women to date and marry white men is on the rise, while the black male/white female dyad appears to be on the decline. Some of the black women in our sample say they are tired of waiting for "Mr. Right"; rather than be alone they will accept a white man. One even disclosed that she had started frequenting places where she could meet white men. Unlike in the past, white men are available and interested in black women. Some of this interest can be accounted for by their growing disenchantment with liberated, sexually aggressive white women. Even with their tendency to be strong-willed personalities, many black women are more traditional than neoliberated white women. Another reason is that for the moment America has become more of an open society. People have the same right to intermarry as they do to become gay, cohabitate instead of marry, and have abortions instead of bearing children.

OTHERS

Americans have a tendency to think in terms of only two racial groups: whites and blacks. Official data forms often list all other racial groups as "other." These others, however, number as many as all the blacks in this country if they are combined. The largest group is Latino, with Asians, Arabs, Indians, Native Americans, and others making up the rest. It would seem reasonable for blacks to date and marry these nonwhite groups—and some do. But most date and marry whites for various reasons. Whites, of course, are more numerous and likely to come into contact with blacks. Many of the other third world groups are concentrated only in certain areas. The Latinos live primarily on the Eastern seaboard, the Southwest, and West Coast. Most of the Asians live on the West Coast, and the rest of the ethnic minorities are isolated in certain areas or widely dispersed throughout the country in small numbers. In the South, for instance, there are basically only two racial groups: blacks and whites.

If the circumstances were more favorable and the numbers greater, chances are that few of the other minorities would date and marry blacks. When racial minorities date outside their group, the outsider is likely to be white, because he/she is the most prestigious and wealthy of all the racial groups. Moreover, the prejudice against blacks held by whites also exists in other minority populations. This is particularly true of Asians who rarely date or marry blacks. As a 29-year-old male artist found, "With this Asian woman alone I was fine, but with her family and friends I felt more of a tolerance than acceptance. I couldn't really relate to the culture, although it was interesting: the dress, food, music, or anything." Among younger Asians there may not be a strong prejudice against blacks as a people. In fact, many have blacks as close friends. Yet there is no frequent occurrence of serious dating because of their family's objection to out-marriages. When intermarriages occur (and they do very often, especially among the women), whites are much more acceptable than blacks. Furthermore, Asian women are not as interested in sexual flings as white women and stay away from black men whom they view as sexually adventurous.

Hispanics are more receptive to dating and marrying blacks. They are already a mixed group, particularly Puerto Ricans, and do not share the color prejudice of Asians. Unlike among the Asians, however, there are not as many status equals for middle-class blacks to choose from. One man, a 41-year-old private investigator, commented on the differences:

Spanish women for the most part are much more family oriented but don't have much education. After sex there is nothing to do. Oriental women are very concerned about pleasing a man in all ways but are extremely reluctant to break the family customs. They become outcasts to their family. This usually causes mental hangups which are impossible for me to cope with.

Many of our single blacks had positive experiences with other racial minorities. A 34-year-old female personnel specialist said, "I have dated a Puerto Rican and a Mexican. I can't recall the circumstances under which I was seeing them. I don't think I had any special reasons other than the fact that I was attracted to them. I had sex with the Mexican and Puerto Rican. My experiences were very rewarding. They were sexually uninhibited and more sensitive to a woman's needs. They seem to have more confidence in themselves." Some of our subjects claimed that the only people they dated out of their race were other third world people. This makes sense because those nonwhite people are generally acceptable in the black community. This could be one reason why marriages between nonwhite populations in the state of California last longer than black/white couples.[16]

One advantage of blacks dating or marrying whites is that the two groups are more culturally compatible. Like it or not, most blacks are thoroughly American in their values and behavior, especially in the middle-class. Hence they may be more comfortable with an American white than other racial minorities. A 34-year-old female college administrator reported:

I have dated an American Indian and an Arab. They appealed to me. There was a lot of chemistry, very spontaneous. The environment was such that race was no issue. I was sexually involved with both men. They didn't seem too different than black men. However, both of them were more dominating than many black males, quite culturally paternal.

We might note that many of the whites that blacks had dated were not Anglo-Saxon or Americans. A large proportion of them were Jewish, a white group that has a very special relationship (both negatively and positively viewed) to blacks. While it may be disputed, Jews generally have held less racist attitudes about blacks than other white populations. Moreover, they are not closely associated with slavery or racial segregation in the South. Some blacks had dealt extensively with Europeans. A 43-year-old male writer observed, "Every rewarding and good experience (somewhat lasting or at least having potential) with someone of another race was with a woman who had experienced a prolonged, extensive involvement in a culture other than that of the U.S.A.; for example, South America, Germany, France. European ladies are cooler than American white ladies whom I don't generally date.''

SUMMARY

Our reading of history tells us that there is no pure race. Since the beginning of time men and women of different cultures and races have been attracted to and married each other. Some of these mixed unions have been voluntary; all too many have been the result of political and economic sujugation of a captive group. While the coercive nature of racial miscegenation is largely a relic of the past in most societies, the notion of superior and inferior racial groups is a legacy of our racist history as a people. As long as racial groups have selfstyled definitions of superior and inferior, and the oppressor and oppressed, biracial unions cannot occur as natural events in the dating marketplace. It is naive and selfserving to think otherwise. In contemporary America interracial relations do not take place in a vacuum. Even the most pollyanic of whites and blacks must have some awareness, however subliminal, of the implications of their actions when they enter into such a socially defined deviant merger.

Realizing the problems involved does not negate the fact that biracial unions can be mutually satisfying for the people involved in them. Given the existence of a society of racial equals, our concern and analysis of interracial dating would be a frivolous effort. At this point in time America's racist past and ethnocentric present do not allow its biracial couples to revel in the joy and pain of a normal male/female relationship. Wishing it otherwise does not obviate the realities of the situation. Moreover, the secondary consequences of interracial coupling are, in themselves, of great magnitude. The fear of black women that white women have taken away all their men is not consistent with the social reality. If you consider the number of black men married to white women, after subtracting the number of black women with white husbands, the number of black men lost to black women totals less than sixty-five thousand. Many more black men are lost to prison, drugs, death, and homosexuality. Yet this heightened fear of white women has left many black women with a collective feeling of inferiority and rejection.

The availability of white partners has still another consequence for our black singles. It prevents them from effective problem-solving of their own internal faults. On the one hand, they stereo-type the men and women of their own race and make the erroneous assumption that they can find a lasting happiness by mating outside their group. What they have found, in many cases, is they simply exchange one set of problems for another set. While the issue was not addressed very often, most of our black singles had experienced difficulties other than external social pressures in their interracial relationships. Additionally, black women may deceive themselves into believing that they are without a mate due to the presence of the white woman, without examining their own responsibility for the male-female conflict that pervades the world of black singles.

As for the future of interracial relationships, it is possible that they will continue to rise as black men and women become more disenchanted with each other and look for other options. Yet the conditions that gave rise to the increase in interracial dating and marriage are beginning to change. Already the number of black students on predominantly white college campuses is beginning to decline. Black people are struggling to hold their own in white-collar positions as racial lines harden over the intense competition for jobs in the 1980s. Those biracial couples who do effect a merger will find the going rough. This is not to say that a black person who finds a compatible white person should await a racial utopia before consummating their relationship. It only means that they should do a cost-benefit analysis before proceeding with all deliberate speed. Would that these factors did not have to be taken into consideration; that people could meet, date, and marry with no concern for the color of their skin but only the content of their character. That day has not arrived, and each race had best put its own house in order.

NOTES

1. Patsy R. McClendon, Letter to the editor, *Essence Magazine* 45 (May 1978): 6.

2. Forrest G. Wood, *Black Scare* (Berkeley, California: University of California Press, 1970).

3. Charles V. Willie and Joan D. Levy, Black is lonely, *Psychology Today*, 5 (March 1972): 76.

4. Joan Downs, Black/white dating *Life*, 28 May 1971, pp. 56-61.

5. Alex Bontemps, National poll reveals startling new attitudes on interracial dating, *Ebony*, 30 (September 1975): 144-151.

6. Ibid., p. 144.

7. Willie and Levy, Black is lonely.

8. David Heer, The prevalence of black-white marriages in the United States 1960 and 1970, *Journal of Marriage and the Family* 36 (May 1974): 246-258.

9. Susan Berman, San Francisco, city of sin: why can't I get laid? *City of San Francisco*, 3 August 1975, p. 10.

10. Doris Y. Wilkinson, Expectations and salience in white female-African male self-other role definitions, in *The Black Male in America*, eds. D. Wilkinson and R. Taylor (Chicago: Nelson-Hall, 1977), p. 269.

11. Gary Schulman, Race, sex and violence: a laboratory test of the sexual threat of the black male hypothesis, *American Journal of Sociology* 79 (March 1974): 1260-1277.

12. Nathan Hare, Division and confusion: what happened to the black movement, *Black World* 25 (January 1976): 20-33.

13. Willie and Levy, Black is lonely.

14. Calvin C. Hernton, *Coming Together: Black Power, White Hatred and Sexual Hangups* (New York: Random House, 1971), p. 135.

15. Calvin C. Hernton, *Sex and Racism in America* (Garden City, New York: Doubleday, 1965).

16. Department of Public Health, State of California, Divorce in California (Berkeley, California: Bureau of Vital Statistics, 1967), p. 29.

Parents as Partners   8

Throughout the history of the family in the United States, it has normatively been conceived as being headed by two adults of opposite sexes. The family unit with one parent as its leader has been regarded as an aberration whose existence must be due to some human tragedy or personal flaw. In the case of a racial group such as blacks, large numbers of single parents have led to the pejorative image of its family system as weak or pathological. Recent historical research has refuted the long-standing myth that black families, in the main, have been headed by women since the demise of slavery. The fairly large numbers of single-parent black families is basically a concomitant of urbanization, industrialization, and migration factors.[1]

The alleged pathology of black single-parent families is a long and complex saga which has been dealt with elsewhere.[2] Our concern is with the middle-class single parent and her/his dating behavior as it is affected by the multiplicity of roles to be filled; for example, as a parent and dating partner. Using the middle class as our subject population means we do not have to focus largely on the economic problems of raising a child alone. While not that economically secure, most middle-class black single parents have annual incomes in the range of $9,000 to $16,000.[3]

Far from being an aberration, the single-parent family is fast becoming the typical black family. As of 1978 it represented 47 percent of all black families.[4] By the year 2000 it is estimated it will be a majority of all black families. Re-

cent trends, which show that two-parent families among blacks declined more in the six-year period between 1970 and 1976 than in
the preceding twenty years,[5] presage the beginning of an era in
which most children will be raised by only one parent during their
formative years. A number of factors are responsible for this transformation of the black family structure; among them, the increase
in out-of-wedlock births as a proportion of all births and a spiraling divorce rate.

In the middle-class black community, almost all the increase in
single-parent families can be attributed to the increased divorce
rate. While some middle-income, single black women are consciously having children out of wedlock and others are adopting
children, they represent a very small minority of the single-parent
group. In the years between 1960 and 1977, the rate for divorces
among blacks rose by 160 percent. Circa 1977 the black divorce rate
for persons between the ages of 25 and 54 was 28.6 percent. In fact
the formerly married blacks represent the overwhelming majority of
those blacks we classify as single. Moreover, the divorce rate
appears to have increased faster among the middle-class group than
all others. Another change from previous divorce statistics of relevance to us is that children are more likely to be involved in the terminated marriage. In 1950 fewer than 30 percent of dissolved marriages involved children, but by 1976, 60 percent of black divorces
involved them.[7]

However, those are statistics for the general black population. If
we consider the middle class alone, a different type of picture
emerges. Based on a number of empirical sources, including our
own, we can construct a profile of the typical middle-class divorced
person. As is true of single parents, the prototype of the currently
divorced is a woman. Divorced women outnumber men by a ratio
of 3 to 1, due to higher remarriage rates for males. Most divorced
women married around the age of 23 years or older and remained
married for less than six years. The median income for the divorcee
living in a metropolitan area is approximately $11,000 a year. She
has two or more years of college or business education, as does her
former husband. Before marriage she had known her husband for
two years or less. They both have urban backgrounds and their

religious preference is Protestant. Almost a majority of divorced black women have no children at the time of marital disruption.[8] This is probably due to the very low fertility rate of black women with some college education: 1.5 children for every married black woman in 1976.[9]

A fact we have not mentioned up to this time is the very high divorce rate of college-educated black women. When we look at the percent known to have been divorced in 1970 by level of education, we find the highest percentage, (28.6) among black women with one to three years of college training. The corresponding figures for those with a high school education is 23.3 percent; and 21.0 percent for those who have completed elementary school.[10] Undoubtedly some of this unexpected disparity is traceable to the tendency of lower-income blacks to use separation as their only form of marital dissolution. Still, the divorce rate among middle-class blacks is twice as high as that of middle-class whites. Again, some of this racial difference may be due to the unseen forces of racism and its ramifications in the marital arena. A more plausible explanation, however, is the unbalanced sex ratio; for example, the excess number of women and the resulting keen competition for men, married or otherwise. In Chavis and Lyes' study of educated black women, while not citing it as a primary reason for their divorce, 56 percent of black women believed their husbands had engaged in extramarital relations.[11]

SINGLE PARENTS AS A LOWER CASTE

Since 98 percent of our single parents are women, our report will of necessity focus on them. When entering the dating game, the newly divorced woman will find that there is a pecking order. All eligible women are ranked according to their constellation of attributes, ranging from physical attractiveness, personality traits, and other values, by the men in the pool of eligibles. All attributes being equal, however, the single mother will rank relatively low. Her low evaluation will generally be associated with her status as a single person who has a child. This attitude is best exemplified in the statement of one black male eligible that "all in all I really don't want to deal with a woman who has crumb-crushers if I have any other choice.'' Some of the problems involved in having a child will be evident later in our discussion. Suffice it to say that the single mother has restrictions on her availability, movements, sexual expression, and the like. Men can ignore some of the liabilities, but others impinge more directly on them and their priorities.

Not all single mothers have child-rearing responsibilities to the same extent. Having a responsible person to care for her child while she dates is easier for a woman who has an extended family network in her local area. But this is more common to low-income blacks than the middle class. Due to their greater mobility, they are less likely to live in an area with kin who can baby-sit for them. Also, since they were formerly married, they may have moved to the husband's place of residence or followed him on a job transfer. Hence, the ability to date may be constrained, more or less, by the availability and cost of child caretakers. However, the ability of eligible men to screen out single mothers from dating partners is undermined by their sheer numbers in the dating game. As a young male Ph.D. reported, ''There are a limited number of quality black women to share my life with, especially those who don't already have children.''

That having a child is becoming less of a barrier in dating opportunities is reported by many of the women in our sample. In response to our question of whether having a child affected her dating opportunities, a 30-year-old psychologist retorted, ''I do not believe having children has much effect, if any, on my dating. There are just as many men that prefer a woman with children as do not.'' In fact, argues one woman, a 35-year-old guidance counselor, ''Some men prefer women with children because they like families and want to play with young kids.'' This may be true particularly of the formerly married man who has limited access to and interaction with his own child. However, by general consensus, these women observe that the free-floating single black male does not want to be bothered with another woman's child.

The attitudes and practices of single parents are influenced by their class. In the lower class there is often the expectation on the part of mothers that they are trading off sexual and domestic services for some financial remuneration if they have children.

While this may occur among middle-class single mothers, it does not appear that common. A middle-class woman is more likely to have a sufficient income, and her child support payments are probably more reliable than the lower-income mother's. Some of the men in our sample do report sharing baby-sitting expenses or buying the child gifts. Lower-class men are known to assume fatherly responsibilities towards the children of women they date. Thus, they often become surrogate fathers to their sexual consort's children while neglecting their responsibility to the children they procreated.[12] Due to the different marital patterns of middle-class blacks and variations in their dating styles, this is not a common practice reported among our respondents.

In addition to bearing the liability associated with having children, the single mother is at a disadvantage because of her age. The typical divorcee is over 30 years of age when she resumes dating. As a result she is victimized by the tendency of men to link physical attractiveness to the youthful age of a woman. This not only affects a woman's opportunity for dates but also her chances for remarriage. This fact is reflected in the statistics on remarriage which show a much higher remarriage rate for middle-class black men than women. And when these men remarry, their new wives are typically much younger than their former wives. Black women who remain divorced have a higher educational level than those who decide to remarry.[13] Many of the black women who remain divorced do so by choice. Their higher incomes make them less dependent on a man for financial support.

Other factors which militate against single mothers in the dating game are more capricious and inconsistently applied. A few men label the single mother as morally stigmatized as a result of sexual relations with the former husband. Others talk of enlarged vaginas stemming from childbirth, which make sexual relations less than satisfactory. On the other hand, many men would prefer a woman with a record as a wife and mother than some of the free-floating single women in the dating game. As one man, an urban planner, said, "Give me a woman who has a child any day. At least she's demonstrated the maturity to handle the responsibility of a home and children. And I strongly suspect that some of these single women can't handle any kind of responsibility."

THE DIFFERENCE A CHILD MAKES

Whatever their chances in the dating game, it is quite clear that single mothers are in it in a different way. In comparison to never-married, childless women, dating is more likely to be an expressive than an instrumental activity. Those who have children simply do not have the ardent desire to get married that characterizes their childless counterparts. Part of this difference can be attributed to their having been formerly married. Rainwater once observed that it was more important to have been married and divorced than to have never married.[14] There are certain attitudes that result from past involvement in the conjugal state. For some women the trauma of the former union can embitter them toward marriage. A number of women commented on the scars left by their marriages. One poignant tale was that of a 37-year-old woman who had helped put her husband through medical school, assisted him in establishing his medical practice, and was abandoned after 14 years of marriage. She comments, "After that experience my level of trust in men is very low. Since my divorce I've accumulated a lot of things, but they will only be used for me and my children."

Our findings on the single mother's desire to remarry is similar to that of other studies. Most of them did not expect to remarry. We might note that this attitude could reflect their desire to avoid discrepancies between their beliefs and social realities. Most may realize that having passed the age of 30, and having one or more children, their chances for remarriage are slim. Hence, they bring their attitudes into conformity with reality. On the other hand, the single mother's attitude toward men may be more positive than her childless counterpart's. If her negative experiences were with one man, she may not generalize the resulting bitterness toward all men but see him as an exception. The never-married woman's negative experience may have been with a number of different men. Thus, she may be distrustful or defensive with all future male partners.

From the statistical data we know that middle-class black women do remain unmarried more than similarly situated white women. However, the remarriage rate is considerably higher for young childless divorcees.[15] This suggests that negative experiences in marriage are not a sufficient explanation for the low remarriage rate. Having children and the age at the time of divorce are also important. Bell's study found that the mother role had more importance to black women than the wife role.[16] It could be that having satisfied the desire to bear and rear children, single mothers find the wife role too unattractive to aspire to for one more try. As a result, we found our young, childless divorcees more eager to remarry. Among our middle-class group they constitute a near majority of the recent divorcees. Another group that remarries at a higher rate are those women with three to five children.[17] Due to the low fertility rate of college-educated women, such women are rare among the group we studied.

In looking at the dating habits of our sample, we saw a number of variations. Most significantly, single mothers did not go out on the typical date as often as childless women. Much of their interaction with men was confined to their homes; having dinner, watching television, or listening to records. A number of women were simply dropouts from the dating game. Almost all of them held full-time jobs and reported that, along with child-rearing chores, they simply did not have time for men. Those who did resume dating after the divorce found they had to make a number of adjustments. The rules of the dating game and the behavior of men had changed considerably. Many who were interested in remarriage discovered that dating was more likely to be defined as opportunities for sexual dalliance rather than chances for courtship. Others expressed surprise at the lack of male etiquette in areas such as opening doors, paying for the date, and transporting them from their home.

Their standards for mate selection often differed from their never-married peers. Basically, they tended to steer away from the free-floating single male. They preferred men who exhibited qualities of stability and responsibility; who could conceivably make good fathers. Some of them even screened out men who had not already been married and had children of their own. Such a qualification is presumably based on the feeling that those men would be more accepting of their children. That is not always the case. Many of those men avoid single mothers because of the perception that the additional cost of more children, should a marriage occur, would be higher than they could bear.

Being a single mother also means discriminating in the selection of friends. As a rule, single mothers can no longer move in the circles they socialized in when married, due to the threat they represent to married women. Also, their interests now are different. Childless single women are often not deemed desirable friends because one cannot get reciprocity in baby-sitting from them since they are too busy dating themselves. Hence, a single mother's friends come from the network of other single mothers. Some women related that they try to keep a set of platonic male friends to use as a male model for their children. They found these men to be more stable than their lovers and thus the women could avoid some of the problems associated with sex that is linked to the nonplatonic relationship.

The problems of being a single parent and being in the singles world are illustrated in the case of a 27-year-old black educator. She had never been married, but had brought her teenage brother to live with her. According to her:

> I found that my single friends perceived me as "too busy" and/or unavailable to socialize at times. Yet, this group of people were my peers, not other married couples or single parents who had either younger children than my brother or who were older themselves with adolescent children. Thus, my single friends discriminated against me, at times, and I felt left out. I could not engage in social activities as frequently due to household management and child-care responsibilities and maintaining a professional career, which was overwhelming at times. This experience served to sensitize me to the position of single parents, particularly if various support mechanisms are lacking.

THE QUESTION OF SEX

Sexual matters must definitely be handled in a different manner for the single parent than her childless counterpart. There is not only the question of whether to have sex with a man but where or when. A main concern of single mothers is the type of sexual values they are transmitting to their children. Parents are often seen as asexual by their children, and some single mothers feel that any expression of their sexuality will brand them as morally loose and deprive them of the respect of their children. Despite the liberalization of sexual values in recent years, many mothers uphold traditional sexual mores for their children. The woman who is too open with her sexual life is fearful that her child will want to have lovers too.

In our study single mothers did not possess appreciably more conservative sexual standards than other single women. Yet, most were paragons of circumspection in their sexual life. Many said they confined their sexual activity to places outside their homes. According to a 34-year-old nurse, "I do have to curtail my at-home activities and limit my sexual expressions to only those that he can understand and accept. I want him to see plenty of affection demonstrated, but that's not always the case." There are numerous cases among our single-parent group where couples have to engage in sexual rendezvous at hotels, another reason why some men rank single mothers as low in the pool of eligible women. Many women cannot afford to leave the children to go off for sexual adventures. A common ruse in such instances is to go to bed with the man in her home, but require him to leave before the child awakes.

Of course, there are some parents who do not particularly care about the sexual model they present to their child. Many long-term divorcees, for example, have distinctly more permissive sexual attitudes than never-married women. Having no desire or chance for another marriage, they do not have to pay lip service to the sexually conservative ideals needed to attract a man. Moreover, they may wish to convey those same permissive sexual values to their children. One such case was that of a 32-year-old airline stewardess. She claims that, "I feel people should have sex with whomever is willing or whomever they please. I don't worry about what anybody thinks when it comes to morals, as long as I don't disrespect my child or carry on in her presence, the sky's the limit for me. I have no hang-ups."

On the other hand, there are single mothers who adhere to very conservative nonmarital sexual standards. Many of these women are past the age of 30 and cannot adjust to the changing sexual standards. In some cases they strongly internalize the sexual mores they convey to their child. To do otherwise, they feel, would seem absurd. They refuse to play the moralist while acting differently. If they concealed their sexual activity, they would feel hypocritical. Single mothers who have very conservative sexual values have a handy excuse with the presence of a child. As long as men attempt seduction in the mother's home, the presence of the child is a convenient rationalization for turning them down. This reason can be used selectively, depending on a woman's desire to engage in sex or not. Some single parents have declined a male request for sex when the only child present was barely months old.

Some single mothers tread a middle course with their sex life. While avoiding open display of her sexual habits, she does attempt to convey to the child that sexual intimacy is a natural expression of a heterosexual relationship. According to a 34-year-old school teacher, "No man has ever stayed one night with my child here. If I'm going to stay overnight with a guy, it will be a weekend trip, in which case my daughter will stay with relatives. I've explained to her that sometimes I'll be spending nights out, and she understands that and doesn't mind it. We discuss it often, and she understands my need as a woman for male company." The problem of sex is not a constant one for all single parents. Often it will depend on the age and sex of the child. Concern is more keen when it is a teenage daughter rather than a younger or male child. Regardless, restrained sexual expression continues to be a burden of single parenthood.

THE MALE SINGLE PARENT

If the female-headed household is considered an aberration, the single male parent is truly deviant. Until recent years men had sole responsibility for their children only in cases of the mother's insanity, death, or incarceration. As a result of recent changes in the woman's role and attitudes toward children, over a million children under the age of 18 are in their fathers' care. Much of the recent increase is due to the phenomena of runaway wives; women who abandon both husbands and children. Approximately 1.5 percent of black children in 1976 were living with their fathers.[18] This percentage is a modest decline from other years because of the growing proportion of black children born to unmarried women. These black single male parents represent a special case because large numbers of them chose to fight for custody of their children in a divorce case. Instead of boarding the child out with relatives, or remarrying quickly in order to have a caretaker, they chose to recognize their own nurturing instinct.

Even when men become single fathers, they avoid many of the problems endemic to single mothers. Whereas the single mother is ranked rather low among all female eligibles, the divorced father is often regarded as more appealing to women. He is viewed as a model of stability and responsibility because he showed he cared about his child. Considering the popular image of black men as not being interested in children, the relatively rare single father is a very attractive figure to many single women. Caring for their children also indicates they are good providers. At the same time they share the liability of many single mothers. Many women who like the glamour of dating and free-spirited activities find the single father's child-care responsibilities unappealing. While this is truer of the free-floating single woman, even other types think twice about a serious involvement with a man who has a "ready-made family."

From a male perspective there are other advantages to the solo parent role. He does not have to pay the cost of expensive dating activity since he can always claim he cannot secure a baby-sitter. Many women will come in and cook for him and the children. Because his interaction with the opposite sex is often confined to his domicile, sexual seduction is facilitated, although he may have the same rules of sexual propriety in his home as the single mother. One of our single fathers claims that he did not allow women to stay overnight after a sexual interlude. Of course, it allowed him to avoid the kinds of commitment that many women seek and the childless single male finds harder to elude.

Because the single father is so rare and seen as such a heroic figure, he receives more sympathy and support from friends and relatives than would ordinarily be given a single mother. People customarily assume a woman's status as a solo parent is normal or her own fault whereas they impute to single fathers a peculiar martyr status. Many of our single fathers claimed they met most of their potential sexual partners through their children. Once a woman seeks a permanent arrangement with a single father, she will attempt to do it through his children, playing with them, cooking, making them clothes, and various other activities. Some men avoid this possibility by limiting her involvement with the child.

As we mentioned earlier, the single male parent shares similar problems with the single mother. His movements are restricted; much of his time must be committed to the child, and his role as a bachelor must be subordinated to his role as a father. Moreover, when looking for a mate he must pay special attention to her motherly qualities. Any intensive involvement with a woman carries a special risk for him. Unlike the single mother's male lovers, his female companion will most likely become very involved with his children. Thus, the disruption of the relationship means more than losing a girlfriend, it can mean the loss of a maternal figure for his children. All in all his lot is still a lot brighter than that of the solo female parent.

Children impinge on a burgeoning romance in a number of different ways. This is true even for the formerly married male whose children do not live with him. Certainly he does not face all of the problems that characterize the lives of single mothers. A typical response to our question about how children affect their dating opportunities was made by a 34-year-old male social worker, "They don't affect my life as a single in any way. They live with their mother." Still, for the responsible male parent there are subtle intrusions on his single life. Even the former husbands of successful career women are expected to contribute to the financial support of children after a divorce. This drains away a male's economic resources which he could expend on his current lover. It should be noted that the costs involved in supporting a child are spread over a longer period for middle-class black parents. Unlike the lower-class parent whose child support is generally terminated by the age of 18 or younger, the middle-class parent is expected to provide his/her child with a college education. For this reason some single women find the formerly married male less than desirable. A number of them reported that a male lover wanted to delay or avoid marriage because of his need to support children by a former marriage.

Again, the sensitive divorced father's time and energy must be divided between a lover and his children. This becomes a thorny matter, in particular, during the holidays. A never-married, young college professor talks of the pain she felt when her current lover went off to Canada to visit his children during the Christmas holidays. Subsequently she found herself at a New Year's Eve party alone and met another man. Due to her feelings of loneliness and rejection, she responded to his seductive gestures and had intercourse with him that night. Women are also aware that men who have children by a previous marriage still remain in contact with their former wives. This 29-year-old male probation officer told us, "Usually, the women you are with are very jealous and don't want you associating with your former wife. And if you spend more than the required time to pick up your child, you are going to be accused of getting too 'social' with your exspouse." This problem of retaining ties to a former spouse is relatively rare for the single father who has his child living with him. Generally, he is raising and supporting the child alone with the former wife totally out of the picture.

WHAT ABOUT THE CHILDREN?

In the case of single mothers the needs of their children are much more than a minor consideration. Their needs, in many cases, are the major consideration. While children may represent a structural impediment to unrestricted dating opportunities, they are also central to the process of forming and maintaining a significant relationship with a man. A serious candidate for the mother's affections must often meet the approval of an older child. In the words of a 36-year-old female college administrator, "Our relationship is such that she feels free to make comments and give her opinion of the guy I may be dating. Everytime my daughter has made negative remarks about a man, she has been right. For a child she has an exceptional ability to judge people and their intentions. Everytime I've not followed her advice the relationship has not worked. She is very aware of the way men treat me."

"While some children may be perceptive in their evaluation of a mother's dating partners, they are also known to make invidious comparisons. Several factors besides keen insight can enter into a child's assessment of the mother's lover. He may be seen as a competitor for the mother's scarce time, energy, and affection. Children living with only a mother often become accustomed to monopolizing her time and attention. The perception of a male intruding on his/her turf can lead to acting out behavior, jealousy, and destructive acts. A 36-year-old claims representative refrained from any dating because, "I felt it was easier to wait until my child was old enough to understand or had left home rather than go through the competition that was sure to be involved."

Another factor that can color a child's perception of the mother's lover is his/her tie to the biological father. Many children retain a desire to have the estranged couple reunited. A serious candidate for the stepfather position threatens the fulfillment of that hope. Sometimes a child will engage in sabotage. Such was the case of a young boy who reported his mother's boyfriend to the police for smoking marijuana. Another single mother reported her sons would constantly barge into her bedroom when the lover was there. Then they would deliberately call him by the name of another one of the mother's male friends. Still, the child's ability to relate to the male dating partner is paramount. If there is an extreme incompatibility, the mother may be confronted with the alternative of abandoning her child or terminating the dating relationship. Given society's norms regarding the maternal role, the outcome is fairly predictable—though no less painful.

A serious dating partner will soon find himself immersed in the mother-child unit. After a few preliminary dates, their activities will become more family centered. This will happen partly because the working single mother will have a limited amount of time to allot to dating and spending time with the child. In some cases single mothers use the male's involvement with the child to escalate the relationship. The transformation of the dyad to a family unit legitimizes a relationship and gives an aura of permanence to it. A male's reluctance to become involved with the child *ipso facto* gives the relationship a less than serious definition. As one woman, a 29-year-old nurse, proclaims, "There is no such thing as a man loving me only. We come as a package. Either he learns to love me and my children or we have nothing in common. He has no alternative."

If an eligible male accepts a woman's children, there are still problems to be resolved. There are, for instance, no clearly defined norms for the role of a male involved in a long-term relationship with a woman who has children. Assuming they do not marry, the male has no legal authority or responsibility for the child. The biological father may retain his paternal rights, although the child's affection may be transferred to the surrogate father. Hence, questions arise about what he should be called, daddy or Joe, and how the children are to relate to him *vis-à-vis* the biological father. Should the male dating partner have children of his own, serious problems can arise when they come together on special occasions. Some of these problems are common to stepparents in general, but the lack of a normative role definition complicates the process of forming a reconstituted family.

IMPLICATIONS OF EXTENDED FAMILY NETWORKS

The role of single parents is a difficult one. They are often entrenched in a situation where the need for economic and sociological support systems is acute. Where possible, the extended family constitutes the most important support system for single parents. When they live in close proximity, extended family members may be parental surrogates for children who are lacking one parent. Since the missing parent is most likely a male, grandfathers, brothers, uncles, and male cousins provide a vital link to the child's perception of the male world. They influence the way he sees his roles in the world, his behavior, his attitudes, and his gestures. It is even possible that children who are free to relate to extended family members have an advantage over those youngsters who are primarily confined to the nuclear family. A child who lives only within the nuclear family must find love and support from two adults or none at all. The child who can relate to an extended family network has a much richer variety of roles from which to choose.

Whereas many of our single parents did not live in the same geographical location as their families, this does not necessarily mean that the crucial functions of an extended family network were not carried out. Through the use of the mail and telephone, many single parents maintain frequent contacts with family members. Single parents continue to receive emotional support through phone calls and letters. Clothes and money are sent via the mail, and a sympathetic ear is only a phone call away. The children often spend holidays and summers with relatives. In this scenario the father can remain a significant figure for the child. Middle-class fathers, in particular, continue to take an interest in the children and their welfare. Among the lower-class group, he is still regarded as a friend of the family who may be called upon for assistance.

While the extended family provides a variety of services for the single parent, a most important one for our group of middle-class divorced mothers is the caretaker role. Even when mothers have the economic resources to hire a baby-sitter, they are more comfortable with a family member taking care of their children. When the caretaker is an older family member, they provide more than a custodial service. They expose the child to a sense of history and inculcate in him/her an understanding of their roots. Through such intergenerational interaction the child maintains a continuity of culture which is crucial to the formation of a black identity. Such a helping pattern serves to relieve the multiple burdens placed upon single mothers. Both she and her children are helped by being allowed time away from each other. It serves to reduce resentment of the children by the mother who may chafe at the burden of being a solo parent. And it can wean the child away from an unhealthy dependence on the mother as the sole source of his life being.

The problem for many single parents is that extended family members are too far away. Genealogical ties, at least for the middle class, seldom dictate a choice of residence. Extended family members are often too far away to ease the daily problems faced by single parents. To satisfy that basic human need, establishing networks that transform friends into family is necessary. Among our single parent group, other women form a valuable fictive kin network. Known as play sisters, they exchange goods, advice, and baby-sitting services. Complications in the dating relationship sometimes exclude male partners as pseudo-kinsmen. In such cases, platonic male friends, whom the women consider more stable, serve in such a supportive role and can be called upon for a variety of services.

SUMMARY

The results of our study reveal a mixed picture of the middle-class black single mother's life in the dating game. She is disadvantaged by the multiple demands placed upon her as a mother, worker, and dating partner. Balancing off these demands and achieving success in each area presents a formidable challenge. It is made no easier by the fact that society and men are often not very sensitive to her unique situation. Her child expects her full attention as a mother, her employer demands a full day's work, and men assume that she can fulfill all the normal functions of a dating partner. Some of these role conflicts can be buttressed by a supportive network of family and friends. In some cases the biological father takes very seriously his nurturant role after he has left the physical environs of his family. Males who choose to date a single mother may be sensitive to the constraints on her time and energy and help her overcome some of the problems of role overload.

While the problems we have described can be formidable, many of our single parents are better adjusted to their single status than their childless peers. They have, for instance, become much more accepting of their unmarried status than other single women. Some do so because they realize their value may be low in the singles market. On a subterranean level, they might wistfully hope to find a loving and responsible man to help lift the burden off their shoulders. Still, they are carrying out essential functions which are very important because there is only one parent. They are raising children who may be no less happy because the father is absent. Indeed, most of our single mothers feel their divorce was a net gain for their children. Since they are not plagued by the economic problems of lower-income single parents, there is little reason to believe the children in such families will turn out much worse than children in two-parent homes. While the children may not fare as well as those raised by two happily married parents, they are probably better off than children in a home with unhappily married parents. Many of our single parents cited the absence of conflict and tension and felt that they had a better feeling about themselves and their children since their divorces.

All things being equal, we would prefer to see black children in a home with two parents. There are certain inherent limitations to the single-parent family. Children can assuage some of the problems of loneliness which seem to be rather acute for our free-floating singles. But they cannot relieve the affectional and communication needs of adult women. We are particularly concerned about those single mothers who have retreated into their family and ceased relating to men. This deprives not only the mother of certain satisfactions that come from a healthy heterosexual relationship, but denies the child a positive model for close relationships outside the family circle. Such a child may find it hard to be liberated in later years from the parental tie.

Regardless of individual or societal preference for a two-parent family, it appears that the single-parent unit is the wave of the future; it behooves us to address the problems that arise from this situation. We cannot continue to regard single-parent families as a form of deviance when their sheer numbers presage that they will be the dominant form of the family in the twenty-first century. It is incumbent of social planners and others to develop support systems for those women and men who attempt to raise their children alone.

NOTES

1. Herbert Gutman, *The Black Family in Slavery and Freedom, 1750-1925* (New York: Pantheon Books, 1976).

2. Robert Staples, Towards a sociology of the black family: a theoretical and methodological assessment, *Journal of Marriage and the Family* 33 (February 1971): 19-33.

3. U.S. Bureau of the Census, Current Population Reports, Series P-20, No. 218, *Household and Family Characteristics, March 1975* (Washington, D.C.: U.S. Government Printing Office, 1976).

4. U.S. Bureau of the Census, Series P-20, No. 84, *Divorce, Child Custody and Child Support* (Washington, D.C.: U.S. Government Printing Office, 1979).

5. Ibid.

6. Ibid.

7. Ibid.

8. William M. Chavis and Gladys J. Lyles, Divorce among educated black women, *Journal of the National Medical Association* 67 (March 1975): 128-134; Marie Peters and Cecile de Ford, The black solo mother, in *The Black Family: Essays and Studies*, vol. 2, ed. Robert Staples, (Belmont, California: Wadsworth, 1978), pp. 192-200. The income figures are for the year 1975.

9. U.S. Bureau of the Census, Current Population Reports, Series P-20, No. 308, *Fertility of American Women: June, 1976* (Washington, D.C.: U.S. Government Printing Office, 1977), p. 55.

10. U.S. Bureau of the Census, 1970 Census of Population, Vol. 11-4C, *Marital Status* (Washington, D.C.: U.S. Government Printing Office, 1971), Table 8.

11. Chavis and Lyles, Divorce among educated black women, p. 132.

12. Elliot Liebow, *Tally's Corner* (Boston: Little, Brown and Company, 1967), pp. 72-102.

13. U.S. Bureau of the Census, 1970 Census of Population.

14. Lee Rainwater, *Behind Ghetto Walls: Black Family Life in a Federal Slum* (Chicago: Aldine, 1970), pp. 45-54.

15. U.S. Bureau of the Census, Current Population Reports, Series P-20, No. 312, *Marriage, Divorce, Widowhood and Remarriage by Family Characteristics: June, 1975* (Washington, D.C.: U.S. Government Printing Office, 1977), p. 10.

16. Robert Bell, The related importance of mother and wife roles among black lower class women, in *The Black Family: Essays and Studies*, vol. 1, ed. Robert Staples, (Belmont, California: Wadsworth, 1971), pp. 248-255.

17. U.S. Bureau of the Census, *Marriage, Divorce, Widowhood and Remarriage by Family Characteristics: June 1975.*

18. U.S. Bureau of the Census, Series P-20, No. 306, *Current Population Survey* (Washington, D.C.: U.S. Printing Office, 1977).

Alternative Life-Styles

9

This discussion has emphasized the complexities of single-hood. To understand its multiple dimensions, one needs to distinguish the condition of being unmarried from single-hood as a way of life. The historical data tells us that the overwhelming majority of Americans do marry at some point in their lives. Only four percent of Americans never marry, and of those who marry and divorce, 79 percent re-marry.[1] Those figures, of course, are based on past patterns and do not represent the attitudes of single men and women who are under the age of forty and never married. Yet, it is my belief that, antimarriage attitudes notwith-standing, almost all of our black singles will eventually marry. And they will eventually marry for a very simple reason: the social structure does not provide any viable alternative.

This assumption may be regarded as heresy by the anti-marriage proponents. Literally hundreds of articles and a number of books have been written which endorse alterna-tives to the traditional marital union. There are several journals, academic and popular, devoted to exploring and justifying these alternative life styles. Support for them comes primarily from whites, women, and gays, for rea-sons unique to those groups. Black endorsement of alter-native life styles has been noticeably absent. This may not last long. Two of the largest black magazines have recently published articles on the advantages of staying single. However, a new journal, *Black Male/Female Relation-ships*, started by psychologist Nathan Hare and his wife Julia, has a promarriage perspective.[2]

Ironically antimarriage attitudes have been prevalent in the black population, especially among women, for a number of years. Over ten years ago Bell noted "that marriage has limited importance to black women at all educational levels," and if education were held constant at all levels, black women would show a greater rejection of marriage than would white women.[3] This finding has to be interpreted in the context of black life in the United States. In the past most white women married primarily for economic security or an elevation of their socioeconomic status. Due to the high rate of unemployment and the low wages of black men, many black women have found marriage a poor mechanism for achieving those goals. Most studies have found black wives to be more dissatisfied with their marriages than white wives.[4] We know that the black divorce rate is twice as high as that of whites.[5]

Even if marriage does not offer security, most black women would settle for the satisfaction of their psychological needs. Yet most men, both black and white, are not socialized to meet the emotional needs of women. There is a generalized discontentment with marriage among those who are married and an anticipation of unhappiness in the conjugal state among those who are not. The unhappily married tend to be concentrated in the lower stratum of the social classes. Still, middle-class black women do not escape the disaffection with marriage, although for slightly different reasons than those in the lower class. They are often unable to find men of comparable status and have to face keen competition for them, both before and after marriage. The official divorce rate is actually higher among middle-class black women although marital breakup is greater among lower-class women, who do not use the divorce courts as frequently.[6] At any rate, there is considerable dissatisfaction with marriage as an institution. But this dissatisfaction will not be translated into large numbers of black women who never marry. Black women will continue to marry until there are viable alternatives.

As for men, particularly lower-class blacks, they also voice antimarriage attitudes. Studies show them to fear public and private fights between spouses; to see marriage as creating problems of how to feed, clothe, and house a wife and child, and inducing anxiety about being able to ward off attacks on the health and safety of their children.[7] These lower-class men are the most likely of all blacks to remain legally unmarried. Middle-class black men, on the other hand, are less inclined to voice antimarriage perspectives. Even the middle-class men in our sample, while claiming to enjoy the single life, believed they would eventually settle down in permanent unions. Unlike the other groups, they saw themselves as having much to gain from marriage. They had an abundance of women of different races and educational levels from which to select. Because of the shortage of men in their category, they could make very favorable matches from the variety of women in the eligible women pool. Since society and their own values allow them considerable flexibility in choosing the women they marry, their pool is infinite, actually ten times larger than the middle-class black woman's. Moreover, marriage for them provides an image of respectability, steady and free sexual relations, regular and better meals, and various other benefits. Within marriage they maintain a certain freedom to pursue their careers and other activities, even to continue the dating of other women. Small wonder that they see marriage in a positive light. They are the group of blacks most likely to marry, and when divorced, to remarry.[8]

Despite their antimarriage attitudes, most black women harbor a desire to marry at some point in their lives. To confine our analysis to middle-class black women, we find that this attitude will vary in intensity by age and marital status. Black women under age 30 are more inclined to be antimarriage and willing to experiment with certain types of alternative life styles. Those over the age of 30 become more concerned about a legal marriage when the problems of having a child emerge as a reality. Since the alternative family forms cannot produce a socially approved parentage, they are more reluctant to try these family substitutes. On the other hand, regardless of age, formerly married mothers seem less anxious about entering a second marriage. Whether it is due to fewer opportunities or less desire, they have a low rate of remarriage. For them, alternative life-styles are more acceptable although they will contain the same problems that beset their never-married counterparts.

Regardless of their espoused commitment to singlehood as a way of life, most of our middle-class women had what we might call a singles career where they have gone through several stages. Few have been free-floating singles all of their life with casual dates every weekend and no committed relationships. To understand this fact is paramount to understanding their attitudes against marriage. In interviewing our never-married women, we found that almost all of them had at least one serious relationship with a man. The relationship was aborted after one of the couple declined to enter into a marriage. The complexities of rejection are such that it is impossible to ascertain who was most reluctant to marry. In all instances we only got the biased report of one party. It does seem clear that the misgivings of the women involved the potential mates, not the institution of marriage itself. Others might say that the two factors are intertwined and without fears of marriage, the males in question would have been acceptable. That could be the case, but the men described to us had such personal flaws that our conclusion seems defensible. Furthermore, a number of women had several such serious relationships in their singles career.

One result of such aborted relationships has been the development of overtly hostile attitudes toward marriage, partly to protect against the painful disillusionment so often experienced by many women. In other words, it is better to expect nothing and achieve something, than to want something and not get it. It is a protective armor against the anticipation of failure in male/female relationships. Yet, these attitudes are not consistent with the actions of these women, as those who enter into serious relationships with them soon find. Four years after this study began, a followup study was done on ten of the women initially interviewed. When possible, the women themselves were contacted. In all cases the original referers were contacted. All the women were in their thirties. Nine of ten women had entered into serious relationships with men where marriage was considered. Four of them had gotten married. Only one of the women was married to a middle-class black American male. And her husband was a married man she had been having an affair with for three years, who finally got a divorce from his wife. Two of them married Africans, and one married a white male. These ten women were selected because they were over thirty and had espoused an antimarriage philosophy.

Given the shortfall of black men of a similar educational and income level, it can be assumed that many black women will have to settle for an alternative life-style. The questions remain: Are there really alternatives, and how viable are they? For blacks in general, many of the alternative life-styles advocated are nothing new. Having a child out of wedlock has long been known to the black community. The latest figures show that 50.3 percent of black children born in 1976 were conceived out-of-wedlock.[9] Raising a child alone is hardly considered an alternative life-style to most black women. About 45 percent of all black households are headed by women, and they have the lowest income and most problems of all blacks.[10] As Harriette McAdoo has warned, "these types of families should not be romanticized out of context. They exist for sheer survival in the face of real and threatening problems and the problems may be becoming overwhelming."[11]

So-called alternative life-styles constitute another problem for middle-class black women. For years "middle-class" or a respectable status in the black community was associated with having a stable marriage and family life. Having children out of wedlock, raising a family alone, and heterosexual cohabitation were all behaviors endemic to the lower classes of blacks. To now enter into such behavior voluntarily is counter to the newly attained middle-class status of many blacks. Yet these very "alternative life styles" are being contemplated and entered into by some, and for very good reason: they seem to have no other choice. Few are willing to be perpetual free-floating singles, and these family substitutes are their ways of achieving the goals generally fulfilled by marriage.

Rather than use the misleading term *alternative life-styles* to describe the behavior of middle-class blacks, it is more appropriate to call them *family substitutes* or, even better, *coping styles.* Alternative life-styles imply that individuals are free to choose within an array of available options. But middle-class black singles, especially women, are choosing within the limits of the existing social structure. They are free to choose between alternatives, but not free to choose what the alternatives should be.[12] In looking at the family substitutes available, we shall see that people are products of their culture and cannot free themselves from it for greater individual freedom unless they first understand the constraints that culture imposes. Monogamous marriage is the culturally sanctioned institution in which the needs of most adults are met in the United States. Family substitutes are inadequate ways of satisfying these human prerequisites. As Etzioni has noted, "the common denominator of all these family substitutes is that they do not last, are highly unstable, and constitute revolving door unions rather than a family."[13]

DEALING WITH LONELINESS

One of the problems that beset individuals with a long tenure in the single status is that of loneliness. While loneliness is certainly not unique to singles, nor are all singles lonely, it is reasonable to expect that people who are unattached to a special person will suffer from periodic bouts with loneliness. Recent changes in the nature of American society almost guarantee that those of us who live in solitude will occasionally encounter feelings of loneliness. Given the fact that most of our black singles live in relatively large cities, places in which they were not reared nor have families, the impersonality of such environments is conducive to feelings of loneliness. Blacks may be particularly vulnerable to loneliness. According to census data, they are more likely to live alone.[14] Among our middle-class group, they do not have a concentration in particular areas of a city, especially in the Midwest and Western parts of the country.

Students of the subject note that it is not living alone that causes loneliness. Rather, it is feeling a painful gap between one's actual life and one's desired life.[15] Our singles may be particularly vulnerable to this feeling because they sense most sharply the gap between the search for intimacy and the failure to find it. Single people are more inclined to feel it is important to attain the romantic ideal, to have a special person in their life. Most of our black singles admitted to feeling lonely at some point in their life. As a 35-year-old female nurse commented, "The times when it's worse is right after a relationship has ended. At that time I find myself feeling lonely even in the midst of crowds. It's not really being alone but a feeling of isolation because I no longer have that one person I could call on. Generally, it goes away after awhile."

However, even people who are in serious relationships can occasionally feel lonely. The most common solution to this feeling and an often-used family substitute is heterosexual cohabitation. The practice of living together without a marriage contract was very common to black people. Some years ago a researcher of black family life found that "a large majority of the Negro families of the rural South are established via common law marriage."[16] These common-law marriages, as they were called during that time, differed greatly from the living arrangements of our black singles. They were entered into because a wedding license and ceremony were regarded as too expensive for people with low incomes. Moreover, they shared with legal marriages a certain stability (many lasted a lifetime) and even a legal status. The central difference, of course, was that they were exclusively found among the poorer class of blacks.

Our group of singles, middle-class blacks, only adopted the practice of living together after it was firmly established in the white community. While many of our older black singles were and are cohabitating, it is more common among college students. In one of the few studies on the subject, Jacques and Chason compared the cohabitating habits of black and white students at two different Florida universities. They found the highest rate of cohabitation was among black males, the lowest among black females. Fifty-one percent of the black men had practiced cohabitation, 49 percent of white women and 48 percent of the white males had engaged in it, while only 21 percent of the black women in their study said they had lived with a man. Among college students, however, cohabitation is often nothing more than a faddish lifestyle. About half of those students who had cohabitated with a member of the opposite sex had done so more than once. Only 22 percent of them had a live-in relationship that lasted longer than a year.[17] The end of the academic year served as the natural finale to many of these relationships.

Some older black singles had their first cohabitating experience when in college. For others it was a postcollege experience. The majority of our sample had never lived with a member of the opposite sex. A disproportionate number who had done so lived in California where cohabitation is normatively regarded as one of the stages in courtship. Whether they had such an experience or not, women had mixed feelings about their own involvement in heterosexual cohabitation. A 33-year-old female teacher said:

> I think living together is a marvelous idea. Marriage today seems to be nothing, once you have that piece of paper things begin to change. By living with someone they can't take you for granted since you always have the freedom to leave. I am very much interested in finding a relationship of this type (a long-term relationship).

As women become older their attitudes toward cohabitation may shift from their previous perspective. It depends on how the aging process shapes their attitudes toward marriage. A couple of examples illustrate this point. A 31-year-old female teacher commented:

> I would not mind living with someone who I do not necessarily plan to marry. As I have been getting older I have been contemplating this more often. Living alone is not all that great, especially in a place like New York City. I would feel better if a man was here with me. Then I wouldn't have to deal with all these creeps I keep meeting.

A 30-year-old female researcher reached a different conclusion as she entered her thirties. According to her:

> In terms of living with someone, I've always wanted to but it never fit into my situation. Now, I'm not into an experimental thing. I don't want to invest that kind of energy, personally, I could not function in the emotional limbo a "living with" relationship would create. I want a binding contract. I figure if people pay $3.00 for a dog license, surely a real man (could) pay $3.00 to marry me. If I'm good enough to live with for any length of time, marry me.

These attitudes reflect the anticipation of what can happen in a cohabitation arrangement. Other women had experienced living with a man. In the main their attitudes were not positive about the practice. A 32-year-old female psychologist declared:

I have "homesteaded" on two occasions and would avoid a repetition. My solitary life-style makes living with anyone a high stress situation. Somehow, the relationships could not stand the strain (they might not have lasted much longer anyway). With no fringe benefits, only a decline in primary advantages, as we got to the getting too used to one another phase, I decided solo was better.

Another woman, a 27-year-old research assistant, commented on her experience and change in philosophy:

I have lived with a man and don't plan to do it again, although I'm glad I didn't marry that particular person. Eventually I hope to marry and raise a family. I think marriage is important for legal and social sanctions, especially for children. It also gives more weight to casual "living with" arrangements that proliferate today. In my opinion a relationship is more than a "split expenses down the middle," sex every night relationship that seems to be in vogue. I really believe in functioning as a unit, emotionally and financially, and I believe that two people should express their personal, family, and community responsibility in a ceremonial manner.

Men, on the other hand, seemed more receptive to entering a cohabitation arrangement. While there seemed little difference in the incidence of cohabitation among the men and women in our sample, few men harbored strong attitudes against the practice. A 34-year-old male college professor told us:

I would consider cohabitation in a nonmarital situation although I question the motivation behind such arrangements, including my own. Mostly it would be to avoid making a very serious commitment to a woman. Also, I have reservations about the kind of psychology such a situation generates. If the commitment is there, then why not actualize it in concrete terms? If the commitment is lacking, then why relinquish some very good freedoms? For me the question really isn't one of cohabitation or marriage. It's more a matter of letting another person enter my private space and all that entails.

One of the reasons for the male/female discrepancy in attitudes toward cohabitation are the different implications of this living arrangement for the sexes. The double sexual standard is still strong enough that women are more stigmatized by entering into such a living arrangement. Many women find they are denied the legitimacy that marriage confers while being subjected to all its constraints. And heterosexual cohabitation has not received total acceptance in American society. Most of our sample who had co-habitated lived in cities other than the ones in which they were reared and their families reside. The women reported that their parents, when they knew, disapproved of their "living in sin."[18] Research indicates that even the male partner in such living ar-rangements shows less respect for his residential mate than other men show toward a woman with whom they have not lived before marriage.[19] For most cohabitating couples, there is still the uncom-fortable problem of the lack of terminology to use in introducing a heterosexual roommate. Most unmarrieds adopt ambiguous terms such as "my friend" or "lover" which are often not descriptive and very awkward to use.

Most live-in relationships begin with little conscious planning or explicit agreements. Generally, they start off as arrangements of convenience, whether the convenience consists of saving rent money or only travel time between two residences. Once in the same domicile, the partners may assume that implicit agreements exist when there are actually only a series of one-sided illusions. Women tend to assume that living together is a prelude to marriage while men may see it as a way of obtaining the benefits of marriage without incurring the legal obligations. One man, a 32-year-old salesman, said, "I feel that I would like living with a woman for about two years at the most and then go our separate ways, without children. I know this is harder on a woman but I would like to be happy as well as making her happy."

There are, however, some black women who see a cohabitating arrangement as time contained. This is particularly true of formerly married women. They tend to follow a strong pattern of separate-ness when cohabitating. Many keep separate bank accounts and use a different telephone number, while some continue to pay rent on their own apartment. In essence they adhere to a philosophy of "nothing lasts forever" and avoid merging into a collective identity with their live-in mate. One woman, a 31-year-old college profes-sor, had such a philosophy, "I would consider living with someone that I'm not married to if I am assured that there will be no strings attached and we both can go and come as we choose, as well as date others.''

Most cohabitation arrangements are rarely that open. We interviewed only a few live-in couples, since their life-styles were unlike most of our singles. Previous research has shown few differences between the relationships of cohabitators and marrieds. As a 28-year-old female dance instructor informed us:

I am living with my boyfriend and have been for a few months. It is nice but also hard after I have lived alone for eight years, with just my daughter. Now I have to suggest, confirm, compromise, listen, share, love, and live with more consideration for everybody in the household. When it was just my daughter, with her being so young, I made all the decisions without any consulting. I spent money, cleaned, cooked, went as I pleased. I am not complaining, but it is just that it is so different and I have to be aware of not being so selfish and not so set in my ways. Frankly, I don't see any difference in this from my marriage.

There are differences, and they create a common and serious set of problems for unmarried couples. An overriding issue, for instance, is one of the partners believing the other is not as committed as he or she is. This feeling is often translated to recurrent accusations about the partner's fidelity. A 37-year-old male social worker complained that:

I've put up with fits of jealousy that no married man would stand for. When you're married you can at least flirt around with somebody and the other partner doesn't get too shaken up if you don't make a big deal of it. But when you're living with somebody, if you so much as dance with another person, your live-in mate makes your life miserable. I'm too young to be stuck with one woman.

Still the differences between living together and being married are far more subtle than the similarities. Cohabitating couples are far less securely anchored. There is more tentativeness about the capacity of the other to sustain hostility or endure a rocky period. Theoretically the easy exit is always available to one of the partners who tires of such a living arrangement. But many such couples do not separate when tension enters the relationship. They do not believe they have more options or more freedom than the married. The attachment is the important thing, not marriage, and they basically form marriages. This is especially true when children are involved. For all practical purposes, the parent's live-in-lover becomes a parental surrogate and his/her departure from the scene can engender the same sort of separation anxiety in a child as caused by the biological father. In recent years there has been a significant increase in unmarried couples seeking help for their troubled relationships.

Given the similarity of marriage to heterosexual cohabitation, one would assume that living together is a foolproof test of marital compatibility. Such does not appear to be the case. An Ohio State University study found that those who had lived together for two and a half years stayed married only an average of two years.[20] Apparently, living together couples maintain the image of being lovers and continue to relate to the romantic model that characterizes dating partners. Marriage creates new models related to the husband/wife roles and based on the assumption of permanence. The unmarried couple may suppress angers, fears, dissatisfactions, assuming the other would walk out. In a marriage such fears are relaxed and more conflictual behavior may emerge. A 31-year-old female teacher commented on the difference:

> I've lived with someone. It differed from marriage in that I was much happier—not because of the institution of marriage. I had a lifelong friendship and love with the man I lived with. Another important difference was that I was being possessed by my husband and loved by my lover.

Heterosexual cohabitation is not really an alternative life-style. It is, in reality, a transient arrangement or transitional stage for most people who enter into it. Researchers of the subject are agreed that most cohabiting couples either marry or break up. This is especially true of our middle-class black singles for whom marriage and parenthood are still strong values. Estimates are that 75 percent of the people who live together eventually break up.[21] In her study of heterosexual cohabitators, Pepper Schwartz reported that she looked for cohabitators who have lived together for ten years or more. She is convinced that they do not exist—people either marry or separate.[22] Even those couples who have lived together for five or more years are often not committed to cohabitation as a way of life. When we asked a couple who had lived together for seven years why they had not married, the woman replied that they had not been able to put three conflict-free months together.

When all is said and done, heterosexual cohabitation is not a viable alternative for black singles because it cannot effectively address the basic issues they face. The male shortage, for instance, means that large numbers of black women cannot find a partner to live with either. Furthermore, the need to share, communicate, and compromise also exists in a cohabitation situation. Those unwilling to do so will continue to encounter problems of male/female conflict. As a 32-year-old female real estate agent informed us:

> I've lived with a man twice. It's the best way to find out if you want a man. Neither one worked. I'm selfish and like living alone. My privacy is important to me. I know me and I'm not giving up anything I have for marriage. Problem is that I don't want to have to tell anybody where I go, who I see, etc. I'm not going to cook, not even once a week. I'm used to running things, especially the business part.

Despite these problems inherent in heterosexual cohabitation, the chances are that more and more of our black singles will experiment with it as a substitute for marriage. Everyone seems aware of the fragility of marriage and the spiraling divorce rate. However, the recent Marvin decision by the California Supreme Court, with all its ambiguity, has introduced legal complications into such an arrangement. It is possible that people may be willing to incur financial losses if cohabitation partners are granted legal rights rather than risk the failure of a marriage. After all, the failure of a live-in arrangement carries nowhere near the continued stigma of a divorce. Children born to live-in couples are still rare, and they avoid that problem associated with divorced couples with children. Still if stability and security are important, and I think it is, most people will find it better to marry than cohabitate.

Other responses to the problem of loneliness are evident but not as prevalent among our black singles. Living with a member of the opposite sex without sex is one of them. In the San Francisco Bay Area this became a common practice due to a shortage of moderate priced housing and the desire to economize on living costs. The Bay

Area, however, may lend itself to such living arrangements because of the large gay and asexual male population.[23] While we did not find any black singles currently involved in an asexual cohabitation, a few reported such experiences in their past. The motivation for entering into cohabitation on a platonic basis varied from individual to individual. One woman told us:

> You either have to be totally involved with someone sexually or not at all. One thing that is important to me is that I not be sexually attracted to him. But I must be able to enjoy him as a person. And I wouldn't pick someone I couldn't stand to look at.

Other women claimed to prefer men as roommates because they are cleaner around the house and are out very often. Most of these platonic cohabitations were short-lived, some for the same reason as same-sex living arrangements. A few of our respondents reported that sex did become an issue with their male housemate and that outside men they became seriously attached to objected to the situation.

A combination of different living patterns have emerged among our black singles. Rare but interesting are the mixed threesomes. This can be any combination of men and women but typically consists of one woman and several men. Some living arrangements exist for sexual motives, others for economic ones. Such an arrangement has been popularized by the television show "Three's Company." The majority we know of are platonic and often are dissolved when one of the roommates becomes seriously involved with one of the other roommates or an outside person. A 35-year-old female public school administrator reported:

> I've lived as part of a trio in an isolated circumstance which lasted about two years. I found that it gave me double sources from which I could enjoy love and attention. Each partner felt free to explore outside the triad for additional interrelating or sexual experiences.

Communes and other collective living arrangements, which were somewhat popular among whites, never took hold among our group of middle-class black singles. One woman, a 31-year-old social worker, contemplated the idea. According to her:

I've considered communal living with several sisters who have children, financial problems, and all wanted to go to school. That was frightening to them—not me because I grew up in a house (five rooms) with seventeen persons. Cooperative economics, collective sharing can bring many families together if they chanced mutual sharing towards growth of individuals and all children involved. It's an opportunity to teach what we know to each other, thus encouraging individual responsibility and collective action toward enhancing the quality of life for blacks wherever we are.

On the other hand, there are those individuals who do not want to and are not capable of living with any other person. This may be especially the case with some of our black singles who have reached the age of thirty without ever marrying or cohabitating. Recently there has been a trend toward buying houses in which to live alone. Some were candid about the selfish motives for doing so. A 31-year-old female attorney said:

My reasons are strictly selfish. I like to do what I want to do when I want to do it. And with no disturbances or value judgements made about it. It gives me independence, and I can work without having my concentration spoiled. I enjoy eating out and don't want to cook meals for anyone.

This, of course, is a national trend, and narcissism is in part responsible for the large number of singles in the black middle class. Many of these individuals simply want the luxury of coming home, turning up the stereo, dropping off their clothes on the floor, and going off for the weekend with whomever they want. Ultimately this need will have to be balanced off against other needs which cannot be satisfied by such an existence.

THE SEXUAL SOLUTION

Finding a sexual partner was not a crucial or pervasive problem for most of our black singles, especially not for the women. Achieving regular sexual gratification within the context of an emotionally satisfying relationship was. One alternative life style that purports to resolve this problem is that of homosexuality. We realize the difficulty of positing this behavioral modality as an alternative to conventional marriage. Still it is an option that is being discussed and in some cases adopted. Whether the increased prevalence of lesbianism is due to the shortage of black men or the conflict in male/female relationships, we do not know. About twenty of the men in our sample are homosexual or bisexual, a rather high number considering there are less than 130 men in the total study. This could be due to the fact that all our interviews and a large proportion of the questionnaires come from the San Francisco Bay Area.* In San Francisco gays compose an estimated 25 percent of the adult population. We interviewed no known lesbians, and our attempts to include them in the study were unsuccessful. Either they did not meet the criterion or refused to talk to us.

Homosexuality is difficult to discuss as an option for black singles because it remains a subject fraught with controversy. Even understanding the nature of homosexuality is problematic because the research is permeated with bias. On the one hand there are those who consider it a genetic disorder and everyone affected by it a pervert. A more recent group are those who declare homosexuals to be similar to heterosexuals, and they use this argument to enhance the civil rights of gays. Some would claim that homosexuality cannot be a viable alternative for our black singles because that tendency is formed in early childhood. However, we are in agreement with psychiatrist Richard Green who suggests that "at the present time the most one can say about the genesis of homosexuality is that it remains unknown."[24] In interpreting the importance of sexual orientation we might keep in mind the words of Erich Fromm, "The very first thing we notice about anybody is whether that person is male or female. And it's the one thing we never forget. Name, telephone number, profession, politics, all of these details may slip from our memory, but never the individual's sex."[25]

Not only have we failed to understand the causes of homosexuality, but we still know little about its nature. It is estimated that 10 percent of the male population is homosexual. Although no reliable figures are available, blacks are assumed to be proportionally representative in that gay population. The majority of gays are assumed to be male, but this may be because lesbians maintain a

---

*The majority of blacks in the study, however, do not live in the city of San Francisco, nor did we recruit most of our subjects from San Francisco. The largest number lived in Oakland, which is a more typical American city.

low profile and are less likely to have come out of the closet. It appears that the majority of black homosexuals, both men and women, have less than a college education although they are well represented, or perhaps more visible, in certain middle-class occupations. Many live in urban locales where they are unlikely to be discovered, although they can be found in all environments. Certainly, those involved in an open gay life-style will live in large cities with sizable gay populations. Today the most hospitable cities for homosexuals in the United States are New York, Los Angeles, and San Francisco.

A recent study entitled *Homosexualities* by Bell and Weinberg has attempted to refute some of the stereotypes about gays. This book provides our most extensive information about black homosexuals. In general Bell and Weinberg found that black male homosexuals tend to be younger than their white counterparts, an average age of 27 in contrast to 37 for white males. They had less education and were employed at a lower occupational level than white gays. Members of the black group more often expressed the belief that their homosexuality and homosexual contacts had helped more than hurt their careers. Over two-thirds of black male gays reported they spent less than half of their leisure time by themselves in comparison to half of their white brethren. Both the black and white homosexual men claimed to have more good, close friends than the heterosexual men did. A similar difference existed in attitudes about job satisfaction. Black and white homosexuals expressed greater satisfaction with their jobs than did heterosexual men. About half of black and white male homosexuals stated they had no regret whatsoever about being homosexual.[26]

It is worth noting that only one-fourth of black gay males said that all their friends were men.[27] The other three-fourths probably constitute the only platonic male friends some of our single women have. They make very good friends for many of these women because they share some of the same interests, and women know they do not view them as sexual objects. A 26-year-old male artist said:

I enjoy women a lot. I enjoy their companionship without emotional entanglements. I prefer having a platonic relationship with a woman rather than a man. Most of my male friends are gay and our interests overlap too much and we become competitive. I go out to dinners, movies, museums, plays and talk on the telephone with my female friends. They help me keep things in perspective and provide me with a balance to my life. However, they tend to lament the fact that I'm a man lost to them.

Another interesting characteristic of the life-style of black gays is the extent of their involvement with whites. Over two-thirds of the black male homosexuals said that half of their sexual partners had been white.[28] One of our respondents believed race was less important in the gay community. However, he acknowledged that whatever their sexual orientation, whites have a certain insensitivity to blacks, and cultural differences present problems. One black male gay declared that the majority of whites who are homosexually interested in blacks are misfits, that they desire a black mate only because they sense an identity between their own feelings of inferiority and the myth of black inferiority.[29] Whatever the reason, there is certainly some element of racism among white homosexuals. As a black woman reported:

I've learned that in San Francisco's gay bars there's real racism—even overt racism—in terms of just being able to get into gay bars. They ask black gays for three pieces of I.D. with their pictures on them, but they don't ask whites for that. Or they have a certain quota and after they've filled it, they won't let any third world people in. And there are still the sexual myths about black people. The myth of the black man as a stud, for example.

If black homosexuals stay in the black community, they do not necessarily find a high degree of acceptance. Blacks may tolerate, but will not openly approve of homosexual behavior. Ministers in the black church have preached that it is unnatural for men to burn for men, and women to burn for women. The A.M.E. church is on record as being diametrically opposed to homosexuality.[30] Black physicians have tried to "cure" homosexuality in black patients. A Howard University newspaper called gays "freaks" and condemned homosexuality as capitalist depravity.[31] However, black male homosexuals were less likely to hide the fact of their homosexuality from their family and friends than their white counterparts.[32] As one black gay reported, "In a lot of ways the black community won't accept homosexuals, but in a lot of ways I feel blacks will accept gays before the white community does—on a gut level—simply because blacks know what it's like to be oppressed.''

Lack of acceptance by the black community is not the only problem faced by male homosexuals. Sexual contacts are often fleeting ones. One-third of these men reported having at least 500 different sexual partners during the course of their homosexual career.[33] Despite those large numbers, two-thirds of them complained of having trouble finding a suitable sexual partner.[34] Just as in the heterosexual world, youth and attractiveness are highly valued. Most younger gay men tended to rate their sex appeal higher than the older men did.[35] As one gay male commented, ''I hope I don't live much past 50. After that, nobody wants to look at you, and you always have to pay for sex.'' There was an interesting racial difference in the psychological adjustment of black and white male homosexuals. The black males were more likely to feel less happy at the present time than five years ago, to feel more tension and to feel lonely more frequently.[36]

With all these problems homosexuality does not seem to be a viable alternative, at least not for black males. Coupled with the stigma of homosexuality is the fact that many problems heterosexuals face are present in the homosexual world. Among them are the problems of finding a compatible partner. A number of our gay males complained they were unable to find a compatible male with whom to establish a meaningful relationship. One male, a 35-year-old social worker, told us:

Yes, I've lived with a lover in a homosexual relationship. The first four years were wonderful, but the last six months were hell. I'm basically a relationship person. But the society reinforces butterfly relationships, where you light one second for sex. He wanted to continue living together but I wasn't willing. He was conventionally middle class while I'm more bohemian. He cares what people think and I don't.

Lesbians share the social stigma of their male counterparts, but there are salient differences between the two groups. One of the reasons they are less visible could be attributed to the fact that lesbians are less socially acceptable in the black community. Or so thinks Audre Lorde, who declared, "If the recent hysterical rejection of lesbians in the black community is based solely upon an aversion to the idea of sexual contact between members of the same sex—why then is the idea of sexual contact between black men so much more easily accepted, or unremarked?"[37] In agreement with her is another black lesbian who cried out:

> As a black lesbian I am in a weird situation. I am oppressed not only by society as a whole, but by the black community too. The black community looks upon the lesbian as blacks do upon whites. This is particularly true of black males who consider lesbians a threat. Black males think that a lesbian is fair game sexually for anybody, because she can't get a man or is turned off by men."[38]

Those black women who chose lesbianism fared better than their male counterparts. They had fewer transient sexual contacts. Most of them had fewer than ten female sexual partners during the course of their homosexual career. Two-thirds of them reported that the majority of their sexual partners had been persons whom they cared about and for whom they had some affection.[39] In the lesbian culture youthfulness did not take on the importance it had among male homosexuals or heterosexuals. Few of the lesbians encountered sexual problems or contracted a venereal disease.[40] Because members of the same sex are more sensitive to each other's sexual needs, many lesbians reported satisfactory sexual experiences. Nowhere was this more evident than in the greater skill of lesbians in performing oral sex than that shown by men performing it on women.[41] More than two-thirds of the black lesbians reported they spent less than half of their leisure time alone.[42] However, black lesbians were more likely to report poorer health and more psychosomatic symptoms, to feel lonely more often, and to display more tension and paranoia.[43]

We know no more about the causes of lesbianism than male homosexuality. A theory that covers both groups is that their homosexual orientation emerges in response to past difficulties in heterosexual relationships. It is true that a half of the black lesbians had been married at least once (compared to fewer than 20 percent of black male homosexuals).[44] Some of our black female singles did report that they would consider a lesbian relationship if their relationships with men did not improve. According to a 37-year-old teacher, "I'm not ready for homosexuality yet. If men keep playing games with me, I might consider switching in later life. Right now, I still know a few cool dudes." Probably a more typical response to lesbianism is that of a 39-year-old college administrator:

Don't worry about me and the Daughters of Bilitis. Somehow I don't think deliberately complicating my life like that would net me anything I'm particularly in need of. For that kind of risk I'd have to be *assured* of something really great. Knowing what I know about human beings of both sexes and many races I have little hope that anybody can assure me of anything. So, I'll take my chances with my present life-style.

Indications are that most black women live primarily heterosexual lives. Some have recently turned to occasional bisexual experiences. Most of them do this in a clandestine manner, frequently between their serious relationships with men. Some have claimed that there is no such thing as bisexuality, only people who are basically homosexual with the ability to perform heterosexually. But our interviews with psychologists, leaders of women's groups, and gay black males confirm a great deal of alternation between partners of different sexual orientations. A number of women reported having sexual experiences with men who were regarded as exclusively homosexual. Some of the women in our sample were formerly married to men who eventually came out of the closet. During the marriage they claimed to have experienced a normal frequency of sexual relations. One of our male subjects, a 37-year-old professor, said:

I have considered an alternate life style involving a male partner as well as legal marriage to a woman. I feel that I could do either and be happy. I prefer to do it with a woman for awhile because I would like children— perhaps later with a man. I'm too conservative to do the both together.

Whether blacks opt for homosexuality as an alternative to the conventional heterosexual marriage is up to the individual. Any person who consciously and voluntarily makes that decision should be aware of the problems involved in choosing such a life-style. It compounds the problem of being members of a racially oppressed group. For women it means being discriminated against on the basis of sexual orientation as well as gender and race. In less tolerant areas gays are still subject to threats of blackmail, and housing and job discrimination. Gay marriages still have no legal standing, and this means stable gay couples do not have the legal rights granted to heterosexual couples. Approval in the black community for homosexual orientation may not be forthcoming soon, especially not for women. It may be an alternate life-style for those who can accept their homosexuality, but it remains one that is fraught with difficulty.

FULFILLING THE PARENTAL ROLE

Socially approved parenthood is another element of life that could, ostensibly, elude our black singles who never marry. Since most black singles were formerly married, having a child out-of-wedlock presented a problem for only a minority of our unmarried blacks. Still, it is a source of identity that is denied them. Or, is it? Some years ago a black woman, writing for a black women's magazine, observed, "Lately I've noticed a strange thing. More and more single black women are having children out-of-wedlock because they want to. Most don't have a man lined up either. In the main, they are taking on the challenge of becoming a single mother, despite the availability of abortions."[45] A similar resolve was expressed to us in the interviews, questionnaires, and conversations with black women. Considering that all of our subjects are middle class, this could be regarded as class heresy. Although lower-income blacks have long had children out-of-wedlock and have had a support system in which to raise them, having children only in the context of marriage was an identifying characteristic of the black middle class. Dollard, for instance, reported in his study of some years ago the case of a man known to have a number of illegitimate children by different mothers. For this reason he was judged to be "not really of the middle class."[46]

As we previously noted, single motherhood is a common status in the black community and is on the increase. In 1960, 22 percent of the nation's black births were delivered by unmarried women, but by 1976 this increased to 50 percent. These single-parent house-holds average only 53 percent of the income of black husband-wife families.[47] Most of these black women were from the lower income strata, and few acknowledged a deliberate attempt to become pregnant.[48] Our black singles are motivated by the fear they may never marry or marry at too advanced an age to take the risk of having a child. Giving birth and raising a child is still a compelling force among many black women who are unmarried. Having a child out-of-wedlock has, again, become more acceptable as middle-class whites tend to give sanction to such practices. Most of these black singles have relatively high incomes, and the child will not be plagued by the poverty that besets other single-parent families.

At this point many black singles are only contemplating the pos-sibility of single parenthood. However, we were told of numerous cases where middle-class black women became pregnant by "accident" and decided to give birth to the baby. In our discus-sions with women we were told that they were evaluating men in terms of their fatherhood potential, that is, looks, intelligence, and other desirable traits. Some even have specific men targeted for fatherhood. As a 28-year-old female attorney revealed, "If I am at age 35, and still unmarried, and if I have reached a level of econom-ic security (which is my five year goal), I would consider having out-of-wedlock the child of a long time friend/lover with whom mar-riage is not part of the friendship expectation."

In general, the designated father was unaware of the woman's plans. When queried about their reaction to being selected as the father of a woman's child, a few responded negatively. A 29-year-old male dentist informed us:

That would depend on the woman. With a few women I wouldn't care and would even help support and raise the child although we're not mar-ried. There are some women I know who have such bad traits I'd feel funny about them raising a child that has my blood. If I wasn't told about it in advance, I think I'd be resentful.

These women also have to reconcile their maternal desires with their career ambitions. A woman raising a child alone will be subject to all the stresses and strains experienced by career wives with children without having the built in supports that marriage can provide. Since many live in cities apart from their families, they do not have the buffer of the extended family support network. A 26-year-old female reporter pondered the problems that could arise:

> I've considered raising children alone. I was pregnant two years ago but had a miscarriage. I thought a lot about having a child alone. But I decided it wasn't fair to the child. It needs as much love as it can get. I would have started out with a handicap having to work. I like the idea of giving life.

Other women consider the problem of raising a child alone without a male role model in the home. Based on the available research, there is cause for concern. One study pointed out that single-parent families entail the greatest risk to the mental health of black children.[49] Representative of this fear is the view of a 28-year-old female college administrator, "I want to have a child or adopt. I sometimes think I am being selfish if I am not married because there would or might not be a male (positive) image in the house for this child. Therefore, I would deny a child something very valuable."

These women might also consider the mental health risk to themselves. In an investigation of the cause of hypertension among black women, Shimkin found raising a child alone to be the one factor that stood out.[50] However, we have to be cautious in interpreting most of these studies on single mothers. Most of them were low-income women, and we might be looking at the effects of poverty, not the absence of a male figure.

Of course, there were some women who simply did not want to have children, for various reasons, in or out of marriage. So reports a 28-year-old college instructor:

> I wouldn't like to have children before I was married. I wouldn't want that responsibility. I value my freedom. Even after I'm married I don't know if I want that kind of responsibility. Besides, children get on my nerves. So I'd never consider this as an alternative. Raising one alone would be strictly a necessity.

Those women who have voluntarily given birth to a child out-of-wedlock may encounter problems to which they have given little thought. Eventually they will have to cope with the issue of what to tell a child about its father. Conversely, some unwed fathers have demanded visiting rights with their child, and a few have sued, with mixed success, for the custody of the child. And despite the more permissive morality in America, being an illegitimate child, particularly in the black middle class, is not a comfortable status. In the lower income group, the out-of-wedlock child is generally not stigmatized by the "sins" of the mother. Within the middle class, however, there is still a curious moral code which permits non-marital sexual activity but condemns the birth of a child from such behavior.

So far men have not figured in our discussion. That is not because none of them wanted to fulfill the parental role. Many had children by a former marriage or sexual liaison. A few claimed interest in adopting a child, but it seemed like an idle dream. Obviously, the father role is not the strong source of identity for men that motherhood is for women. In an earlier chapter we looked at single fathers, but all of them sired their children in a marital context. Fatherhood does not seem such an urgent task for men because they do not have to meet the biological deadline of the female sex. They can still sire children at an advanced age, and most of them will eventually marry or, at least, have a better option to do so than black women. A 29-year-old male insurance adjustor commented:

> I thought about raising a child alone briefly, because there are so many orphans. I basically don't like children. I don't like to be touched and children do a lot of it. I came from a large family and had to baby-sit and change diapers. So, I don't like it. I think this is an unhealthy attitude to have, so I'm going to change it.

Whether many of our women will opt for single motherhood remains to be seen. Only those 35 years or older have to make it a serious concern. The problems for both mother and child increase greatly when a woman reaches the age of 40. What is more likely is the continuation of another practice that has existed for a number of years. It is obvious that some of the post-30-year-old women have recently married men who do not meet their standards. They may do so in the hope that such a union will last but with a willingness to accept its failure. Often they have a child and then get a divorce. Cases abound of black women marrying long enough to have a child and subsequently obtaining a divorce. While other forces may be at work, the coincidence is too great to overlook. Some black women attempt to adopt a child but generally have more trouble adopting than married couples. Adoption agencies may give preference to white couples over single black women in the adoption of a black child. And for many it is the experience of giving birth that is important, not the rearing of a child. This is the one thing that continues to elude many women who remain single.

DEVIANT PATHS TO A NORMATIVE GOAL

Individuals who find the above alternatives undesirable may choose to pursue the goals of marriage via unconventional means. Probably the most common of the unconventional ways is that of polygamy. Having more than one spouse is an old and sanctioned practice in many societies throughout the world, including the ancestral home of most Afro-Americans—Africa. In America, however, monogamy is not only the normative form of marriage but the only one that has a legal status. The classical form of polygamy does exist among Afro-Americans. Mostly it is limited to polygyny (a man and several wives) and is probably rarer among Afro-Americans than among Mormon adherents of the philosophy. Polygyny differs from the earlier mentioned mixed threesome because the individuals involved assume the more traditional roles of husbands and wives in a marital context. We were unable to find any for our study, although we did talk to persons who knew those practicing polygyny. Many of the polygynists were members of black cultural nationalist groups or possessed a pan-African philosophy. From the second-hand accounts, we learned that many of the polygynous marriages had failed. The main problem seemed to be that of women with monogamous values embedded in a polygynous structure. As the friend of one black woman involved in a polygynous marriage informed us, "She split after discovering that he just wanted two women to work for him instead of one."

A practice which is found more often and which has considerable support is what we call informal polygyny. These living arrange-ments are described by sociologist Joseph Scott as a pattern of interaction, which lasts for several years, wherein two women agree (willingly or unwillingly) to share a man between them in a familial context.[51] Basically they agree to be consensual husbands and wives without the benefit of religious or legal approval. Scott maintains that the imbalanced sex ratio requires black women to resort to this type of polygynous arrangement in order to cope with their sexual, companionship, and maternal needs. According to him, "With the shortage of black males, biological genocide could be a reality for blacks if black women choose to be celibate and not have chil-dren by the males who are still available."[52]

Many of these polygynous males were legally married to one of the women. In all cases they shared different households, with the male alternating between each residence. He occasionally shared parental and financial obligations with each woman although the nonlegal wife was sometimes self-supporting. Many of the women disliked the situation, but for a variety of reasons accepted it. In most cases they believed an exclusive relationship was impossible. Some of the married women did not complain about sharing their husband because they believed a part-time husband was better than no husband at all. A polygynous-like arrangement could serve as a tension reduction device for marriages which were in emotional and sexual trouble. Scott claims that companionship needs, sex needs, and needs for affection supersede legalities and conventions for most women of childbearing age.[53] Whether that is an exaggeration of the tendencies of most black women or not, the sharing of men is not of recent origin in the black community. The imbalance in the sex ratio has existed since the turn of the century. Even then in most Southern black communities there were examples of polygynous-like living arrangements. Perhaps we can agree with Scott's conclu-sion that:

Until there is some way to correct the sex ratio imbalance and until blacks control the economic and welfare institutions in such a way to stop the breaking up of black monogamous relationships we cannot be too harsh on black men and women who find some satisfactory adjustments in sharing themselves and their economic resources in a new, at least for this society, family form which meets their most basic needs.[54]

Black women could at least improve their chances of finding a monogamous mate if they were willing to violate certain norms of the selection process. One of them is the taboo on marrying men of a younger age. In recent years there has been a discernible increase in black women dating and marrying younger men. We have no idea of the success rate of such age discrepant marriages. Certainly, there are problems inherent in such marriages. Whether they outweigh the benefits to be derived from expanding the pool of eligible men, we do not know. A 29-year-old female teacher commented, "It makes good sense in biological terms for a 40-year-old woman to hook up with an 18-year-old male, since women reach their sexual peak in their forties. As you know, with men it's all downhill after the early twenties." Yet older women/younger men marriages may not last. A psychiatrist notes that, "As a woman grows older and loses her beauty, a younger man may begin to see her as a mother figure and have difficulty relating to her sexually." Moreover, differences in maturity level, salary, and attitudes about having children may all generate conflicts in such marriages. Still one woman summed up her view about the benefits and costs, "Seeing the track records of marriages today, what guarantees that I would have a longer-lasting marriage with someone my own age?"

Another ostensible option for middle-class, single black women is that of marrying foreign-born black men, from Africa and the West Indies. This is already occurring, especially among black women with postgraduate degrees. Many women meet foreign students on college campuses. One finds, however, a continuing reluctance to consider African men as mates. One woman, a 28-year-old psychologist, informed me, "Most black women want to marry a man who meets their ideal. And marrying an African is not one of their ideals." Anyway, large numbers of highly educated black women are marrying foreign-born blacks. Most of the men are Africans. They strongly value black women with a higher education who possess "western ways." Since most Africans who receive college degrees are men, there is a dearth of homogeneous women in their homeland. West Indian men, being closer to their native country and having more educated West Indian women to choose from, are less inclined to marry Afro-American women. African men also are willing to marry Afro-American women who have a high level of education and income because they do not feel threatened by them. It has been said they are not threatened by them because they view *all* women as inferior regardless of their income or educational level.

Marrying an African is by no means a panacea for single black women. Although Africans represent a disproportionately large number of blacks who have college degrees in the United States, there are not enough of them to compensate for the shortfall of black men in the bachelor pool. And despite the rhetoric about blacks being an African people, there are considerable differences between African and Afro-American culture. An Afro-American woman who marries an African, for instance, may have to face the possibility of eventually living in Africa. And that, according to Bernadette Kayode, "requires adaptability, a tremendous amount of patience and a willingness to understand customs that differ from those that shaped her values. Emotionally, she has to be able to accept the contradictions of 'returning home'."[55] She will have to accept the fact that Afro-Americans are outsiders in African cultures as well as a lack of creature comforts she has come to take for granted in the United States. Refrigerators, television sets, and telephones are still a luxury on the African continent. Kayode, herself once married to an African, has observed, "There are no figures and it is difficult to hazard a guess, but a significant number of Nigerian/Afro-American marriages fail. Influenced by factors playing on any marriage in any society, the Nigerian/Afro-American marriage carries additional burdens that may repeatedly intrude and never be fully resolved."[56]

SUBLIMATION

If none of the aforementioned options are acceptable, there is always the process of sublimation. This is the act of transferring psychic energy into socially acceptable channels of endeavor. We suspected that many of our single women were trying to divert their attention away from their interpersonal relations or lack thereof. To occupy themselves they were taking yoga classes, joining organizations, devoting full time to school, doing anything to keep them busy and distracted from their single status. A favorite organization was the black church. Many black women have returned to organized religion after a long hiatus. For some of our singles, this came across in the religiosity expressed in the answers to our questions. Most, however, did not change their life-style or values as a result of rejoining the church. It is mainly a way of seeking spiritual regeneration and achieving a feeling of belonging to some group. Surely, it is not a ruse to meet eligible men since black churches tend to be top heavy with women and children. The men that are there can best be characterized as being in the advanced age category.

Joining organizations and taking up hobbies are favorite sublimation techniques. Some women return to school to seek an advanced degree. Those who have attended college know, that even in the most difficult fields, studies do not have to preclude involvement with a member of the opposite sex. Yet there were women in our sample who claimed that school consumed all their time. What they meant was that a relationship with a man can take up too much psychic energy and distract them from the goal of achieving a graduate degree. In some cases, especially after the end of a relationship, they were just taking a vacation from men. Such was the case of a 42-year-old female nurse:

> At this time I am in graduate school and my time and energy is fairly limited to what I can give to a male/female relationship. I feel that I want a special relationship and should give full attention to it, in order to have the best possible growth. Good relationships, long lasting relationships do not just happen.

Full-time preoccupation with a job is a common diversion from relationships with a man. Some women claimed that their work just preempted all their time. Very few men made a similar claim. One could assume that black women have harder jobs and simply put in more time on them. This was somewhat contradicted by other black women who held comparable positions, and faced many demands on their time. Unlike some white women, few black women have obsessive desires to be career women. Our research, as well as that of others, reveals that most black women prefer to combine their occupational role with a family role. Their history and role models are such that they expect to work full time but see no conflict between that and fulfilling the wife and mother role. A 31-year-old female biochemist declared, "I would prefer a blend of marriage and a career. If I could only have one, I would choose neither but would choose to work awhile and then stay home awhile, trying to achieve a balance by alternating the choices."

Lately it has become fashionable to look upon a career as the sole source of a woman's identity. Such a view is shortsighted because it ignores the fact that few men opt for such a choice. Jobs, no matter how rewarding, are often a major source of tension in an individual's life. This is particularly true of the occupations in which most middle-class black women are lodged. Social workers, teachers, and nurses are all in constant and sometimes hostile contact with people. They can be victims of job burnout, where they develop a profound and lasting dread of going to work. It can mean mental and physical depletion, ranging from fatigue to a full fledged nervous breakdown. And most people do not have the types of jobs which grant them a great deal of autonomy or recognize their humanity and individuality. Having to work year after year just to survive without any other source of satisfaction can be emotionally debilitating. Predictably, three out of every five Americans say work is not their major source of satisfaction; leisure and their family is.[57]

We have one empirical study of black women's attitudes about how they will cope with the male shortage. In a study by Marie Smith, she selected 135 respondents from the black single female population of Baltimore, Maryland and Washington, D.C. Her subjects had a median age of 29.6, an average annual income of $12,208, and a median educational level of 14.3 years. Most had positions classified as professional. She elicited the following information from them:

1. Eighty-three percent expected to eventually marry a black man.
2. Thirty-nine percent believed that sharing a man with another woman was better than having no man at all.
3. Fifty-nine percent would prefer a foreign-born black man as an alternative sexual partner to an Afro-American. The third most preferred group were white males (13 percent) with Asians (3.1 percent) and Puerto Ricans (4.6 percent) ranked last. In total, 57 percent of them

would date men of other races as an alternative to not finding a black man.

5. Less than 5 percent of the women surveyed would accept lesbianism as an alternative to the black male shortage.[58]

SUMMARY

In our examination of alternatives to the conventional monogamous marriages, few, if any, appear desirable or viable. Some cannot be regarded as legitimate alternatives for blacks. Dedication to a career seems irrelevant to a group of black women who have been in the labor force for the last hundred years. Raising a child alone has become a traditional, and often undesirable, life-style for too many black women. Those who realize the burden it imposes on both the mother and child are hardly inclined to view single motherhood as something they want or happily choose. Other alleged alternatives contain flaws because they do not address the basic cause of black singlehood: the shortage of black males and the conflict between the sexes. Heterosexual cohabitation, for instance, does not increase the number of males available nor does it alter the ability of men and women to live in a harmonious relationship. Ironically, two of the most mentioned alternatives, homosexuality and interracial marriages, are used more often by men, thus compounding the problems of black women seeking a heterosexual mate within the race.

However, not all is lost. Black people have coped with the shortage of men for a number of years and have managed to marry. Through a variety of coping mechanisms, they have been able to establish a marital union and raise children. Much of this has been accomplished through the pattern of serial polygyny, that is, a male marries more than one woman in his lifetime. Whether this will continue or not depends on how many black women choose to redefine their options and priorities. Noted black feminist Patricia Bell Scott believes we will see a different type of black woman in the future:

I say that the breakdown in clear definitions as to what is expected of men and women in intimate relationships has created more intrapersonal conflict for both. I see lesbianism as a life style that is sure to increase. I also believe black women are likely to choose several life-styles during a lifetime. In other words, we are going to see women who opt for a casual, heterosexual relationship at one point, but then choose lesbianism at a later point. I'm not trying to be facetious, but "gray lesbianism" is a logical alternative. Gray lesbians are women over 65. Since the Black aged population is largely female, this is a viable alternative.[59]

The situation of black singles is much too fluid, and the research on them too sparse, to pontificate about the direction of their family life-styles. Given the present circumstances, it is difficult to hold out much hope that the majority of black women will marry and stay with one man their entire lifetime. The theory of alternative life-styles is conceptually flawed, however, because it does not take into account the effects of social structural forces over which most individuals have minimal control.[60] Not only does American society fail to provide structural supports for persons engaged in alternative life-styles but it can and does punish individuals who violate its norms. Furthermore, the greatest punishment is administered by the individuals themselves, when there is any incongruity between their life-styles and the values they have internalized. In the past the black community provided some support for the coping mechanisms of its members. But middle-class blacks increasingly are outside the cultural borders of the black community and are more subject to the norms of their class and the wider white community. In the past, middle-class blacks were an integrated part of the larger black community and shared its values. Presently, they are a diffused group that is beholden to middle-class values of individualism and materialism. Whether the reality of the black community can be accommodated to their new found values is an unanswered question.

NOTES

1. U.S. Bureau of the Census, *Marital Status and Living Arrangements: March, 1976*, Current Population Reports, series P-20, No. 306. (Washington, D.C.: U.S. Government Printing Office, 1977).

2. John Stark, Scenes from a happy marriage, *Black Male-Female Relationships* 1 (June-July 1979): 13-15.

class women, in *Black Family: Essays and Studies*, vol. 1, ed. Robert Staples (Belmont, California: Wadsworth, 1971), p. 254.

4. Robert Blood and Donald Wolfe, Negro-white differences in blue collar marriages in a northern metropolis, *Social Forces* 48 (September 1969): 59-63; Karen

Renne, Correlates of dissatisfaction in marriage, *Journal of Marriage and the Family* 32 (February 1970): 54-67.

5. Paul Glick and Karen Mills, *Black Families: Marriage Patterns and Living Arrangements* (Atlanta, Atlanta University, 1974), p. 14.

6. Ibid., p. 13.

7. Robert Staples, Educating the black male at various class levels for marital roles, *The Family Coordinator* 30 (April 1970): 164-167.

8. Glick and Mills, *Black Families*, p. 9.

9. Half of black children born to unmarried women, *The Washington Post*, 4 May 1978, p. A1.

10. U.S. Bureau of the Census, *Divorce, Child Custody and Child Support* (Washington, D.C.: U.S. Government Printing Office, 1979), p. 2.

11. Blacks' fresh trials, *Newsweek*, 15 May 1978, p. 77.

12. Noel Cazanave, Social structure and personal choice in intimacy, marriage and the family alternative lifestyle research, *Alternative Life Styles* 2 (August 1979): 331-358.

13. Amitai Etzioni, Marriage and maternity as endangered species seen in perspective, *Human Behavior* 3 (1974): 10-11.

14. Glick and Mills, *Black Families*, p. 22.

15. Suzanne Gordon, *Lonely in America* (New York: Simon and Schuster, 1976).

16. Sister Frances Jerome Woods, *The Cultural Values of American Ethnic Groups* (New York: Harper and Brothers, 1956), p. 223.

17. Jeffrey Jacques and Karen Chason, Cohabitation: a test of reference group theory among black and white college students, *Journal of Comparative Family Studies* 9 (Summer 1978): 147-165. Census data and other studies show a higher incidence of cohabitation among non-college Blacks.

18. Cf. Elizabeth Toupin and Zella Luria, Some cultural differences in response to coed housing: a case report, *Mental and Physical Health Problems of Black Women* (Washington, D.C.: Black Women's Community Development Foundation, 1975), pp. 126-135.

19. Judith Lyness, Living together: an alternative to marriage, *Journal of Marriage and the Family* 34 (May 1972): 305-311.

20. Living together first may not help marriages, *Jet Magazine*, 30 December 1967, p. 52.

21. Richard R. Clayton and Harvin L. Voss. Shacking up: cohabitation in the 1970s, *Journal of Marriage and the Family* 39 (May 1977): 273-284.

22. Pepper Schwartz interviewed on the Sunday Times Television Show. KRON, 8 July 1979, San Francisco.

23. Cf. Susan Berman, San Francisco, city of sin — why can't I get laid? *City Magazine*, 3 August 1975, pp. 10-12.

24. *San Francisco Chronicle*, 27 October 1976, p. 16.

25. *San Francisco Chronicle*, 19 May 1979, p. 33.

26. Alan Bell and Martin Weinberg, *Homosexualities* (New York: Simon and Schuster, 1978), pp. 34-215.

27. Ibid., p. 173.

28. Ibid., p. 85.

29. Levi Benton, Case history: I'm a black homosexual, *Sexology*, March 1972, pp. 15-18.

30. Religious leaders say black church untouched by gay rights crusade, *Jet Magazine*, 13 June 1978, p. 8.

31. Jocelyn Johnson, Faggots, freaks and macho men, *The Hilltop*, 9 February 1979, p. 5.

32. Bell and Weinberg, *Homosexualities*, pp. 63-4.

33. Ibid., p. 85.

34. Ibid., p. 117.

35. Ibid., p. 104.

36. Ibid., p. 207.

37. Audre Lorde, Scratching the surface: some notes on barriers to women and loving, *The Black Scholar* 9 (April 1978): 34.

38. Ann Allen Shockley and Veronica Tucker, Black women discuss today's problems: men, families, society, *Southern Voices* 1 (August-September 1974): 18.

39. Bell and Weinberg, *Homosexualities*, p. 93.

40. Ibid., p. 105.

41. Sex team finds few surprises in new study, *San Francisco Examiner*, 17 April 1979, p. 6.

42. Bell and Weinberg, *Homosexualities*, pp. 183-184.

43. Ibid., p. 215.

44. Ibid., p. 167.

45. Joyce White, Single motherhood, *Essence*, November 1972, p. 54.

46. John Dollard, *Caste and Class in a Southern town* (New Haven: Yale University Press, 1937), p. 265.

47. U.S. Bureau of the Census, *The Social and Economic Status of the Black Population in the United States: An Historical View 1790-1978* (Washington, D.C.: U.S. Government Printing Office, 1979), p. 119.

48. Frank Furstenberg, Premarital pregnancy among black teenagers, *Transaction* 7 (May 1970): 34-42.

49. S. B. Kellam et. al., Family structure and the mental health of children, *Archives of General Psychiatry* 34 (1977): 1012-1022.

50. Demitri Shimkin, Personal communication, 9 January 1975.

51. Joseph W. Scott, Polygamy: a Futuristic family arrangement for African Americans, *Black Books Bulletin* 4 (Summer 1976).

52. Joe Scott responds to criticisms, *Black Books Bulletin* 4 (Fall 1976): 78.

53. Ibid., p. 80.

54. Ibid.

55. Bernadette Golden Kayode, African/Afro-American marriages: do they work? *Essence* 10 (July 1979): 81.

56. Ibid., p. 129.

57. *San Francisco Sunday Examiner and Chronicle*, 20 August 1978, pp. A-12-13.

58. Marie Smith, *Black Female's Perception of the Black Male Shortage*. Masters' Thesis, Howard University, April, 1978, Chapter 5.

59. Patricia Bell Scott, Personal Communication, 1 February 1978.

60. Cazanave, Social structure and personal choice.

Conclusion

Recently black singles have emerged as a majority of the adult black population. It is without historical precedent that such a large proportion of any racial group should be unmarried across all age ranges. When we include all the blacks defined as being unmarried, we find that at any given point in time, about 54 percent of all adult black females, and 47 percent of black males are not married and living with a spouse.[1] Based on the present trend, we can realistically predict that by the year 2000 the majority of adult blacks, male and female, will continue to be unmarried. Hence, this is not an esoteric group of people we are discussing. Perhaps more important than why there is such a large unmarried black population is how significant this group is to the functioning of the black community.

Before exploring the answers to those questions, I wish to make my own position clear. A white colleague of mine has conducted a study of white singlehood as a viable alternative to marriage.[2] That is not my perspective. Most blacks do not see their singleness as a viable choice but as a condition forced upon them by certain vicissitudes of life in America. This does not mean that black singlehood is a pathological form or that black marriages are that happy or functional. What it does signify is that being single and black is problematic. It requires coping with certain problems that either do not occur in the conjugal state, or happen with less frequency, and for which solutions are more readily available to married people.

Let us be clear at the outset that not all people are single in the same way. Some may be living with another person and the relationship takes on all the qualities of a marriage, others have children who occupy their time and satisfy certain emotional needs, and a number of them may be wedded to a career. At the same time there are those who are actively involved in the dating game and ardently pursuing a spouse. The bottom line of all these different configurations are conflicts in the male-female relationship. Remaining unmarried or dissolving a marriage is the most fundamental expression of an inability or unwillingness to resolve that conflict.

If it is not already clear, it is necessary to understand that not all black singles are narcissistic or in conflict with members of the opposite sex. At any given point in time they may be in a warm, loving relationship. Somehow those relationships are not consummated, and the primary reason is a perceived dissimilarity of values, interests, and goals. The problem is partially a demographic one with strong class overtones. While marriage rates for middle-class black males are high, there simply are not enough eligible men to insure a monogamous marriage for women in that class cohort. Still, the conflict between black men and women is more real than apparent. That does not mean they are irretrievably alienated from or hate each other. It does suggest that they continue to define their needs in very different ways, and that attaining the delicate balance between varying world outlooks is increasingly difficult to achieve.

At the same time the society is now structured to make singlehood a more viable option for many of our group. The increased educational and occupational options for women mean that marriage is more of a free choice for them. Ironically, while they are no longer economically dependent on men for a standard of living, other forces have given rise to an elevated desire for class homogamy in marriage. This has occurred at the same time as the pool of eligible men has broadened their own options by marrying women of other races, homosexuality, and other alternatives. Still, the singles world is no longer a pariah in American society. Much of the discrimination against singles has abated. In the black community their numbers are so large that they can form a support network among their members. While these aspects of singlehood can be reassuring, they remain secondary to the urge to mate.

Despite some misgivings, I have confined my analysis to what might be called the black middle class. Excluding lower-income blacks means I do not have to deal with the economic forces which pervade so much of their existence. It is also my feeling that singlehood is handled in a very different and perhaps more effective way by lower-income blacks than by the middle class. Few black women in the lower class, for instance, are never married or childless. Most of them will raise children with the help of the biological father and an extended family system. The free-floating black single is much less common in this group. As to the significance of black singlehood for the functioning of the black community, there are certain ramifications which are felt collectively. In contrast to the ideology of singlehood as a viable alternative, it must be interpreted as a symbol of role failure in the normative sense. Perhaps we need some redefinition of roles. But nobody has yet come up with a known workable alternative. Alternative family substitutes such as open marriage, communal living, heterosexual cohabitation, have been tried and found wanting. And middle-class blacks were never into those family substitutes anyway. Being single and living alone is not a role that relates to any other role. It is the ultimate expression of individuality in a society that is based on a vital togetherness. And that is one reason why the society is geared toward families, not single individuals. There are few social rewards that go to the perpetually single and quite a few punishments.

There is also the problem of emotional stability. Singles do have the recurrent problems of loneliness and other emotional crises, situations which they often have to endure without a buffer to cushion their impact. This is not to say that all married persons have an accessible person to provide them emotional support and no single persons do. Many married people are lonely and frustrated, and a number of single individuals have an informal network of support structures. But I am not juxtaposing marriage to singlehood as a sum-zero proposition. Indeed, it is the opposition to the problems of marriage that constitutes the raison d'etre for much black singleness. In a way similar to many presidential elections, people are voting against rather than for a particular option. Some are willing to settle for a troublesome life of celibacy rather than accept a conflict-ridden marriage.

These problems of singlehood are cited with the clear knowledge that many marriages are unfulfilling. Some women in particular seem to suffer greatly while married. Many of the difficulties, however, arise from unrealistic expectations about what marriage can provide. Whether marriage ever provided much personal happiness for its members is questionable. As far as blacks are concerned, it did serve certain functions which have not been filled by other groups or institutions. Among those needs serviced were the rearing and socializing of children, and sanctuary from a racist and hostile society. While those functions can be carried out in a structure other than marriage, there seems to be no evidence that this is happening in the black middle class.

Some of these statements run counter to prevailing ideologies of a creative singlehood. Personally, I am not a partisan of the traditional nuclear family, nor am I advocating a return to woman's domestic and subservient role. All that is being said here is that certain vital cooperative and sharing functions of marriage are being eroded for an individualistic singlehood. And I am not at all sure that blacks as an oppressed racial minority can afford that luxury. Witness, for instance, the increase in the gap between black and white family incomes. From 1970 to the present black family income declined vis-à-vis white family income. In part this decrease was a result of the reduction in the proportion of black families with two or more workers. We know that there are fewer black families with two workers because of the decrease in the number of blacks married and living with a spouse.[3] The income of individual black workers vis-à-vis individual white workers has actually increased, albeit slowly.

What is the significance of the finding that blacks are more likely to live alone than whites are? The fact that this trend is becoming so pronounced has its own implications. How is the black community to develop when its most educated members fail to marry, and those who are married have such a low fertility rate that they are not reproducing themselves? Using a cost-benefit analysis, what are the costs to the black community of individual expression and gratification?

Given the gradual resurgence of racism and the erosion of black gains from the sixties, the price may be higher than black people want to pay. There is no easy solution to this complex dilemma. Marriage is often a very fragile and conflict-ridden institution for many blacks. From my observations many black singles enjoy a higher level of education, income, and emotional well-being than some of their married brethren. This seems particularly true of women. But this is not a study of black marriages. Somehow and somewhere we must find a happy medium between the two "evils." Meanwhile, let us examine what brought us to this point.

As was true of white families, black families were primarily an economic unit in the nineteenth century. Unlike many white wives, black wives worked outside the home, particularly in the South. In 1900 approximately 41 percent of black women were in the labor force, compared with 16 percent of white women.[4] A notable exception were middle-class black families who preferred that the wife stay home in order to avoid the licentious behavior of white men. During the nineteenth century most blacks were concentrated in the rural South. The middle class was a very tiny and specialized segment of the black community. Most were schoolteachers, morticians, doctors, and ministers. A college degree was essential for most blacks aspiring to middle-class status. A significant deviation from the white culture was the large number of black women who went to college. One of the reasons for this unusual pattern was the limited options open to black women. Either they received college educations and became schoolteachers or worked as domestic servants in white households. Black men had a greater range of occupations open to them.

In the twentieth century blacks migrated to the cities of the South and the North. In the Northern states, blacks increased their numbers in the middle class as more opportunities were opened to them. It was not until the 1960s that any significant economic gains were made by blacks. As a result of the civil rights movement, black student protests, and affirmative action programs, the middle class underwent a great expansion. By 1974 about 20 percent of all black families had incomes over $15,000 a year. Thirteen percent of blacks between the ages of 25 and 35 had completed four or more years of college.[5]

Today's black middle class is primarily an urbanized group. Many of them have their roots in the South and received their education in a predominantly black college. They can be found in a number of different occupations rather than the traditional ones of teacher, social worker, or doctor. The greatest concentration are still in the helping professions although some are newscasters, architects, journalists, or occupy other careers. As a result of certain historical factors, the majority of them are women. They have incomes ranging from ten thousand to fifty thousand dollars a year.

The social structure of middle-class blacks in New York, Chicago, Los Angeles, San Francisco, and other large Northern cities is considerably more complex than was found in the rural or urban areas of the South. With their move to the urban North and exposure to higher education and different cultural values have come different behavioral modalities. They are by far the most acculturated of the black population. In fact many of the problems in black singlehood are no different than the ones whites are also facing. There are, however, unique problems that black singles face. As one observer noted, the problem has changed from living in a racist, segregated society to coping with a racist, integrated society.[6]

Living under different constraints and facing another set of cultural imperatives, many middle-class blacks have adopted the lifestyles and value system of middle-class whites. Among these values is the subordination of group needs to individual desires. This value is easily maintained in an urban setting where the social sanctions on individual conduct are negligible. So each individual is doing his or her own thing. A primary reason for the black involvement in individualism is the decline of the black movement. Without a leader, ideology, or movement to guide their behavior, many blacks have been forced to fashion their life-style and values on their own. Hence they have acquired the ones presented to them by the dominant culture as representing the good life.

In conjunction with those changes have been the influence of the women's movement and ideology. Few black women consider themselves feminist and a lesser number are actively involved in the women's movement. But the influence of feminist ideology is pervasive and obviously reflected in the rapid increase in black women's organizations, consciousness-raising groups, and the everyday resistance of black women to what they perceive as black male chauvinism. It is possible this may be the paramount factor in black male-female conflict. On the other hand, the women's movement may be only a consequence of sex-role conflict rather than a cause. Whatever the relationship between the women's movement and black singlehood, it is very much evident in the changing relationship between the sexes.

We have already discussed the implications of singleness for blacks. There are certain additional structural conditions which make singlehood such a distressing status for this group. One must point to the past history of racism and even to its present form for the existence of some of these conditions. It is the legacy of racism which has created the imbalance in the sex ratio among middle-class black singles. Upwardly mobile black families were forced to send their daughters instead of their sons to college to save them from the degradation of domestic work. The end result of this practice is an excess of black female college graduates. In 1978 there were approximately 100 college-educated black males to every 118 black female college graduates over the age of 25, although the original reason for the imbalance no longer exists.[7]

This imbalance was formerly dealt with by college-educated black women marrying men of lesser education. In one study conducted over twenty years ago, it was found that over half of these women were married to men employed at a lower socioeconomic level.[8] A generation later we find that college-educated black women are much less willing to cross class lines in seeking a mate. One finds a curious pattern in the characteristics of never-married blacks. There are actually a larger number of men between the ages of 25 and 35 who have never married than women. But the largest proportion of those men are at the lowest socioeconomic level while the greatest proportion of never-married women are at the higher socioeconomic level.[9] Moreover, the divorce rate has increased most among higher-status blacks, and the women in that group are least likely to remarry.[10]

If we add the two factors together—the high number of college-educated black women who never marry and an equally large proportion who are divorced—the sex ratio in the eligible pool of mates for college-educated blacks is as low as three women for every man. There are other forces which tend to lower this ratio

even further. Although there are no reliable data on black homosexuality, it is generally agreed that the overwhelming majority of
them are male. Fewer cases of black lesbianism are known to the
community. Another decrease in the eligible male pool occurs
through the much larger proportion of black men who marry
women of other racial groups. While the percentage of blacks married to whites is estimated to be less than 5 percent, it is known to
occur more often in the high status group.[11] The tendency of
college-educated black males to marry women without college
educations reduces the men available even further.

Racial tokenism in employment plays its role in creating impedi-
ments in matching up black singles. One study of white singles
found work was the most frequently cited institutional setting for
meeting persons of the opposite sex.[12] Due to the practice of many
white employers hiring a token black to prove they are equal opportunity employers, a number of blacks work in settings where there
are no other blacks. And the more educated and talented a black is,
the more likely is this to be the case.

In many large cities, particularly outside the South, there is
literally no central place where middle-class black singles can meet
each other. Unlike whites they do not frequent singles bars or live
in predominantly black singles apartments. There are few black
organizations where singles are likely to encounter each other.
Whereas whites have formed dating services, singles' organizations, and even advertise for mates in newspapers and magazines,
much of black dating is circumscribed. Because contacts are limited,
many blacks find themselves dating people in a very small clique
and unable to broaden their options.

Changes in black residence patterns have heightened the isolation
of black singles from each other. Although Los Angeles and San
Francisco have a sizeable black population, the middle-class group
is beginning to be dispersed in predominantly white apartments
throughout the two areas. Moreover, where there is no large concentration of blacks in a given setting, there are likely to be few
facilities which cater to them. Thus, in San Francisco, which has a
very diffused black middle class, one is hard pressed to point out
one place where they congregate. And class and racial boundaries
are rarely crossed by middle-class blacks, especially not by the
women.

There are other forces at work, some too complex to delineate in this brief conclusion. Problems in finding a compatible mate are much more complex than in times gone by. The interests and values of blacks were much more similar in the past. Nowadays, they may be looking for somebody who is into opera, skiing, or Zen Buddhism. Some of them in specialized occupations may want somebody who can relate to their field of endeavor. Thus, a woman banker may seek a man who understands the intricacies of international finance. These changes, coupled with the other barriers to a successful interpersonal relationship, complicate the exodus out of singlehood for many blacks.

What we are witnessing in the year 1980 is the end product of the black liberation movements that probably reached a peak around 1973. It is the formation of a small elite class that has behaviorally assimilated into the values of the dominant majority. They form about 25 percent of the black population in the United States. And they are not the inauthentic black bourgeoisie that E. Franklin Frazier wrote of so pejoratively twenty years ago.[13] A number of them have gone to the top white and black universities. Some have traveled and studied abroad, mostly in Europe. They occupy, in part, the role of native elites in a colonized nation. I categorize them as elites because their status and way of life is vastly different from that of the black masses who remain undereducated, poorly clothed, fed, and sheltered.

They are estranged from the black majority, not only in terms of education and income, but in life-styles. However, their assimilation is not a completed process. They are still part of a separate black community, but it is a milieu which, with a few exceptions, has not developed any institutions or values of its own. They are truly marginal people who exist on the cultural borders of both the black and white community. This is not a role they have chosen but one forced upon them by the peculiar character of American society. The black majority still has many of its traditions and values. In the black community, or ghetto, the stores, restaurants, and nightclubs belong to them. They are more likely to have other support institutions that sustain them such as their churches, an extended family system, and friendship networks.

Many recent changes in the lives of middle-class blacks are endemic to the urban North. In the cities of the South, middle-class blacks are a more cohesive group. Due to the hard lines of racial segregation in that area, the black middle class is more likely to live in the same environment as always and to have developed organizations and facilities that cater to their special needs. Many of the elite blacks in the South attended predominantly black colleges and joined fraternities and sororities which serve as social centers after graduation. This, too, is changing as the black middle class in the South is beginning to disperse into former white enclaves. Some are frequenting predominantly white recreation and amusement centers. Of course, the presence of too many blacks in these settings often change their racial character, and whites respond by moving into other settings or impose an informal quota on the number of blacks that may enter.

Our basic perspective of the world of black singles is that it constitutes a market or exchange system. In concrete terms this means that men and women form relationships on the basis of their ability to bargain or negotiate for certain values. Traditionally the most common transaction was the exchange of female sexual access for male economic resources. This occurred on many levels of society despite the ideology that people dated and married on the basis that strong affection or love was present. However, it is a complex process which takes on a number of different dimensions, depending on who does the buying and selling and which values are most highly desired in a partner.[14]

What we see is that bargaining still occurs between men and women who come together in the dating game. The traditional exchange values have been supplanted by another set of priorities. As a result of changes in American society, men have much greater access to female sexuality and the economically independent woman has much less need for the financial support of men. Thus, the parties involved may be bargaining for the satisfaction of certain psychological and physiological needs. But certain characteristics of the exchange system remain constant. Particular attributes are still more or less valuable in that market and a certain class of individuals have more options than others.

The conditions under which middle-class blacks select their mates and their standards have changed. In the 1980s the number of black female college graduates will far exceed the number of comparable males. Yet most of these women will accept nothing less than a mate of similar educational level. This is a function of their acceptance of Euro-American emphasis on status homogeneity as the basis for marriage. Not too long ago less educated males were acceptable as mates if they were hardworking and possessed other positive qualities. Yet the middle-class black male also falls victim to the lure of Euro-American values in his standards for a wife. As he rises into middle class and acquires some power and income, his standards begin to mirror those of his white counterpart. What he wants is a woman who fits into the Euro-American definition of womanhood (for example, dependent and submissive). But the majority of black women did not have these role models as children nor did the imperatives of black survival allow them to acquire such traits.

In the white community, people's roles were consonant with their socialization and cultural reality. Women were supportive and deferential because the men could reward such behavior through their superior economic position and more powerful status. Thus, the woman's compliance was assured through the role models in the family, her socialization into a feminine and docile image, and the reinforcement of such behavior by the stratification of gender roles. As a consequence of a rising feminist consciousness, many white women have penetrated the facade of male paternalism. Since white women are increasingly joining the labor force as workers, their role model, and that of their children, may emulate the one exposed to black women for more than a century.

When all is said and done, both singlehood and marriage are what we make them. Certainly, racism and the machinations of a capitalist society create formidable barriers against the building and maintaining of harmonious interpersonal relationships. But those same forces have coexisted with much better relationships than we have in contemporary American society. In the past the family was a buffer against those oppressive forces. Today it is decimated by them, partially because individuals have succumbed to their most pernicious values. Human relationships have become one more commodity in a society permeated by individualism and materialism. Only the test of time will prove whether the spiritual values of a nation will prevail over the end products of industrial capitalism.

Hence, the crisis of the black family stems from more than

poverty alone. It is also due to the problem of acculturation, the acceptance of values—alien values—which do not conform to the structural context of black society. Despite all that was said about the lack of acculturation being the major cause of black family weakness, it is becoming all too clear that their unique cultural moorings were functional for a unique situation. Now we stand at the crossroads of a major decision about which way we will proceed to order our lives. Will it be the organic family unit built on a black ethos or the materialism and individualism of Euro-American culture? Whatever that decision may be, we should not be deluded into believing that the consequences are individual ones. The future of the race may be at stake.

NOTES

1. U.S. Bureau of the Census, Current Population Reports, Series P-20, *Marital Status and Living Arrangements, March 1978* (Washington, D.C.: U.S. Government Printing Office, 1979), p. 1.

2. Peter Stein, *Single* (Englewood Cliffs, N.J.: Prentice-Hall, 1976).

3. Lester Thurow, The economic status of minorities and women, *Civil Rights Digest* 8 (Winter-Spring 1976): 4-5.

4. Rayford Logan, *The Betrayal of the Negro*, (New York: Collier, 1965), p. 162.

5. U.S. Bureau of the Census, *The Social and Economic Status of the Black Population 1974* (Washington, D.C.: U.S. Government Printing Office, 1975).

6. Charlotte Robinson, Black marriages—victims of the affluent rat race. *San Francisco Examiner*, 25 April 1976, p. 24.

7. U.S. Bureau of the Census, *Money, Income and Poverty Status in 1975 of Families in the United States and the West Region, by Divisions and States* (Washington, D.C.: U.S. Government Printing Office, 1978), pp. 21-22.

8. Jean Noble, *The Negro Woman College Graduate* (New York: Columbia University Press, 1956), p. 108.

9. Charles W. Mueller and Blair Campbell, Female occupational achievement: a research note, *Journal of Marriage and the Family* 39 (August 1977): 587-593.

10. Paul C. Glick and Karen M. Mills, *Black Families, Marriage Patterns and Living Arrangements*, (Atlanta, Ga.: Atlanta University, 1974).

11. David Heer, The prevalence of black-white marriage in the United States, 1960 and 1970, *Journal of Marriage and the Family* 36 (May 1974): 246-259.

12. Joyce R. Starr and Donald E. Carns, Singles in the city, in *Marriage and Families* ed. H. Lopata, (New York: D. Van Nostrand, 1973), pp. 148-153.

13. E. Franklin Frazier, *Black Bourgeoisie*, (New York: Collier Books, 1957).

14. William Goode, *World Revolution and Family Patterns*, (New York: The Free Press, 1963), p. 8.

APPENDIX A

A Methodological Note

In seeking to investigate the sociodynamics of the black singles world, we started out with no preconceived theories or hypotheses. All we knew was that statistically they were a large group and were experiencing problems in their relationships with the opposite sex. Our first task was to determine who would make up the sample and, second, to decide on what research methodology to use. This chore was made easier by the fact that we were all members of the subject population (black and single). Time and financial constraints were another consideration. The author had studied black families for over fifteen years and knew well the literature on them and their situation. It was obvious that using lower-income blacks would entail an analysis of poverty, crime, education, racism, and other social problems that impact on their marital status. Since the majority of blacks live in or around large cities, it made sense to concentrate only on urban blacks. We used a restricted age range (25 to 45) because our preliminary tests indicated that those individuals who fell outside the age range were significantly different from our age cohort. We did collect data on the younger and older age groups, which will be used for a future comparative analysis. At this point, those data only serve to confirm our decision to exclude them from the sample.

Having decided to confine the study to urban, college educated blacks, between the ages of 25 and 45, we formulated a tripartite approach to studying the world of black singles. The writer and a black male interviewer would conduct in-depth interviews with black singles in the San Francisco Bay Area. Our main understanding of their situation came from the interviews. Since we lived in and knew the area, we were able to use some purposive sampling. When our sample seemed deficient in certain types of singles, we were able to make conscious efforts to contact and interview them. This happened in the case of men, women over the age of 40, very attractive women, and other categories. As questions arose about certain responses, we made special efforts to have future interviewees elaborate on them. In some cases we checked the responses of women with men and vice versa.

Our main concern was obtaining the most honest responses we could from the subjects. Being unmarried is a situation that forces many people into a great deal of face saving. Thus, there have to be two levels of observation, what people say and what they feel and do. While our personal interviews followed the general format of the self-administered questionnaire, we did much more probing and follow-up on the questions in order to obtain clarity and assess any contradictions. After doing a certain number of interviews, we would pause to analyze the responses we were getting and make special efforts to probe deeper on some questions. One of the questions that needed clarification was the role of opposite-sex friends for women. After further exploration, we found that most of the cross-sex friends they claimed were more realistically described as casual acquaintances, or fell into the typology we developed.

Since the interviews were initially conducted by two young and single black males, we decided to use a female interviewer for our women subjects. After reading her interview data, no significant differences emerged. It might be naive to believe that being male and single had no influence on our responses, but whatever effect it had seems to be negligible. Similarly, those people unfamiliar with the San Francisco Bay Area may believe our interviewees constitute an atypical sample. However, the blacks living in that area tend to be more traditional than the whites, although the liberal ethos of the Bay Area may exert some influence on their values and behavior. Moreover, most of our subjects did not live in San Francisco proper. The majority lived in Oakland, which is similar to other East Coast cities with a large black population. Many of them were not natives of the area but had spent the major part of their lives outside the state of California.

The main control we had for bias in the interview sample was the self-administered questionnaire. This questionnaire consisted of some demographic items and open-ended essay questions. Key people were identified in the twenty-five largest standard metropolitan areas in the United States. The key people were those individuals we knew who had access to individuals fitting our sample description. Sometimes they were college professors who were active in their community. Others may have been leaders of, or active in, organizations which contained members of our subject population. The responses were tabulated by Standard Metropolitan Areas and monitored. If one SMA was not represented, we sent the questionnaires out again to another key person to distribute. We did not seek randomness in the questionnaire sample, only adequate representation. The questionnaires elicited interesting and valid data but did not constitute the major source of our interpretations. While the quotes in the text are a mix of the interview and questionnaire subject's responses, the questionnaires mainly served as a cross-check on the interview data. Some people may have given more honest responses on the questionnaire because it was totally anonymous. However, we were not able to follow up on the questionnaire responses nor to obtain extensive answers to some of the questions.

Our third method was field research. This consisted of going to places and events that singles frequented. They included churches, restaurants, house parties, discos, membership clubs, and other locations. The chapter, "Where the Action Is," is heavily laden with interpetive analysis because it reflects the author's observations. The observations were made in the San Francisco Bay Area and the cities of New York, Detroit, Los Angeles, Chicago, Washington, D.C., Atlanta, New Orleans, and Boston. Observations were systematically recorded and compared to the responses of interview and questionnaire respondents. In some places the author was identified as a researcher on the black singles life-style. At other times he was just another participant in the particular activity.

In doing this study we attempted to check the validity of our responses and interpretations by using a representative group of subjects and making comparisons among them. What we sought to do was to discover the categories and properties of relationships among and between black singles. While qualitative analysis may generate theory, it does not seek to verify it. Only in a few cases have the data been reported in statistical form. To do so would have been pointless. Our purpose was to report the range of the black singles experience and aspects of that condition. The first priority was to seek an understanding of the black singles world and express it in comprehensible form. The crucial element in this task was to analyze structural conditions, processes, patterns, norms, and consequences and report their manifestations. What we understand is more important than how we came to understand it. While we are aware that our approach is vulnerable to criticism from colleagues in the academic world, the ultimate test of the value of our work will be the subject population's comparisons of our conclusions with their own experience, and those of others they know and how well our reported material jibes.

APPENDIX B

Tables

Table 1   SEX RATIOS, BY AGE AND RACE: JULY 1, 1976
(Total including Armed Forces Overseas. Males per 100 Females)

Age	Total	White	Black
All Ages	95.2	95.7	91.4
Under 5 years	104.5	105.0	102.1
5 to 9 years	104.1	104.7	100.8
10 to 14 years	104.0	104.6	101.2
15 to 19 years	103.2	103.6	100.1
20 to 24 years	101.4	102.6	93.5
25 to 29 years	99.2	101.2	87.7
30 to 34 years	97.9	99.9	84.7
35 to 39 years	95.4	97.5	82.5
40 to 44 years	95.5	97.4	83.6
45 to 49 years	94.9	96.0	87.6
50 to 54 years	92.6	93.3	86.5
55 to 59 years	91.3	91.7	86.3
60 to 64 years	87.9	88.3	82.1
65 years and over	69.0	68.4	72.3

Source: U.S. Bureau of the Census Current Population Reports, Population Estimates and Projections, Series P-25 No. 643, January 1977, p. 5.

**Table 2   YEARS OF SCHOOL COMPLETED BY BLACKS, AGES
25 TO 54, AND MARITAL STATUS, MARCH 1977**
(Numbers in thousands, noninstitutional population)

	4 years of college	5 years of college or more
25 to 34 years old		
MALE	123,000	89,000
Single	43,000	14,000
Married	74,000	44,000
Wife present	60,000	40,000
Widowed	—	—
Divorced	5,000	2,000
FEMALE	136,000	69,000
Single	33,000	22,000
Married	91,000	39,000
Husband present	86,000	37,000
Widowed	2,000	—
Divorced	13,000	8,000
35 to 54 years old		
MALE	65,000	62,000
Single	4,000	8,000
Married	55,000	53,000
Wife present	50,000	50,000
Widowed	—	2,000
Divorced	6,000	—
FEMALE	131,000	81,000
Single	10,000	4,000
Married	98,000	61,000
Husband present	80,000	53,000
Widowed	6,000	1,000
Divorced	18,000	15,000

Source: U.S. Bureau of the Census, Current Population Reports, Series P-20, No.
314, Washington, D.C., 1978, p. 31.

Table 3 TWO-PARENT AND ONE-PARENT BLACK FAMILIES:
1978, 1970, AND 1960

Type of Family	1978	1970	1960	Percent Change 1970 to 1978	Percent Change 1960 to 1970
Two-Parent Families	52.2	67.0	77.0	− 3.2	16.4
One-Parent Families	47.8	33.0	23.0	79.6	92.3
Maintained by a:					
Woman	45.0	30.6	20.7	82.7	97.8
Man	2.7	2.4	2.3	39.4	42.0

Source: U.S. Bureau of the Census, *Divorce, Child Custody, and Child Support*, Series P-23, No. 84, Washington, D.C., U.S. Government Printing Office, 1979, p. 9.

Table 4 PERCENT OF BLACK CHILDREN
LIVING WITH BOTH PARENTS, BY FAMILY INCOME, 1975

	Own Black Children Percent Living With	
	Both Parents	One Parent
Total Own Children	54	46
Under $4,000	17	83
$4,000 to $5,999	29	71
$6,000 to $7,999	51	49
$8,000 to $9,999	66	34
$10,000 and over	82	18
$10,000 to $14,999	79	21
$15,000 and over	86	14

Source: U.S. Bureau of the Census, The Social and Economic Status of the Black Population in the United States: An Historical View 1790-1978, Series P-23, No. 80, Washington, D.C., U.S. Government Printing Office, 1979, p. 108.

APPENDIX C:

Questionnaire

Dear Friend:

This questionnaire is being sent to you by a black researcher as part of a study of black singles. I am conducting it without foundation funds or organizational support and am soliciting your cooperation. The number of black singles is rapidly increasing and we know practically nothing about the reason why, or the nature of this prevalent state of black people. It is my purpose to find out how blacks are coping with their single life-style and what, if any, problems they encounter. You can help me by answering honestly and clearly the questions contained within.

All answers are confidential. Do not put your name anywhere on the questionnaire or return envelope. We are interested *only* in the collective response, not in identifying specific individuals. Please return the questionnaire to the person who gave it to you, or to me. My name and address are listed below.

Thank you for your cooperation.

Sincerely,

Robert Staples

Graduate Program in Sociology
UNIVERSITY OF CALIFORNIA
San Francisco, CA 94143

Sex _____

Age _____

Name of the city and state in which you spent most of your life.

_____

Occupation_____

Father and Mother's Occupation_____

_____

_____

Your educational background _____

_____

_____

City and state in which you presently live _____

_____

Marital status (never marrried, divorced, etc.) _____

_____

Are you the mother or father of a child?_____

Do you have children of your own living with you? If so, how many?

_____

Are you living alone? If not, what is the relationship with the person(s)
living with you? _____

_____

What is your income range (e.g., $5,000-$8,000; $8,000-$11,000; $11,000-$14,000, etc.)? _____

How would you describe yourself in terms of physical attractiveness? (below average, average, above average, exceptional) _____

Unless the question is totally irrelevant to your situation, please answer at length. If necessary, answer on a separate page. If you are pressed for time, just answer the questions of most interest to you.

1. Why are you presently unmarried?

2. Describe what, if any, problems you believe are unique to unmarried blacks who are seeking a mate.

3. How do you spend your leisure time?

4. What qualities are you looking for in a mate?

5. Do your standards for a more casual dating or sexual partner differ from the above? If so, describe them.

6. What role do friends of the same sex play in your life?

7. What role do friends of the opposite sex play in your life?

8.   As an unmarried person do you experience feelings of loneliness or sexual deprivation? If so, how do you deal with them?

9.   Describe your feelings about whether you should engage in sexual relations with people you date and under what conditions.

10.   What is your overall evaluation of the women/men you go out with socially?

11.   Where do you meet most of the people you date? Where do you go?

12.   Have you noticed any change in what women/men expect or do on dates nowadays?

13.   Have you ever considered, or adapted an alternative life style such as living with someone you are not married to, homosexuality, dedication to a career, raising children alone, etc.?

14.   If you have children, how does this affect your opportunities for going out on dates, the type of person you can date, and any other aspect of your life?

15. Have you ever dated a member of another race? If so, why? How would you describe your experience?

16. How would you describe the experience of being black, single, and male/female?

Selected Bibliography

Adams, Margaret. *Single Blessedness: Observations on the Single Status in Married Society.* New York: Basic Books, Inc., 1976.

Aldridge, Delores P. The Changing Nature of Interracial Marriage in Georgia: a Research Note. *Journal of Marriage and the Family* 35 (November, 1973): 641.

Bass-Hass, Rita. The Lesbian Dyad. *Journal of Sex Research* 4 (Winter, 1968): 108-126.

Bayer, Alan E. College Impact on Marriage. *Journal of Marriage and the Family* 34 (November, 1972): 600-610.

Bell, Allan. Black Sexuality: Fact and Fancy. A paper presented to *Focus: Black America Series.* Bloomington, Ind. Indiana University, 1968.

Bell, Robert. The Related Importance of Mother and Wife Roles Among Black Lower Class Women. In *The Black Family: essays and studies* 1st ed., ed. R. Staples. Belmont, Ca: Wadsworth Publishing, 1971, 248-255.

Benton, Levi. Case History: I'm a Black Homosexual. *Sexology* 39 (March, 1972): 15-17.

Bernard, Jessie. Marital Stability and Patterns of Status Variables. *Journal of Marriage and the Family* 28 (November, 1966): 421-439.

Bianchi, Suzanne and Farley Reynolds. Racial Differences in Family Living Arrangements and Economic Well Being: An Analysis of Recent Trends. *Journal of Marriage and the Family* 41 (August, 1979): 537-552.

Black Scholar. The Black Sexism Debate. *The Black Scholar* 10 (May-June, 1979).

Black Women's Community Development Foundation. Mental and Physical Health Problems of Black Women. Washington, D.C., BWCDF, 1975.

Brain, Robert. *Friends and Lovers.* New York: Basic Books, 1976.

Broderick, Carlfred. Social Heterosexual Development Among Urban Negroes and Whites. *Journal of Marriage and the Family* 27 (May, 1965): 200-203.

Brown, Prudence et al. Sex Role Attitudes and Psychological Outcomes for Black and White Women Experiencing Marital Dissolution. *Journal of Marriage and the Family* 39 (August, 1977): 549-562.

Campbell, Angus. The American Way of Mating: Marriage Si, Children Only Maybe. *Psychology Today* (May, 1975): 37-43.

Cazanave, Noel. Social Structure and Personal Choice in Intimacy, Marriage and Family Alternative Lifestyle Research. *Alternative Lifestyles* 2 (August, 1979): 331-358.

248   *Selected Bibliography*

Chavis, William M. and Gladys Lyles. Divorce Among Educated Black Women. *Journal of the National Medical Association* 67 (March, 1975): 128-134.

Christensen, Harold T. and Leonor B. Johnson. Premarital Coitus and the Southern Black: A Comparative View. *Journal of Marriage and the Family* 40 (November, 1978): 721-732.

Clark, Milton R. The Dance Party as a Socialization Mechanism for Black Urban Preadolescents and Adolescents. *Sociology and Social Research* 58 (January, 1974): 145-154.

Clayton, Richard R. and Harwin L. Voss. Shacking up: Cohabitation in the 1970s. *Journal of Marriage and the Family* 39 (May, 1977): 273-284.

Crouch, Stanley. The Myth of the Black Male. *Soul Illustrated* 3 (Spring, 1972): 21-23.

Cox, Oliver. Sex Ratio and Marital Status among Negroes. *American Sociological Review* 5 (1940): 937-947.

Davis, George. *Black Love.* Garden City, New York: Doubleday, 1977.

Day, Beth. *Sexual Life Between Blacks and Whites.* New York: World, 1972.

Drake, St. Clair and Horace Cayton. *Black Metropolis.* New York: Harcourt, Brace and Johanovich, 1945.

Dickinson, George E. Dating Behavior of Black and White Adolescents Before and After Desegregation. *Journal of Marriage and the Family* 37 (August, 1975): 602-608.

Edwards, Marie and Eleanore Hoover. *The Challenge of Being Single.* New York: The New American Library, 1974.

Ellis, William A. A Sexual Crisis. *Essence* 4 (October, 1973): 41.

Editorial. Black Man/Black Woman—Closer Together or Further Apart. *Essence* 4 (October-November, 1973).

Frazier, Franklin E. *Black Bourgeoisie.* New York: Collier Books, 1957.

Gebhard, Paul, et al. *Pregnancy, Birth and Abortion.* New York: Harper & Row, 1958.

Geis, Gilbert, et al. Interracial Rape in a North American City: An Analysis of 66 Cases. A paper presented to the Inter-American Congress of Criminology Meeting, Caracas, Venezuela. November, 1972.

Glick, Paul and Karen. *Black Families: Marriage Patterns and Living Arrangements.* Atlanta, GA: Atlanta University, 1974.

Glick, Paul. Some Recent Changes in American Families. Current Population Reports Series P-23, No. 52. Washington, D.C.: U.S. Government Printing Office, 1975.

Greenberg, Judith B. Single Parents and Intimacy: A Comparison of Mothers and Fathers. *Alternative Lifestyles* 2 (August, 1979): 308-330.

Greenwood, Nancy A. What's A Nice Person Like You Doing in A Status Group Like This?: An Analysis of Singles as an Emergent Status Group in American Society. Unpub. ms., 1977.

Grier, William and Price Cobbs. *Black Rage.* New York: Basic Books, 1968.

Gustarvus, Susan and Kent Mommsen. Black/White Differentials in Family Size Preferences Among Youth. *Pacific Sociological Review* 16 (January, 1973): 107-119.

Gutman, Herbert G. *The Black Family in Slavery and Freedom 1750-1925*. New York: Pantheon Books, 1976.

Halsell, Grace. *Black-White Sex*. New York: William Morrow Company, 1972.

Hare, Nathan. For a Better Black Family. *Ebony* 32 (February, 1976): 62.

———. What Black Intellectuals Misunderstand about the Black Family. *Black World* 25 (March, 1976): 4-14.

Heer, David. The Prevalence of Black-White Marriage in the United States, 1960 and 1970. *Journal of Marriage and the Family* 36 (May, 1974): 246-259.

Herton, Calvin. *Coming Together*. New York: Random House, 1972.

———. *Sex and Racism in America*. New York: Doubleday and Co., 1965.

Henriques, Fernando. *Children of Conflict: a Study of Interracial Sex and Marriage*. New York: E. P. Dutton, 1975.

Himes, Joseph. A Value Profile in Mate Selection Among Negroes. *Marriage and Family Living* 16 (August, 1954): 244-247.

Jackson, Jacquelyn. *Aging and Black Women*. Washington, D.C.: College and University Press, 1975.

———. But Where are the Men? *The Black Scholar* 3 (December, 1971): 34-41.

Jackson, Lorraine B. The Attitudes of Black Females toward Upper and Lower Class Black Males. *The Journal of Black Psychology* 1 (February, 1975): 53-64.

Jacques, Jeffrey M. Mate Selection among Southeastern Black Americans. *Journal of Social and Behavioral Sciences* 23 (Spring, 1977): 112-135.

Jeffers, T. The Black Woman and the Black Middleclass. *The Black Scholar* 4 (March-April, 1973): 37-41.

Karenga, M. Ron. In Love and Struggle: Toward a Greater Togetherness. *The Black Scholar* 7 (March, 1975): 16-28.

Kiser, Clyde and Myrna Frank. Factors Associated with the Low Fertility of Non-White Women of College Attainment. *Milbank Memorial Fund Quarterly* 1 (October, 1967): 425-429.

Kronus, Sidney J. *The Black Middle Class*. Columbus, Oh.: Charles V. Merrill, 1971.

Kulesky, William and Augelita Obordo. A Racial Comparison of Teenage Girls' Projections for Marriage and Procreation. *Journal of Marriage and the Family* 34 (February, 1972): 75-84.

Ladner, Joyce. *Tomorrow's Tomorrow: the Black Woman*. Garden City, New York: Doubleday, 1971.

Larue, Linda. The Black Movement and Women's Liberation. *The Black Scholar* 1 (May, 1970): 36-42.

Lewis, Diane R. The Black Family: Socialization and Sex Roles. *Phylon* 36 (Fall, 1975): 221-237.

Lewis, Hylan. *Blackways of Kent*. Chapel Hill: University of North Carolina Press, 1955.

Liebow, Eliot. *Tally's Corner*. Boston: Little, Brown, and Company, 1966.

Mack, Delores E. The Power Relationship in Black Families and White Families. *Journal of Personality and Social Psychology* 30 (September, 1974): 409-413.

Mayo, Julia. The New Black Feminism: a Minority Report. In *Contemporary*

Sexual Behavior: Critical Issues in the 1970s eds. Joseph Zubin and John Money. Baltimore: John Hopkins University Press, 1973, 175-186.

Milner, Christina and Richard Milner. *Black Players.* Boston: Little, Brown, and Company, 1972.

Morton, Carol. Mistakes Black Men Make in Relating to Black Women. *Ebony* 30 (December, 1975): 170-175.

_____. Mistakes Black Women Make in Relating to Black Men. *Ebony* 31 (January, 1976): 89-97.

Noble, Jean. *Beautiful, Also, are the Souls of my Black Sisters: a history of the Black Woman in America.* Englewood Cliffs, NJ: Prentice-Hall, 1978.

Parrish, Milton. Black Woman's Guide to the Black Man. *Essence* 4 (April, 1974): 56-57.

Pettigrew, Eudora. Women's Liberation and Black Women. *Journal of Social and Behavioral Sciences* 23 (Spring, 1977): 146-162.

Porterfield, Ernest. *Black and White Mixed Marriages.* Chicago: Nelson-Hall, 1977.

Poussaint, Alvin. Blacks and the Sexual Revolution. *Ebony* 26 (October, 1971): 112-122.

_____. Sex and the Black Male. *Ebony* 27 (August, 1972): 114-122.

Poussaint, Alvin and Ann Poussaint. Black Women/Black Men. *Ebony* 33 (August, 1977): 160-163.

Poussaint, Ann. Can Black Marriages Survive Modern Pressures. *Ebony* 29 (September, 1974): 97-102.

Rainwater, Lee. *Behind Ghetto Walls: Negro Families in a Federal Slum.* Hawthorne, New York: Aldine Publishing Co., 1970.

Reed, Julia. Marriage and Fertility in Black Female Teachers. *The Black Scholar* 1 (January-February, 1970): 22-28.

Rooks, Evelyn and Karl King. A Study of the Marriage Role Expectations of Black Adolescents. *Adolescence* 8 (Fall, 1973): 317-323.

Rose, La Frances. Relationships between Black Males and Females—toward a definition. In *Women and their Health: Research Implications for a New Era.* Washington, D.C.: U.S. Department of Health, Education and Welfare, 1975, 62-72.

Roscow, Irving and Daniel Rose. Divorce Among Doctors. *Journal of Marriage and the Family* 34 (November, 1972): 587-599.

Sawyer, Ethel. *A Study of a Public Lesbian Community.* M.A. Thesis, Washington University, 1965.

Schulman, Gary. Race, Sex and Violence. A Laboratory Test of the Sexual Threat of the Black Male Hypothesis. *American Journal of Sociology* 79 (March, 1974): 1260-1277.

Sizemore, Barbara. Sexism and the Black Male. *The Black Scholar* 4 (March-April, 1973): 2-11.

Snell, Dee. *How to Get and Hold your Black Man in Spite of Women's Lib.* Baltimore: Ceegul Publishing Co., 1974.

Staples, Robert. Sex Life of Middle Class Negroes. *Sexology* 33 (September, 1966): 86-89.

_____. Educating the Black Male at Various Class Levels for Marital Roles. *The Family Coordinator* 19 (April, 1970): 164-167.

_____. Towards a Sociology of the Black Family: A Decade of Theory and Research. *Journal of Marriage and the Family* 33 (February, 1971): 19-38.

_____. The Myth of the Black Matriarchy. *The Black Scholar* 2 (June, 1971): 2-9.

_____. The Myth of the Impotent Black Male. *The Black Scholar* 2 (June, 1971): 2-9.

_____. Sex and the Black Middle Class. *Ebony* 28 (August, 1973): 106-114.

_____. The Black Dating Game. *Essence* 40 (October, 1973): 92-96.

_____. *The Black Woman in America*. Chicago: Nelson-Hall, 1973.

_____. Has the Sexual Revolution Bypassed Blacks? *Ebony* 29 (April, 1974): 111-114.

_____. The Myth of Black Sexual Superiority. *The Black Scholar* 9 (April, 1978): 16-23.

_____. Race and Masculinity: the Black Man's Dual Dilemma. *Journal of Social Issues* 34 (Winter, 1978): 169-183.

_____. The Black Family: *Essays and Studies* (vol. 2). Belmont, CA: Wadsworth Publishing Co., 1978.

_____. Race, Liberalism, Conservatism and Premarital Sexual Permissiveness: A Biracial Comparison. *Journal of Marriage and the Family* 40 (November, 1978): 733-742.

_____. The Myth of Black Macho: A Response to Angry Black Feminists. *The Black Scholar* 12 (March/April, 1979): 24-36.

_____. Black Feminism and the Cult of Masculinity: The Danger Within. *The Black Scholar* 10 (May-June, 1979): 63-68.

_____. Can Black Women Go it Alone? *Black Male/Female Relationships* 1 (June-July, 1979): 25-27.

_____. Beyond the Black Family: The Trend Toward Singlehood. *Western Journal of Black Studies* 3 (Fall, 1979): 150-157.

Stein, Peter. *Single*. Englewood Cliffs, NJ: Prentice-Hall, Inc., 1976.

_____. A Typology of Singlehood. Paper presented at the National Society for Women in Sociology Meetings, San Francisco. August, 1978.

Steinman, Anne and David Fox. Attitudes toward Women's Family Role among Black and White Undergraduates. *The Family Coordinator* 19 (October, 1970): 363-367.

Stewart, James and Joseph Scott. The Institutional Decimation of Black American Males. *Western Journal of Black Studies* 2 (Summer, 1978): 82-92.

Turner, Barbara and Castelleno. The Political Implications of Social Stereotyping of Women and Men among Black and White College Students. *Sociology and Social Research* 58 (January, 1974): 155-162.

Tyson, Richard and Joanne Tyson. Sex and the Black Woman. *Ebony* 33 (August, 1977): 103-113.

U.S. Bureau of the Census. Marriage, Divorce, Widowhood, and Remarriage by Family Characteristics: June, 1975. Series P-20 No. 312. Washington, D.C.: U.S. Government Printing Office, 1977.

_____. Fertility of American Women: June, 1976. Series P-20 No. 308. Washington, D.C.: U.S. Government Printing Office, 1977.

_____. The Social and Economic Status of the Black Population in the United States: an historical view, 1790-1978. Series P-23 No. 80. Washington, D.C.: U.S. Government Printing Office, 1979.

_____. Marital Status and Living Arrangements: March, 1978. Series P-20 No. 338. Washington, D.C.: U.S. Government Printing Office, 1979.

_____. Divorce, Child Custody and Child Support. Series P-23 No. 81. Washington, D.C.: U.S. Government Printing Office, 1979.

Wallace, Michele. *Black Macho and the Myth of the Superwoman.* New York: Dial Press, 1979.

Washington, Joseph. *Marriage in Black and White.* Boston: Beacon Press, 1970.

White, Joyce. Single Motherhood. *Essence* 4 (November, 1973): 54-55.

Wilding, Stephen and Jason Winters. Sex in the 70's. *Essence* 7 (February, 1977): 54-55.

Wilkinson, Doris, ed. *Black Male/White Female.* Cambridge, MA: Schenkman, 1974.

Young, Louis. Are Black Men Taking Care of Business? *Essence* 4 (April, 1974): 40-41.

Index

About the Author

ROBERT STAPLES is Associate Professor of Sociology at the University of California, San Francisco. He is the author of *The Black Woman in America, Introduction to Black Sociology, The Lower Income Negro Family in St. Paul*, and *The Black Family: Essays and Studies*.